Saddletramp

From Ottoman Hills to Offa's Dyke

Jeremy James

MERLIN UNWIN BOOKS

Published by Merlin Unwin Books 2015
First published by the Penguin Group 1989

Merlin Unwin Books
Palmers House
7 Corve Street
Ludlow
Shropshire
SY8 1DB

A CIP record of this book is available from the British Library.

Printed in the UK by Jellyfish Print Solutions Ltd

ISBN 978 1 910723 00 5

Contents

To my mother,
and anyone who has ever been bitten,
been kicked by, is frightened of,
or has fallen off,
a horse.

Acknowledgements

I would like to thank a lot of people, like Teresa Watts of the Woodlands Riding School, Parkmill, Swansea for sitting me straight in a saddle and for falling about laughing when I told her what I wanted to do. Thanks to Altman and James of Bridgend for the superb cotton headcollar bridles and saddlebags that drove me bonkers. Thanks Joanna Jones for your White Light, Patrick Kemp for Radiasthesic Long Distance healing. Thanks Dell Round and Johnathan John of the Swansea Psychic Centre for showing me how to see. I thank Ifanca James, iridologist in Swansea for herbal compounds that set me up without a single moment's illness. Thanks Sally Stud in Cardiff for teaching me how never to say no. Thank you Hugo Evans old chum, for betting me a quid I wouldn't do it: you still owe me. Thanks Athene English, saddler in Hay-on-Wye, fairest stitcher in the land for all the top quality leather clobber, you're a doll, honeybunch. Thank you Owen Humphrys for the loan of that ancient leather jerkin, and Chumpie, Cecilia Humphrys – never said so at the time, but you're a brave girl, thanks for hanging round. Also Marco Windham for your company in the Alps, and dozens of splendid photographs – here's to the next time.

I thank humbly and with all my heart, all you wonderful, kind and open people who helped me on my way, fed me and my horses – there's not one of you I shall forget. Thanks Bob Bennet for finding Maro when she scarpered, Rex and Penny in Greece for first class horsemanship, endless hospitality, for seeding the idea in the first place all those years ago.

Thanks Min Murray Thriepland for being crazy enough to take on Punch, my bull terrier while I was away, and Rupert Sanders, the ever patient solicitor, for sorting out the mess I left behind, and for keeping me out of the nick. I thank Sarah Hayes of International Horse Services for sorting out my papers, getting Gonzo and me safely to England. Mario Sivilieri and Dino Gatta, I never realised at the time what a magnificent job you did in supplying me with an armful of unarguable-with paperwork.

Thanks Frank Champion of Hipavia for sorting out that last snag in France. Thank you Grenville Collins for believing in me: I left your beautiful gift on a riverbank in Turkey: now I shall always know where it is.

Elaine Barry: when I struggled to write all this down you've no idea how much your encouragement meant to me: I just could not have done it otherwise. Thanks Leszek Kobiernicki for being hard on me when I needed it most, for good guidance.

Richard Chester-Master and Tom Vesey thanks for Tack Barn.

But most especially, I would like to thank Providence for the hand she held out to me night and day all the way: I'm sorry when I doubted You, but You see it takes some handling. Thanks Nick Murray Wells: I know you would have approved.

My last and everlasting thanks go to Ahmed Paşa, Şimşek, Maria and Gonzales da Mendoza: four wonderful horses, who made me laugh, brought tears to my eyes, made me angry, gave me rope burns, caused me grief and brought me the tenderest moments of my life, and who never once let me down.

A little Turkish

Çal is pronounced 'Chal'
Ahmed Paşa is pronounced 'Ahmet Pasha'
Şimşek, 'Shimshaik'

1

The Search for a Horse

Until one is committed there is hesitancy, the chance to draw back. Concerning all acts of initiative (and creation) there is one elementary truth, the ignorance of which kills countless ideas and splendid plans: that the moment one definitely commits oneself, then Providence moves too. All sorts of things occur to help that would never have otherwise occurred. A whole stream of events issues from the decision, raising in one's favour all manner of unforeseen incidents and meetings and material assistance, which no man could have dreamed would have come his way. Whatever you can do, or dream you can do, begin it. Boldness has genius, power and magic in it. Begin it now.

William H. Murray, mountaineer, author and soldier

He stood high above us in his filthy trousers, shouting 'Haydi gel!' and waving his arms about. He'd gone up like a mountain goat and was watching us three struggle up after him. No idea what he said. Yildiz and Ali were slow: the climb was killing them too: it was a real effort.

Stopping for a breather, I turned to look out to sea. The sun dazzled hard on the water. You could see the bottom just below the rocks, looking cool. I turned, climbed on. It was hot on that slope. Curry spice and sage grew in patches and a whiff of pine hung around, from all along the coast. There couldn't be a horse in a place like this. I'd looked at them in queer places, never on a cliff face. Someone had shown me one that morning. He was black, a four-year-old, eaten alive with lice and worms. Just leather draped round a skeleton – pitiful. Now we were half way up this hill, after another. I squinted at the man above, just a dozen yards more. Yildiz and Ali had stopped in a clump of erasmus on a crumbling terrace, in the rugged shadow of an old olive.

I reached the plateau, surprééised to find it covered in grass. Suleiman was sitting on the edge. He offered a cigarette, pointing to a small cave at the back of the clearing. Taking a long pull his eyes watered as he coughed out, 'At ... beygir.' And gobbed.

Seemed he reckoned there was a horse in there.

Pretty unlikely. Sweat ran down his face; the climb hadn't been that easy for him either. Then the other two joined us, sitting down for a smoke. Ali still carried the head collar and a stick from somewhere. They talked amongst themselves for a while, sharing a joke. I didn't understand, just looked out to sea, to the little fishing boat below us, the man paying a long net out into the water.

They got up. Suleiman said 'Heidi gel!' again.

They stubbed out their fags and went cautiously to the cave. I couldn't think what all the fuss was about. Why not just get him out, pack in all this silly creeping around?

Then I heard him. There *was* a horse in there.

The grass had been grazed – I hadn't taken it in before. There was dung about the place: he'd been there a while. I couldn't make out anything inside: it was black as sloes. They shouted at me to get back. What were they all so scared of? One of them lobbed in a stone and ran back quickly. They were all oddly agitated. The horse snorted and stamped his feet. I heard him moving around: it sounded as though there were a few of them in there. Ali threw in another stone, went to the entrance, brandished his stick, shouted at the top of his voice and shot inside. Suleiman winked at me. What was he saying? Yildiz, still near the cave entrance, giggled nervously. A terrific din broke out: I heard running, stamping hooves. A man shouted, somewhere between courage and fright. A thwack of stick on hide. Yildiz shouted at me to get back. Suddenly, a wild horse, ears flat against his head, dazzled, came plunging out into the clearing. He went for the first man he saw. No wonder these blokes had been so cagey. Yildiz was his target. He made a break for it over the rocks at full tilt with the horse right on his heels. Then he fell. The horse switched his attention to us two, standing in the open in the middle of the plateau. He came back at a speed straight for me. I'd never heard of this sort of thing, and it wasn't easy running on that stuff, but that horse had it off to a tee. I felt there was something loony about this, then took a purler into the rock, just like Yildiz.

Back on the clearing Suleiman was shouting and yelling. The horse spun back at him, then another one was flushed out from the cave: a mare, just as crazy. For a moment they prowled, arching necks, snorting. They came to an uneasy halt on the grass. This was their patch: we were the intruders. There was a tense and short-fused respite – prickly.

'Beş yuz bin lira!' Suleiman shouted. He'd given me a price, 500,000 lira: £400-odd. I wasn't sure that was what I wanted. Ali threw me the head collar. Surely they didn't expect me to grab one? They pointed at the stallion.

'At guzel!' they said – beautiful horse. He was. Just not quite 'one hundred per cent traffic, box, clip, shoe, perfect gentleman' that's all. I did what I was told. Stole up to him just as quietly as I could. The mare watched me closely, blowing a warning snort, turned her back end on me, giving me bad jitters. The stallion looked like he aimed to kill.

Now I don't pretend to be much of a horseman, and the next step took a bit of courage. Being by profession a country bumpkin, I know to go gently with skittish livestock. With the head collar in my right hand, I crept up on these edgy young horses at snail's pace. I got close to the mare: she must have heard my heart thumping. My friends nodded, signalling me to creep up on the stallion, pop the head collar on. Just like that. I tried.

I felt the wind of a hoof just past my right ear, saw the underbelly of one of them in a cloud of dust, flash of teeth, and a horse turn sharp on his hindquarters. I remember slinging the head collar at him and bolting downhill. The others scattered across the hillside. I didn't stop until I reached the shore. They joined me, tense and light headed, all lit up from the thrill. The two horses loped back up. Suleiman grinned. 'Iki yuz bin lira!' The price had gone down to 200,000.

Some horse that young stallion. Not a chance of getting near him, never mind riding him. If I had a glass, I would have toasted him, and he whinnied his victory all over us. Him up there, tangled, windblown, ferocious. Small wonder the mare had fallen for him. They'd stay up there breeding savage little horses. No one would ever ride them, or put them in a cart. I'm glad there are animals like that. It's good that blood comes savage sometimes: it makes you remember nature occasionally aims to keep things that way.

But that was it. I'd looked at all the horses in Kiskalessi. Now there was nothing to go along the coast with after my borrowed horses from Tarsus. I could have gone east to look for horses, on the Syrian border. But then I reckoned it was going to take nine months to get to England on horseback anyway, and I didn't want to be in the Alps in October. Going east was the wrong way. Nor did I have somebody else's money: it was mine, and it was limited.

I had been in Turkey about three weeks and had looked for horses first in Adana, helped by Suna Caglayan, my only contact. She had been secretary to a chum of mine who had worked in Turkey a few years before. Suna took me round all the horses in Adana, Tarsus, Mersin as far as Kozan. I'd ridden dozens. She thought the idea of riding to England perfectly stupid, and said so. 'Why go on a horse? It'll take months! Why not go in a Porsche, like everybody else, you'll do it in a week.' I never really got my reasons through to her. Nor me. Now I was here, and still hadn't got one.

My local friends had been patient with me because I didn't know what I wanted anyway. I hadn't tackled a long trip before. Other than some advice in England about buying a horse with a leg on each corner, I didn't have a lot to go on, beyond plain hunch. Displaying ignorance can be gruelling at the best of times, but not being able to express your intentions as well doesn't exactly clear the picture.

I thought I really needed a biggish horse. With all my equipment I was packing just short of seventeen stone. I had a long distance saddle, canvas saddlebags, two cotton head collar bridles, a groundsheet, bedroll, army leather panniers mounted on the front of the saddle, an ex-army leather jerkin belonging to a friend, a Ghurka felt hat I bought in Swansea for two quid, a pair of leather chaps which doubled as a pillow at night and a long tether rope for the horse. On top, I carried a grip full of medicines, a couple of books, green oils, cornucrescine, hoof picks and other bits my vet John Killingbeck had supplied, together with some remark about working for a living.

It was too much. 'Twice the money and half the kit,' I'd read dozens of times: it pulled my arms off every time I had to lug the stuff about. As to the ride: it was a whim. You only regret the things you don't do – up to a point. I had a little cash and would sooner spend it on something like this than all the faddling unit trusts you could chuck at me. My route was equally sketchy. By track, path and any other means barring tarmac, towards England, or more accurately, Wales. For navigation, I had a 'compass – military-marching 1939' bought in a junk shop, probably duff. That, and a tourist map of a part of Turkey I wasn't in. I spoke pidgin French, a dollop of childhood Swahili and a handful of Arabic, not worth a light in Turkey.

My first obstacle was an appalling winter which blighted my chances of going anywhere anyhow. Now it was March, spring was moving and I was horseless. I couldn't think what my next move would be.

I just had to go on looking. I had asked everyone in the whole area about horses. They began to call me 'Teşekkür – yok', meaning 'thank you – no' since that was all I ever seemed to say when looking at horses. Abashed as I was, that robbed me of any confidence that remained.

Late in the afternoon I went down to the beach and threw pebbles into the sea. There were no other tourists. Most things were still closed down for the winter. I'd been pretty lucky to get a room there – plain and simple with good Turkish cooking. To my mind, that's amongst the world's best, and a price to suit.

At dusk, I walked into a higher part of the village on the main road. In an empty café, a blind man was drinking tea. I had seen him there before. He was the only person in the place I hadn't talked to. I sat down. To pass the time, I said 'Marhaba', thinking thereafter it would be a one sided conversation. That was most of my Turkish used up. Or I could use the pocket dictionary nouns-only technique. It drives you mad in quarter of an hour. Every word has to be dragged painfully out of this minutely printed piece of work which needed a search light and microscope to read. Guaranteed to pull the most challenging conversation down to turgid banality. My grammarless nouns-only Turkish could clear a room in minutes.

'Marhaba,' ('Hello') I said.

To my astonishment, he answered in English. For a moment I wondered if he were nouns-only. I prepared myself for an exceedingly strenuous following few minutes.

His face bore no expression. He gave no hint of his next move. His next remark stumped me.

'I know where you can find a horse.'

No one had spoken to me in English since I had been with Suna. I wasn't sure if he had actually said it, or if I was going a bit soft in the head. I hadn't spoken to him before, obviously he hadn't seen me, and now he, a blind man, was going to sort it all out.

'You speak English,' I said, immediately wishing I hadn't.

Rubbing it in, he didn't answer. It was my turn.

'How do you know I want a horse?' It came out in fits and starts. 'Everyone knows.' He sighed, making me feel worse. I was glad he couldn't see me crawling up the wall.

'Yes,' I managed, 'I've looked at dozens but can't find the one I want.'

'If you come here at this time tomorrow, I have a friend who will take you to the gypsies. They'll find one for you.'

This simple assurance put new lead in my pencil. He was very likeable. It was good to converse with someone freely. I spent the rest of the evening in his company. His name was Adil Altinkaya, blind from birth. Only when I talked to him did I realise how much we, the sighted, rely on aids to memory, unreliable at that. Not once did he forget my name or ever mispronounce it, although I mangled his several times. He fully recalled my comments to him, gently pointing out my own contradictions.

He spoke of his own quiet philosophy of life, and how the handicapped in Turkey suffer. He spoke of the appalling misery in Adana, wretchedly maimed beggars, men with no limbs at all wheeled daily to the roadside in boxes, propped up behind, forced to sit there in silence as the traffic went by. For his own disability, he didn't give a fig.

He talked of mathematics, history, stars and religion. He knew Christian doctrine, philosophy and could quote from the very book I carried, *The Fusus*, by Muhyiddin Ibn 'Arabi, which he understood – I didn't. He spoke of Islamic mysticism, the whirling dervishes of Konya, of Mevlana Jaleddin Rumi. 'If a man is happy, it is because he has provided happiness to someone else,' he was quoting Mevlana. 'If he is miserable, it is because he had made someone else unhappy. God exists in every particle of nature, and a human being is a mirror of Him.'

Mevlana was more broad-minded than many of our teachers today. 'Come again' Mevlana said 'come again whoever you are, come again whether you are non-Muslim, pagan, Zoroastran or Christian . . . come again, though you have broken your vow a thousand times.'

He was fascinating to listen to, so much of it talk I had not heard before. The wonder of it was that he had not read a word of it. The whole of the next day I spent looking forward to the evening: I've never known a longer wait. Walking all over Kiskalessi, through groves of pine, along cliff tops, through unmarked, defaced, overthrown sarcophagi, I was intrigued by the Turkish landscape and its history. St Paul had come from Tarsus, not far away, and near by, he is reputed to have made his first convert, St Ayatekla, who was denounced as a Christian. Lions wouldn't eat her, flames wouldn't burn her, so the story goes, and she died in Iasuria.

Along this coastline Alexander's armies moved, Crusaders from the north, armies from the east, Parthians, Persians, the traffic of the Romans. Each left a mark, carving their culture into the stone as they went, leaving images of their gods, knocked faceless by the Selçuks.

By nightfall, I sat waiting for Adil, looking out over the castle. I saw him appear with Tahsin, his friend. We were introduced. Adil acted as interpreter. Tahsin asked the right questions. What kind of horses? How tall? Did I want an Arab? How much could I afford? Questions not asked before. He told me that I would be unlikely to find horses where we were. Either I should have to go east, or much further west. I told him that east was out of the question, and anyway, he said I should have to pay a high price for a good horse on the Syrian border. He said he would take me to the gypsies, they would know what was about and where. I would then have to follow their advice. Agreeing, we left the çay shop, picked up my kit, chucked it in the back of his truck. Adil and I squeezed into the front seat alongside him, and we drove through gathering darkness. I liked Tahsin. He was open and no messing. A welcome change from the kind of character I had been accustomed to dealing with. They had all been far more interested in their side of the deal than mine. When things are like that, you don't deal. Refreshing to find someone able to understand I was not aiming to pay the most for the least – just the right price for the right horse.

We clattered along dirt roads for a couple of hours, arriving in a small village with a street bazaar. We shuddered to a halt, and a cloud of dust rolled into the headlight beam. Tahsin got out, Adil and I followed. He walked swiftly through the crowds. There was an earthy smell of aromatic herbs and huge fresh vegetables. We walked past butchers' stands, whole carcases hanging on hooks, while behind, calves waited on tethers for their turn. There were stalls of cloth, pots, pans, harness, leather goods and crawling litter. Adil never betrayed his blindness. His quiet confidence astounded me.

There was a loud noisy group of people just beyond the market, around a fire. Some stood, some squatted: all were shouting. As we approached one or two turned round to see who we were. On recognising Tahsin and Adil, they responded in obvious delight.

'Hoş Geldiniz!' they said – welcome. We were jostled up to the fire. Boxes and rugs were dragged out for us to sit on. They crouched round, full of questions, throwing me looks, and grinning black-toothed grins. They were a diverse lot. They were filled with vivacity and energy, immediate and infectious. In their company I felt high, charged. Some of the women were beautiful, with intricately tattooed faces. A striking young girl smiled at me revealing a hideously overgrown upper gum ending in jagged little black teeth. There was a woman with a goitre like a melon, men with only three fingers, no space for more. Grubby, beady-eyed children came to cheek us, mock and laugh. The men were drably dressed, but the women wore bright baggy trousers, richly patterned tight bodices brocaded in gold thread and small tasselled hats. I found them irresistible. I loved their irreverent dash, their explosive emotions, their chancy charisma. They pushed, squeezed, argued, belted each other and gobbed. Someone dropped a chunk of hot fried meat into my hands, and handed round little glasses of tea. Smoke from the fire blew all over us.

The talk got loud, and it sounded to me as if a major punch-up was about to break out. It didn't sound as if anything was going to be resolved. A fat man, called Gengkis leaned forward. He shouted something at Tahsin, then looked at me nodding. Adil leaned toward me.

'You are in luck. Gengkis is going to Istanbul tonight. He'll take you to a place where there are horses. But they all say it's a bad time to buy horses now after the winter. They say you can go to Urfa with them, and then buy a horse in Syria in a month.'

I caught myself thinking hard. What if I just did stay with them? Maybe these people had the very thing I treasured most. What if I just forgot about everything and went with them? Not easy that. You can dream and maybe sometimes have your dreams: I wondered just how much of a prisoner of my upbringing I was. Could I ever fit in with these people? Were there things I would miss more? I don't know to this day if I did the right thing but said I would go with Gengkis.

As we talked, some music struck up in the bazaar. A pipe was playing in a harsh minor key, an arresting sound. The man was playing to another fellow slumped in a chair. He caught everyone's attention. We all fell silent, listening to the sound, lilting, angular, strange. The pace quickened. Adil said it was a send-off – a man was leaving for the army.

His friends had come to wish him goodbye. I guessed the conscript was the man in the chair: the bloke with the crestfallen look, green and miserable out of the mountains off to an army, garrisoned in some place he didn't want to be. He rose: danced to the music. The thing got going, the gypsies started swinging in time, their faces flushed and they caught the mood. Men started clapping, wolf whistling, girls egging them on. Then a boom from a drum, and the rapid chatter of the tambourine gave an easy beat to the wandering note of the pipe, in that crowded dark bazaar. The air was thick with smoke and dust while the man squared the ground in this melancholy dance, like solitaire. A fellow with a fiddle picked up the measure loud and strong in the hurrying night air, and loose-limbed gypsy girls threw themselves into the dance. Their dancing was not self-conscious, awkward and stiff, but full blooded with thrill. Hips rocked, shoulders shook and arms stroked air. A glorious girl with oil-black hair, coiled her way through the dancers, shimmering. The pace sharpened, men shouted, clapped, whistled to ululating voices. They caught each other's passion, in the beat and rhythm while dust rose thick, glowing gold and orange round the whirling dancers.

Children pulled me up to dance, all caught up in movement and rush. A hunk of greasy bread was stuffed into my hands full of chilli and gooey meat: I didn't care, danced with them. When the pace eased off, I slumped back on the bale of rugs, hot and sweaty. They whirled on. It looked like the party had just started. Tahsin came over.

'Haydi gel!' Those words again.

Now what. He pointed to a car coming up to us. A big old Chevy, bulbous, tatty, belching smoke. Gengkis was inside. On the back seat all my luggage – I'd clean forgotten. He shouted. I'd no idea where I was going. I looked for Adil. Everything was happening too fast: I didn't want to go then, I wanted to talk to him more, learn a bit. In the time I'd known him things had got a lot better, taken on a new light. I'd met these crazy gypsies, enjoyed a bit of their lives. Now because of him and Tahsin I was off to get a horse – I'd got plenty to thank the man for.

'Haydi gel!' Gengkis again.

'Adil,' I said, messing it up. My head went empty. No idea how to say it – what to say. He stood in front of me, expressionless, just like when I met him. I thanked him. It sounded terrible. I didn't have anything to give with my thanks: I felt for him in his blindness, yet knew how much it advantaged him over us somehow. I grabbed his hand and felt that surge of emotion that leaves you stuck without words: they're not what you mean to say. But you've said it then: just feels empty. Perhaps I should wait, go with the gypsies? Stay and learn from Adil? Didn't matter a damn if I did or didn't go back to England did it? But I said I would go and there was the car.

'Güle-güle' he said quietly. It's a lovely Turkish expression: it means 'go laughing'.

'Allaha – ismarladik' you say in answer: but I didn't know what it meant.

Gengkis booted the machine into life, and we rumbled away. I waved, hanging out the window, heard them shout 'gule-gulae: saw them held in the glow of the fire, then they were gone.

I can't remember much about the journey. I had no idea of direction, where we were going. Gengkis spoke no English: my Turkish was non-existent. We struggled then gave up. I dozed, thinking about Adil, Tahsin.

Shapes passed us in the darkness. Trees ghosted above, held in the headlights for a moment then vanished. We crossed roads, drove on rough tracks, through valleys, past rocks, I don't know where. I slept some of the time, my head filled again with the whirr of the pipe, the tambourine and the drumming of the midnight wind. I remember going through a dingy deserted town. About three or four kilometres later, in a dark back street the car stopped.

Gengkis got out, knocked on a door. A lamp was lit and a huddled old man answered. My baggage was unloaded. Gengkis refused any payment, just shook my hand, nodded, grinned, drove away.

Watching the rear lights of the car disappear, I didn't know where I was, who I was staying with, and I didn't care. He handed me an oil lamp, showed me to a room with a palliasse on the floor, said goodnight and closed the door. I lay down, watched the lamp's wick draw a shadow dance on the ceiling. I heard a dog bark once.

2

Ahmed Paşa

Between the idea
And the reality
Between the motion
And the act
Falls the shadow

T. S. Eliot

Genghis had driven me to Western Turkey. I found myself near Çal a small market town north of Denizli. It was reputed to have supplied horses to the Ottoman Empire: a promising history. It was a good starting point, giving me a time advantage. I could now count on being in the Alps before the snow. I could buy a horse there, ride down to the sea, where Chumpie – she's my girl – would join me near Bodrum to ride up to the Greek border. It meant two horses. I decided to confine my search for one horse locally, looking out for another on my way down to the coast. That settled, I wandered round Akkent, the village I was in, as the sun came up.

It was poor and shabby. Open drains oozed, supurating into polluted holes where chickens picked. Mangey pariah dogs slunk about, begging scraps– the lot of a dog there was a bad one.

I made my usual enquiries by way of pocket dictionary, drawings and noises, which made me feel like a man setting himself up just to be knocked down. I had no other way. The first horse I was shown was a shrivelled thirteen hand pony: pushed to say whether he was dead or alive: they're tough on their animals. Someone took me to a shed at the top of the village where there was an 'at güzel' – another 'beautiful horse'. The man who owned this 'at güzel' was a type I had met before. I saw the dollar signs revolve in his eyes. He led me off to his horse in a mighty silence, no doubt wondering by how much he could rip me off.

Reaching his place, he'd settled for a figure and disappeared into a foul black shed. I followed him, only to re-emerge retching. No idea what lived in there, but it fairly stank.

He came out leading a very comely young Arab colt, black as a rook, with a white blaze and three white socks. He was exceedingly pretty. 'Beş million lira!' the man hazarded, rapidly cashing in on my look of approval. The little horse jumped about delighted to be out of that shed, and as he danced the man tried to light a cigarette, lost the rope and the colt beat it out of Akkent at full bore hot on the road for Istanbul. There followed a full-scale swearing contest with me as its object. They all bellowed at me. Realising I hadn't been holding the horse anyway and that their abuse was unlikely to encourage a sale, they became all charm, fawning and grinning with black teeth, offers of tea and cigarettes. I told the man his 'at' was 'çok guzel' – very nice – but a two-year-old, unbroken, untried hot-headed Arab, never mind how pretty, was not on. He dropped his price from £4,000 to £600, said I could take him there and then. If I had a lorry, I would have.

The streets then filled with horses of all shapes. Broken down cart horses, mangey little street ponies fit to drop. Every one was headshy: every one had been badly hit about. One or two nice little creatures trotted out, but they were too small. Someone suggested trying Çal market and not being in a financial position to hang about, I did.

Çal is a friendly little market town, surrounded by undulating hills. The farms roundabout produce vegetables, olives, grapes, maize and sunflowers. There's a big raisin industry. It's prosperous by local standards. An unpretentious place catering for the farming community rather than tourists. I liked it. In the town that day, I was like a magnet to iron filings to anyone who wanted to sell a horse. In no time, my search had been extended by a whole gang of helpers seeking out animals on my behalf. The long, the lame, short and shrivelled were paraded in front of me with enthusiastic eulogies of their many talents. Lame street horses, tiny ponies, all 'guaranteed', were trotted, paraded, dragged out protesting, shown bouts of loving attention usually denied them, for the benefit of this empty-headed tourist who would never know better. Every quadruped in Çal was brought to my attention.

But they soon bored of my failure to turn cart horse into cash, dispersing for lunch, a lie down or loaf about. I shared a little fruit with a wretched donkey in the corner of a crumbling building: he refused an apple, but took the orange I offered.

I wondered about buying a camel. I asked. Ten minutes later I was looking at one. She was a whopping great thing with a mountain of luggage on board which looked as if it had been there for centuries. I expect it had. No idea how old she was. She stank. No citronella would keep flies off her. She had a total absence of charm and the filthiest manners, belching vile green bubbles which burst in long oily strands and which she wrapped round my face each time I went near. Not sure how much of that I could stand. I didn't see myself as another Lawrence. I don't know a thing about camels, no idea about the veterinary aspect. She was hideously expensive. And I have to admit, she scared the goolies off me.

Things weren't that rosy. What made it particularly difficult was my inability to express what I wanted, and, having been shown a horse, why I hadn't wanted that one.

I went round the çay shops in Çal, drank a couple of bucketsful of sweet tea, ate stale bread, oily meat, gooey halva, sat in smoky rooms and spent the rest of the night throwing up.

The following day, I tried the horse races I had heard about at Yumurtaşköy, about a hundred kilometres away. A few people were going in a minibus from Çal and I joined them.

There must have been two thousand people at the races. They were all out on the plain surrounding the track, which was about a kilometre round. They had arrived on foot, tractors, lorries, motorcycles, cars, buses, horses and carts. Many of the cart pullers turned out to be competitors themselves who, after the races had to pull their owners back home.

There were Barbs, Arabs, Arab crosses, a few thoroughbreds and one matronly old English mare. They wore an eccentric assortment of tack, from elaborate high Kurdish saddles, to simple cloth things, cavalry saddles with silver chasing and tassles. All horses wore blue Mashallah beads to keep off the evil eye. Most of the tack was held together with bits of string, and the whole event had an air of a wild jamboree rather than a day at the races.

Proceedings started with a prayer as the Imman gave thanks to Allah. The sun climbed steadily in the sky and the plain began to heat. A strong smell of horse, kebab, diesel and dust. Food and drink were sold behind the spectators, but no alcohol.

There were no lavatories. Those who needed to, took a long walk. You had to watch where you were going after a while. The chap who was silly enough to park his tractor a convenient distance from the crowd found that out on his return. I don't know how he got on it. The races were pacing races, that is to say, both legs on the same side of the horse are raised at once. It looks a strain for the horse. It was considered, and still is in some parts, the correct way for a horse to run. I am told it's a comfortable gait; it doesn't look it.

To prevent the horses breaking into a canter they are hobbled, or the riders lean right back pulling hard on the reins, their feet acting as fulcrum in front. It was like this they tore about the track, whooping and yelling as they went, cheered and encouraged by the ecstatic crowd. Great jiggling men on tiny ponies went beetling down through the dust, jackets flapping, cloth caps flying off, hanging in the saddle by the grace of God alone – Him, and the sheer velocity of the horse. They would suddenly come spilling off on corners, cartwheeling into the crowd, who cheered wildly as the riderless pony, now unrestricted in his gait, galloped on to win the race lengths ahead, hot and uncatchable. There was no formal dress. Jockeys wore whatever they turned up in. Some wore stylish leather accordion boots, traditional Turkish cavalry. Others chanced it in sandals, and their trousers worked up their legs with the pacing action of the horses, stripping their calves of hair, rubbing legs raw. Frightened little ponies charged about under their yelling riders. Noses bled from overspent horses. Chestnuts rubbed clean off, and horribly swollen tongues proved cruel horsemanship. Between heats, horses stood around under the midday sun, unhaltered, untended, ridden again and again. The races were concluded by a bareback thoroughbred race, the best event of the day since the horses ran a natural gait, the jockeys good to stay on.

When the day was over, these poor creatures were bundled into unsteady vehicles or back into harness without food, water or a word of praise. It left me feeling rather sick. I hated the cruelty, the lack of compassion. Where was all the goodness Adil had talked about? Why hadn't these people read about their own culture? What of their Prophet Mohammed and how he had exhorted them to care for their animals, that God is well acquainted with how you treat them? Disillusioned, I walked away from the track, the stench of diesel fumes wafting off the hot dry plain, watching exhausted horses whipped as they struggled to draw overloaded carts.

Wasn't I wasting my time? Suddenly I wanted to leave Turkey. I wanted to scream justice. I didn't want to share their lives, their wretched horses, their bus back to Çal. I was appalled by the ignorance, the unthinking brutality, bored of my prison of incomprehension.

Hot and angry, I walked away and glanced into an irrigation channel, saw the spawning life of spring. Tadpoles black as commas squiggled in the warm green water in inky abundance. My anger left me. I wished I was just a frog calling to his lady love in some tepid Turkish stream.

The following day, I decided I was on a loser. I had drawn a blank. I made up my mind to leave when I heard there was a street fair in Çal, where horses were sometimes sold. I thought I might as well pack up my belongings, leave Akkent, take everything back to Çal where I could either take the first bus out, or look at this fair. In any event, I had to pass through Çal, so nothing would be lost. I left my kit in a çay shop, asked about horses. There were none for sale. Someone said it was early, some might arrive later. The bus to Izmir left at 3.30 that afternoon. I had a full day with not much to do in a town which was not much fun.

I felt about as energetic as you can when your world has just caved in. Drank sweet tea, cups of coffee, wandered about like a sheep lost in fog. The street fair was buoyant, good natured and busy. I looked for things to take home: harness, Mashallah beads, cloth, baggy trousers. When you are down the only thing that will pick you up is the thing that has flattened you: ironic. I found nothing. By three o'clock I was waiting for the bus, beaten. A young lad came up to me and introduced himself as Ozün. There was one horse for sale. I didn't know this boy, nor how he knew me. Should I see this horse? Wait for the bus? I had half an hour. He explained where the horse was. I could get there and back in that time. I decided to kill the time. Just one horse.

I bought a bit of fruit in the market for him: they don't give treats to horses in Turkey, can't afford it. I walked down through the stalls, the bags of grain, wheat, barley and oats, through the harness stalls and bric-a-brac. I rounded the last corner, the horse and I saw each other in the same instant. My heart leapt within me and I knew this was the horse I had sought. I knew it at once. He was big. Big for a Turkish horse: 15.2 hands. He was Arab. White. Stallion. He had faults: he had been hit about the legs, had cuts and bruises, a cracked hoof, and he was about as fit as I was: pretty unfit. At least he was road hard. He was being used to pull a cart. I had seen Arabs ploughing in Turkey. He would be traffic-proof.

I asked who owned him. A man stepped forward, introduced himself as Ahmed Zohran, a decent looking bloke, with a droopy moustache and floppy black hair. I asked to take off the breeching so I could see the horse clearly. Under the saddle pad he had a spine sore – not too serious. He led him out of the shafts, walked him away, turned, trotted him back.

The horse floated in front of me as only an Arab can. He was light-stepped and proud. Held his head up, tail high. He danced like a unicorn: this was some horse. I wanted to ride him, try his paces. No question of a field or school and no saddle. Ahmed Zohran wanted an answer. I couldn't afford to lose this one.

The man looked anxious. The horse was a stallion used to harness not saddle work: he'd never been ridden. He was twelve or so. Too old to teach new tricks? Something said 'Ride' and I was legged up. He moved smoothly. He knew nothing. He had no idea of leg instruction. He was only just controllable on the bit. He sort of neck-reined. But he felt right. Could I afford him?

'How much?'

I thought he said 500,000 lira. I could. I wrote it in the dust at the horses feet. He crossed it out. Damn! I must have misunderstood. To my surprise, he wrote 350,000 lira in the dust. I was so overwhelmed, I crossed it out and wrote 300,000 We settled on 325,000. About £270. Not a word was said but the deal was done. Took my hand, shook it, spreading his arms in a gesture of ownership passing, his horse Ahmed Paşa was mine.

I gave the horse the fruit. He refused the apple, but took the orange. I could scarcely believe what had happened. Now what? Ahmed Zohran wanted his money. He expected me to take delivery of the horse straightaway. Befuddled with all the unexpected chain of events, I tore off to the bank, which was shut. They opened it, cashed my traveller's cheque, and I gave him the lira. Then had to go to the belidiye – municipality – to register the horse, otherwise without a receipt, I could stand to lose the horse.

It was getting late. The sun was already low in the sky. I hadn't made any plans and had no idea what would happen next and ran round like a decapitated hen. Someone gave me a cup of tea which I poured straight down my chest. Scalding. I had a headful of agonising questions. Would the saddle fit? Would the head collar bridle fit? What if he dies in the morning? Where am I going? After all, I planned to ride to England, but where did I actually go from here? Step one? What if he has some unbelievably horrible vice? He's never been ridden! Was I just tossing money away? No question of vets there either. Maybe he had some dreadful Turkish disease, galloping horse-rot? The list went on. My anxiety grew.

By 5.30 I was standing beside him with all my kit. I shook with apprehension. A gang of onlookers didn't help. What on earth had I done? I put the head collar bridle on; it fitted. It was a copy of a nineteenth century cavalry piece, and fully adjustable, but it went up to the last hole. Phew! So far, so good. I eased the snaffle into his mouth, kinder than the mean thing he had been wearing. Now for the saddle. I couldn't bring myself to try it on him. I wormed him instead. Oiled his hooves, dressed his spine sore, checked his shoes. He had bad manners. Tough. What if the saddle didn't fit? I could hardly just ring up Athene English in Hay-on-Wye and get another. I was definitely funking it. I sorted out the medicines. I packed the saddlebags, took everything out of the grip and looked at the huge pile of stuff I was carrying. It was ridiculous. Too much! Started giving things away, like Oxfam hand-outs. Eager hands came forward. Did I want the saddle? What about those green bags? That rope? I was getting in a twitch. I had to do it. I bunged on the numnah, closed my eyes, prayed hard as I lowered the saddle onto his back. It fitted, three fingers clear. Fair a fit as any made to measure. I

19

slung the saddlebags on the D rings, lashed on the bedroll, tied on the panniers and looped the tethers.

I led Ahmed Paşa away from where he stood, when a man appeared from nowhere with an offer of feed for the horse. We followed him to the top of the town where in the street Ahmed Paşa got a light feed of oats, barley and saman – traditional horse food of chopped hay and straw. Ozün appeared again, insisting I eat. I was too wound up. Nevertheless, he took me to a friend's house, forced a salad on me. He asked me what I planned to do: he gave me space, time to think. I still had too much kit. The saddlebags were bulky, uneven. I would have to prune things down tighter.

I decided to make for an old mill I had seen in the distance, on the river Menderes a few days before. It was in the right general direction, about two hours ride. The people would probably help, glad of a sudden windfall by way of healthy cash payment. I felt high, like chucking money around.

Back at the horse, I gave Ozün two pairs of cotton jodhpurs, spare leathers, two shirts, my book on Gurdjieff – dear to my heart though I had no idea what it was about – and my bundle was reduced. I had what I stood in plus a spare shirt, a few medicines, sleeping bag, grooming kit, liniments, citronella. I was ready. At 6.30, perhaps too soon after his meal, I mounted Ahmed Paşa and rode him out of Çal.

There was barely an hour's sunlight left. Children ran alongside rolling steel hoops, people shouted 'gule-gula cowboy!' The sun gold threaded Ahmed Paşa's mane. I waved to everybody, everything. We were on our way.

Uncertain of his rider, Ahmed Paşa high stepped, arching his neck. I felt like a Rajah on an elephant. He trotted high, a little unsteady. I was not sure if I was in control, about to be pitched off or what. We were making good time. Be at the mill in two hours easy.

The sun set in picture book colours, edging the hills pink and silver. Then night fell in one cold drop. Stars clung frostily in the endless black sky and Ahmed Paşa stopped dead in his tracks.

Not for love or bribes would he budge. I urged him on: he refused. I dismounted to lead him: he wouldn't have it. He looked back forlorn to the twinkling lights of Çal, whinnied a lonely whine.

I had taken him away from all he knew. He had spent his life in Çal and never been further than this. Certainly never with a stranger speaking no known tongue. His work was in the safety of the town. At a stroke, I had robbed him of his stabled security, led him alone into the hobgoblin night, and he wasn't going. I wouldn't hit him: never a good way to treat a horse. He wouldn't be ridden or led, all I could do was blindfold him. A horse will follow anywhere in a blindfold – if you can get it on.

Anxious moments as I struggled to tie my jersey over his eyes. I got the knot and the jersey secure, then on we trod like Christian and Valiant for Truth, blind, as ever. I circled him a few times to confound his direction. If he got away, he wouldn't know where to run.

When the lights of Çal disappeared, alone in complete darkness, I took the blindfold off. He winced in fear: I heard his bones rattling. There was nothing there. Just the hollow empty night, sighing wind and eerie rustle in crowded thicket.

I could see the picture building up in his mind. Things had taken a bad turn for the worse. Got stuff piled all over him, sat on, torn away from home without so much as a by-your-leave, tricked by blindfold and now in the deep of night there was nothing between him and the Great Horse Lucifer himself! That, and no offer of dinner. I felt the full weight of that lot. Would I ever gain his trust? Would he ever get to like me?

Then we seemed to be going in the wrong direction. What were we doing messing around in the middle of the night? Compasses are useless in the dark. Definitely going in the wrong direction. Then just as I was certain we were, I heard water, running water. We were near the river: we were going in the right direction after all. Help would be near. I looked out for a light. If I saw a light I'd go for it. No light.

Then I saw the outline of a building. It looked pretty dark. I called out.

'Is anybody there?'

Like *The Traveller*, no one answered.

'Hello! Merhaba!'

Silence surged softly... the place was abandoned. Damn! Why hadn't I realised it was abandoned? Why hadn't I had the sense to check it out first, get a taxi a few days ago? Hell, I didn't know I was going to be there in the middle of the night with a terrified horse! Why wasn't I properly sorted out?

No question of food there. No shelter, no stable, no welcoming bright little fire. No nothing. Just this clammy air. Huge creepy place. I led the horse into the courtyard, and all round, grey obscure buildings raised grim ugly heads. It would have to do for the night. We would have to stay. No blasted alternative. Didn't know where we were, no idea of how to get back or the foggiest notion of where the next village was. Just have to roll out my sleeping bag against one of these horrible walls, tether the horse and he could graze. On what? No grass.

I could just make out the whites of his eyes. He was inches from real terror. Tried to calm him, catching the unsteadiness of my own voice. His breath became short, sharp, steamy. He was freaking me out. He was shivering. What was the matter?

I tethered him to a tree on a short rope, unsaddled him, took the sleeping bag off, and lay it down against a wall. A dead branch like a fleshless talon clawed the air over my head. My heart thumped. What was it with this place? Rustling, indistinguishable noises came from all round, just audible through the roaring water. It was loud. Why did it make such a din?

Ahmed Paşa blew a thin frightened sound. Something dreadful scuttled away beneath my feet. The air grew damper, intense, cold, mischievous, black. What a dreadful place. Tried to talk myself out of it. It looked all right in the day: warm, summery. But now, we'd been tricked. A djinn! That was it! And darkness crouched in there, a living thing.

Ahmed Paşa jumped. I jumped. Another dismembered sound. The water raged louder, writhing, frothing. I paced up and down. What could we do? My heart was bursting in my chest. What was the matter with me?

On my very first night I'd made a howling mess of it! The horse was scared clean out of his wits, so was I, we had nothing to eat, nowhere to sleep and had wound up in this hell hole. Branches screwed upward, something vast plunged in the water, and that was enough.

I hurled on the saddle, bridled and packed him, tossed on the bags, strapped on the bedroll, vaulted straight on him, cut through the tethers and bolted! Phantoms chased us, djinn shooed us - we were tearing headlong over rocky ground. Pitch black, but barely discernible paths opened up for us and like a beacon a distant light shone brilliant. We made for it just as fast as his feet would go. I heard him panting, gasping for air and we danced wild with relief into a lit village square at eleven that night.

I slid off in a pool of sweat. His sides heaved, I loosened the girth. Men quickly surrounded us, pouring out of the çay shop, houses, astonished to find a half frenzied foreigner in their midst on a boiling hot stallion in the middle of the night.

Kind hands took the tack. The crowd patted his panic away. We were led to a stable, thick in old straw where he rolled in ecstasy and was fed a meal fit for Pegasus himself.

I rubbed him down until the sweat was dry and he was calm. Gazed at him. If he hadn't been ridden before, he had now, and given some account of himself. In the dark of that stable I knew no other horse would do: this was the one I had come to find. I wondered what he thought of me.

I was taken to the çay shop where again, with my dictionary, I struggled to explain why I was there, where I was going, the fearful place from which we had come. Then I was taken to a farmer who fed me bread, olives, eggs and tea. It was a feast: I'd expected to go hungry that night.

Their welcome was overwhelming and they bore out to a letter all that I had heard about Turkish hospitality. They pressed into my hands a barrel of goodwill and set a pattern that lasted until I reached the shores of Normandy.

3

Villagers

For the gods oft take animal form to spy on men, and of their pleasantries, or evil, make design to profit or plague them.

Yemajar Mesej

The hubristic shrill of a posse of cockerels drowned the cries of the morning muezzin and dawn crashed blaring into my head, jostling me awake from a contorted dream.

I'd barely slept a wink anyway because of this revolving dog. He'd gone round and round yapping a three beat monotone, fading as he reached the far end of the village. Then back again. This idiotic yelp drove me into psychotic frenzy, inches from murder. Now, as I was drifting off, this bunch of cockerels crowed their heads off, the man in the mosque yelled his head off and I was exhausted from the late demonic night. There was a long way to go with my new horse and I lay there, feeling fresh as a fag end.

I looked at my watch: five thirty. No point in staying where I was, so I grubbed about for my clothes and slipped out to feed Ahmed Paşa. It was lighter outside, the sun rising dim, red, hot. Men were scuttling their buttoning way to the mosque. Smoke from early morning fires swirled in the chilly air.

I passed the cockerels, strutting about like some half witted brass band after a night on the booze, trumpeting wild vibratos with blazing heads. Ahmed Paşa was in an effulgent frame of mind, much taken by the novelty of his surroundings. He whickered a genial greeting, more particularly at his breakfast than at me. I poured the oats into his trough and watched him eat. He chewed slowly, drooling in myopic satisfaction, accenting his gluttony with a lazy pink erection. Bit of a lad, my travelling companion.

I groomed him, gave the saddlery a quick check over. None of it had worn holes in him, seemed to fit well. But I begrudged having the saddlebags: spiteful things: I didn't like them. There was nothing I could do about them so I left Ahmed Paşa to his breakfast and went off to find mine.

It was lighter. I could see the village, piles of wood, shacks and little cottages dotted about. I couldn't see the mill from the night before, nor quite work out where we had come from. There was the mosque with its squat minaret where the muezzin had just done all his shouting. No sign of the revolving dog. Must have gone to earth: or someone cudgelled him.

I ate bread, eggs and honey again with my cheery hosts, who had obviously slept soundly, unaware of the dog. We grappled for conversation: nouns-only. There's a limit to how much of that you can inflict on people, let alone how little the brain can stand. Within the hour, Ahmed Paşa was saddled and packed, all set to go.

I offered a few thousand lira for my keep and livery. They refused. 'This is Islam,' and 'Siz Yolcu,'– you, a traveller. Me, the tourist. I looked for something to give, some keepsake. I had nothing but my camera – the answer.

They lined themselves up in grand pose, one minute like a party of buffalo hunters, the next, stern and tight lipped with noble-brow-staring-profound-about-to-do-great-deeds looks. I snapped a dozen photographs, promising to send them prints – I did.

When the pantomime was over, I mounted Ahmed Paşa a bundle of nerves, expecting him to do something dreadful. Someone shoved a bag of raisins into the saddlebags. We strolled out of Yukarişkoy with children running alongside. I waved to everyone.

'Güle-güle!' they shouted.

'Kwa-heri!' I answered in Swahili.

Once out of the village we emerged into a broad, rough landscape arcing away in a long sweep upward to imposing peaks. The scale was impressive. Daunting. I knew how Odysseus had felt when he saw Scylla and Charybdis: the odds looked grim.

Full of apprehension, we sallied forth with slackened step. The country all about was forbiddingly proportioned. None of your nice cosy

Welsh hills. I eyed the rock for the best route, while Ahmed Paşa cast about for something to funk at, wishing to end the whole business there and then. He lit on an advancing figure and up went the alarm. Ears pricked he gave a thin snort, losing his nerve by degrees, moving away in a half pass to the right. The figure, a shepherd, three parts sheep himself, crouched shiftily, scrutinising us with equal suspicion. He crabbed away to the left, Ahmed Paşa giving him a hard look, checked his pace and turned to make a doughty bolt for home. I caught him in time, jumped off and blindfolded him again. The shepherd disappeared in amongst his sheep, remaining indistinguishable.

I was bugged that my plans for an early morning's hack across the mountain had been brought to such a swift close by an agoraphobic horse.

The thought hit me like a train.

Agoraphobia! It was the second time in so many days the horse had given up outside a village. Was he genuinely agoraphobic? Do you get horses like that? Was this his particular bête noire, which for me was the worst possible sort? I could put up with kicking, biting, bad behaviour, but over a phobia I was powerless. The only idiot in the world who had an agoraphobic horse, and daft enough to buy one. No wonder he was cheap. And I was planning to take him on thousands of miles of ride.

There was no alternative other than test the theory. What better then than walk him to the top of the mountain in a blindfold where I would find out if his problem were real, in which case he would go berserk; or imaginary, in which case he would not. I set myself to the job and we went scrambling, stumbling up this pathless incline. I wondered if Alexander had had to blindfold any of his horses. History would hardly have recorded that. I bet he did. I bet he had sweat with revolving dogs, cockerels, let alone people actually attacking him, throwing things. I expected that was a thrill I had yet to come.

I was worried about the wisdom of this experiment with Ahmed Paşa. Wasn't it cruel to lead a horse quite so far in a blindfold? What happens if he does go berserk? Just how berserk is berserk? Then what? No one would want to buy a mad horse. I had. Maybe I would spend the rest of the summer running over the mountains trying to retrieve my baggage from The Crazy White Horse of Çal? Perhaps I would have to ride him all the way to England in a blindfold? There was definitely something wrong with that plan.

Torn with misgivings, up we went. The climb was rough and steep. Pestered by doodlebug-sized horse flies, the sun hot in a clear sky. I talked to him all the way, encouraging him. I felt for him in his blindfold, but dare not take it off for fear of a mad dash downhill. He followed like a lamb, trusting completely.

On the top, I circled him in figures of eight trying to confuse his direction. Ever so gently, fearing the worst, I took the blindfold off. He stood blinking, panting, dazzled. I clutched the reins expecting to be galloped off my feet and felt like Buster Keaton holding a sizzling bomb at arm's length, waiting for the bang. Like Buster, I didn't know how big the bang would be. Maybe Ahmed Paşa would just flake out from sheer fright? He stood stock still. Gazing. I took a firmer grip on the reins, tensed against the imminent lunge. His jaw dropped, he relaxed, eyes nearly out of their sockets. For a moment I thought he was dying. But he wasn't. He was awestruck. Following his stare, I looked out. We were high.

Way below us the great long plains of Anatolia stretched out in marvellous tapestry, sequinned with pearl white houses, oyster shell towns, silver threaded by the wandering river Menderes, its banks of grey-green poplars all sparkling in the dewy morning light. He gazed on, spellbound by this glorious tableau. Relief washed over me. I breathed out my thanks. He was fine. I stroked the soft hair on his neck, sharing the *'keyif'* – the delight of the moment for its own sake. When he had done, we turned, suffuse with the rhapsody, and walked on.

From that moment he walked forward confidently, never looking back wistfully for a long-gone home. Whatever imaginings had shaded his mind with apprehension had been completely removed by the spell of some moment just past. Free from these fetters, he whinnied his release to the high world we moved in.

For hours we picked our way through the naked mountains, stopping here to adjust the saddlebags, pulling up there to drink from brooks. At midday, we rested in a pretty spot, where a stream ran beneath willows in a warm green valley. I unsaddled him, putting him on the long tether, with no idea if he had been on a long line before. Attaching it to his head collar, I looked into his dark eyes, stroked his muzzle.

'Here I am with a beautiful white stallion alone on a mountain in Turkey.' A dream come true: a precious moment.

I let him run to the end of his rope. It pulled him up short. I doubted if he had been tied by a head collar before: more likely by the foot. He tried a run on the rope again. Then he knew its length.

We shared the raisins, he broke away to graze. I stripped, bathed along with all the frogs in the stream, fell asleep in the sun. In the afternoon after our break we continued our way through high empty passes, hills blown with the strong smell of pine. I fought the saddlebags, pulling them this way and that, adjusted them, levelled the load a dozen times.

The afternoon wore on, the light waned. Black clouds of evening smudged the short horizon, the sun dipped in a perfect day's sky. Darkness swirled in valleys below us. Nothing around but the empty mountain, patches of snow. The distant mew of eagles going to roost and my anxiety grew with the failing light. We fumbled through gloomy dusk. With something not unlike despair, we scrambled up a hill, down into a dry valley, skirted another hilltop and as if by magic, found a path that led us toward sheep bells, and barking dogs. A sad little village about four miles further on.

We walked through a deserted street, past decaying stone cottages, propped up by columns, some by cut quoin stones, signs of a noble ancestry – there were no other clues. A village lost in time. No electricity: no vehicles: no road greater than the one we were on.

I had found another abandoned village – seemed to have a knack for it. I swore. And a man slipped out of a shadow, like a gecko. Hair prickled on my neck. 'Going to be done in,' I thought. Good time to do it. I was dog tired, hungry and aching, in charge of an equally tired and hungry horse. Neither of us was likely to put up much of a scrap.

The man loomed out of the darkness, walked slowly towards us, glued in our tracks. We both watched him. Couldn't see his face: wondered if he had one.

'Merhaba,' he said in a low voice. A fag glowed in the dark.

'Merhaba,' I answered.

There was a pause: he stopped in the road: I could only see his outline: I got ready to spring on Ahmed Paşa and bolt.

'Nasilsiniz arkadaş?' he said, and I knew we were safe. 'How are you, my friend?' he had asked.

He led us to the mukhtar – the village chief – who lived in a higher part of the place in no grand style. His cottage was surrounded by rough lean-tos. A strong smell of sheep and goats. Water trickled into an old stone trough. He pointed to one of the lean-tos and by candlelight, led Ahmed Paşa in. He tipped a full basket of saman into a wooden trough and Ahmed Paşa ate greedily, watched by a little black donkey, goats and chickens.

A pretty little girl in a headscarf and baggy trousers that all the women wear, led me to the water trough, giving me a knotty bundle of herbs to wash with. Strange and coarse, giving off a bitter scent, they frothed like soap. She waited, then led me to the mukhtar.

Five of us sat down in a dingy room heated by an old wood burning stove, filling the place with smoke. A meal was provided by an old woman who sat down on the floor behind us, watching. We ate stone ground flat brown bread, eggs, honey, olives, pears and ginger. The men eating with me had hard, rugged features. They led lives of subsistence farming, hard manual toil. Their clothes were threadbare, the cottage furniture-less: no possessions. They were not interested in mine. The thing that caught their real attention, was the price I had paid for the horse.

It seemed that whichever way you looked at it, I had been done. That I thought I had a bargain was utterly immaterial. I was a mug. No one but a mug paid that kind of money for a horse. What's more, I didn't know a thing about horses, I had all the wrong stuff, I had no idea how to tie him, that the correct way was by the foot, and why didn't I carry a stick? Why didn't I just give him to them, and get on a bus like a proper tourist?

My difficulties were eased by the opportune arrival of Groucho Marx's double. I was glad he broke up the conversation. He was introduced as the English teacher.

'Hello,' I said, standing up.

'Stand up! Stand up!' he said.

He was definitely Groucho Marx's double.

'I am standing.'

'Stand up! Stand up!' he said, sitting.

This was diverting. Maybe he wanted to find out if I was a man or a mouse, was about to roll a piece of cheese on the floor to see.

'Oh!' I said, twigging, 'You mean sit down!' And as I sat, he stood. He *was* Groucho Marx. I liked him.

He took out a packet of cigarettes, dropped them scattering all over the floor. 'Sorry! Sorry!' he said, 'Stand up!'

We spoke a comparable amount of each other's language, so the mukhtar put us together, finding himself spared the ordeal of having to house some foreign tourist for the night.

Groucho lived in a house on the outskirts of the village in total blackness. He led the way fumbling, apologising for the dark. Once inside his home he lit a candle. I looked about. There was a bed, a table, a few bottles of raki. In the corner a door leading off somewhere, which he pointed to, and very graciously asked, 'You are wash in toilet?'

He gave me a box of matches, pushed me through the door. I lit up to find myself in something not a lot bigger than a cupboard. There was a candle, which I lit, a bar of soap, a jug, a saucepan, a hosepipe in the ceiling and a hole in the floor .It took a moment to work it out. But you could squat, have a shower, wash your teeth and cook your dinner all at the same time in there. An ingenious place. A tremendous range of uses for a room so modestly furnished. Mean times, Groucho was digging around on the other side of the room. He found a bottle of raki. Took great gulps from it, which improved the flow of his English but not its content. He offered me a pull on the bottle. Raki makes me throw up on the spot, so I couldn't help. He seemed relieved, content to steam up his specs all alone.

After a little noisiness, he drank himself into a soporific state, curled up on the floor, hiccupped himself to sleep in booze sodden oblivion. In the morning I fed Ahmed Paşa early, left on the path Groucho showed me leading towards Karahayet, where I planned to spend a few days before going on down to the sea. I thanked him for his hospitality. He nodded: he looked as though he felt as if he had just been exhumed.

The morning air was sharp and fresh as we passed through pine woods. Pools of light hit the forest floor, birds sang in green canopy over us. We followed dirt tracks through trees, meeting other tracks at spidery crossroads, confounding all sense of direction. We branched off on promising looking routes only to end up in fleece-thick undergrowth, having to retrace our steps to another path, on another bearing. We fiddled on in this way all morning. But it was lovely soft riding, the surroundings gentle.

Just on the brow of a hill, the forest ended in a long swing of land, and a path guided us to a homely village. A mob of children ran in front of us, giggling, pointing, hiding in doorways. All gaily dressed, they danced about like butterflies watching Ahmed Paşa and me. He was beginning to react to situations like this, showing off, trotting along in half pass, first one side, then the other, completely of his own accord. He tucked his head in, snorted his flashiest self. Don't suppose anyone had ever given him a second look before. They certainly hadn't me. But both together, they looked at us out there, up in those mountains. Being a bit on the thin side I wasn't sure quite what he looked like with me on him. Nasty suspicion we looked as incongruous and silly as Don Quixote and Rozinante.

We blew through the village snorting and prancing when a midget of an old woman stalked out directly in front of us, slap in our path. She brought Ahmed Paşa to a direct halt.

'Pah!' she shouted.

She grabbed his bridle, shrieked a string of oaths at me. Funny old thing, headscarf pulled down tight on her forehead, all four feet of her in great jolly coloured trousers, yelling her head off. No idea what she was bawling about. She must have been pretty in her day. Now she was toothless, audible, eccentric. She signalled me to get off. I did. As I ran up the stirrup leathers, she led the horse away.

We went round to a stable behind one of the cottages where a classic quantity of grain had been poured into a trough. She started to take all the kit off, still yelling. I was puzzled, didn't know what it meant. Was she lifting my horse off me? Maybe he was a stolen horse in the first place, and I had obliged by riding him straight back home, unaware that he was leading me? All I had done was feed him on what might otherwise have been a hungry trip. I had no clue. Then she turned on her heel, stalked out and with a toss of her head, had me following.

Outside a pretty cottage she pointed to my shoes which, as is the custom, I took off, and followed her inside. It was clean as a pin. Freshly painted walls, blue and red striped kelims on the floor and a cushion with a tray in front of it. A fire crackled brightly in an unsymmetrical hearth where a saucepan bubbled out a delicious whiff of hot spicy soup. She pointed at the cushion. Assuming it set for someone, I dithered. She pushed me into it, together with another tongue lashing. She ladled out a bowl of soup, a chunk of gritty bread, a few olives, and wittered on, not a word intelligible to me.

As I ate, three of her friends came in to stare, as one might gawp at an ape in a cage. I felt exhibited. She pointed at me, then smiled with her arms folded as if to say, 'there, I told you so.' The others nodded. I struggled to my feet for politeness' sake, and they all fell silent, so I sat down again. She came over, patted my head. Felt even more like an exhibit.

Then they left. She became all conspiratorial, talking in whispers, pointing after them, opening her eyes wide, nodding. I nodded. We agreed. She showed me her collection of Roman coins: real ones. She delighted in them, turning them over and over in her hard old hands, holding them up to the light, cleaning them with the sleeve of her jersey. Thrust them deep into her trouser pocket which is where they were going to stay.

Then she bustled me out to the horse. I repacked him, offered her 2,000 lira for my meal, which she snatched, eyes twinkling, pointing to Ahmed Pisa's belly, lest I overlook his feed. A further 1,000 lira secured her pleasure. 'Bir dakika!' ('One minute!') she said, scurrying back into her cottage.

I waited for her, children hanging onto their mother's clothes coyly peeping through sticky fingers. The old girl appeared again in giggles, rocking from side to side. Made me close my eyes, open my hands. The kids shrieked in delight. I did as asked. She dropped something spiky into my palms. Opening my eyes I saw it was a huge scarab beetle. She smacked the back of my hand and he shot upward. He hung fleetingly suspended before taking wing and buzzing off. She watched him closely, unsmiling, with her cheeks drawn in. As soon as he flew, she burst into a wild cackle.

'Çok güzel!' ('Excellent') she tooted and whanged a helicopter of snot into the dust. She handed me a tiny ring, which I still have: it's big enough only for a child and I have no idea of what it is made.

I mounted Ahmed Paşa, who was very full of himself after his unexpected treat, and we trotted away waving, watching her windmilling a farewell behind, and I swear I heard that beetle fly past.

We both felt on top of the world after her delicious grub. I sang right out loud as the horse trotted a willing strong step through that rolling landscape high up there on those windblown hills. We passed a family driving mules carrying faggots. Went through a village surrounded by cultivated fields where horses and tractors ploughed and harrowed, all of whom were courted by Ahmed Paşa's unending challenges and flirts.

Hailed passers by, were salaamed, marhabad, waved to. A wonderful day's ride. The road widened through stony hills and at four o'clock that afternoon, we stood high above Pamukkale, the Cotton Fortress: Hieropolis, to give it its classical name. Karahayet lay below us, five kilometres west of Pamukkale. Beyond, lay Denizli, snug beneath the grand snow-capped mountain range of Ak Daglari, spanning the horizon east to west a granite barrier, square in our path.

4

Over the Mountains to the Sea

The hot springs of Heiropolis have drawn people there for centuries. Founded in 190 BC by Eumenes, King of Pergamon, it lasted until the great earthquake of 1334, when it was abandoned. A sacred city, people enjoyed the healing properties of the waters while others came to die. The realm of Pluto meets the world at this spot. The hillside of Pamukkale – the modern Turkish name, the Cotton Fortress – is a fabulous natural sculpture, having a poetic image of Titan's cotton crop drying in the sun.

It's a fabric of shallow basins fringed with stalactites dropping veils of milky warm water into basins beneath in ever-spreading scallop shapes. The place bristles in historic relic from the Greeks to Seljuk Turks, and great parts of the old city remain: a triumphal arch, huge theatre, baths, columned waterways of travertine stone. Sarcophagi lie all around, once filled with the bodies of those who came for an early form of euthanasia to enter Plutonium, Kingdom of the Dead. Toxic gases seethe in a vaulted underground tunnel in which those who tired of life walked to breathe their last, surrendering their lives to Pluto, reaper of the dead.

Now, in our plastic-coated century, Pamukkale village is geared to tourism. Littered with tackily thrown-up hoardings: carpets, knickknacks, fakes, trinkets, sausages and sandwiches – the stuff of a dollar harvest reaped by the Plutos of our time, and just as deadly.

On the road to Karahayet is the necropolis. For a kilometre or more, crowded sarcophagi, mausolea and funerary monuments of the one-time wealthy lie willy-nilly, ransacked, strange and eerie.

The scent of thyme hangs about, and I passed a young shepherd boy in a great wool coat sitting on a tomb playing a reed flute, as his sheep grazed around him. He was lost to his music, never saw me, but the sound and the place made my senses reel.

The crowd that surrounded us as soon as we arrived in Karahayet were interested only in the price I had paid for Ahmed Paşa. Where we had come from, where we were going, what we needed was of no consequence. I could have been a Martian for all they cared, and if he had arrived on a purple horse with sixteen heads, all they would have asked is how much did he cost.

I was in no mood for this. I lied.

'100,000 lira,' I said thinking it would get them off my back. I was asked if I would sell him for 50,000. Someone said they'd seen a much better one for much less. He was a rotten horse, why didn't I give him to them, get a good one?

It was always a difficult time of day. At your most tired, most hungry, anxious about your night's lodging, food for the horse and a stable, you have also to be at your most charming. It's not an easy marriage. A man took Ahmed Pisa's halter rope to show me how to tie a horse properly. Lashed him to a rusty pole with a couple of good granny knots. One quick tug from Ahmed Paşa, and they seized firm. For people so wise in the ways of the horse – which I was constantly told – they showed a lamentable lack of common sense. I could have crowned that man.

I struggled to undo the rope and asked for sarman for the horse. No one moved. I tried again. Said I was perfectly willing to buy some for a good price. A few of the crowd walked away shaking their heads. Others looked at me with knitted brows, then drifted off in silence. Now what had I done?

I asked a little girl of about ten years old standing near to me. She disappeared arriving back a few minutes later with a large ginger cat. She handed him to me, demanding a thousand lira. No idea what all this was about. 'No thanks darling, sarman,' I said, pointing to the horse's mouth 'Eat.' Her eyebrows shot into the back of her head, snatched back the cat, ran off in tears.

Bewildered, I carried on pulling away at the knots. A young lad perched up on a wall chewing a stick, introduced himself as Orhan. He explained that Ahmed Paşa needed some food. I could have crowned him too. He watched me fight the knots. 'Saman,' he giggled. 'Yok sarman!'

I just heard the difference. He was revealing a secret. I rooted around in the saddlebags for my dictionary. Flipping the pages, I found 'sarman'. It said, 'Huge yellow cat'.

I got the picture. So I had the only cat eating horse in Turkey. No wonder they all pushed off. Orhan fell off the wall, convulsed with laughter, unravelled the knots. Found the whole thing so funny could hardly walk. He led us to his father's pansyon, found Ahmed Paşa a stable, produced oats and saman, took me to my quarters. He adopted me like an English child might adopt a wounded blackbird, treating me just the same. Attended to my needs with constant offers of feed. Ahmed Paşa got the same treatment, which tickled him to the tips of his hooves.

The room I was given was stark in its admirable simplicity. No gadgets, no fuss. Just a bed and a chair, which is what I like. Steam wafted out of an adjoining bathroom where a four foot square red-stained hot spring tub gurgled and popped. I undressed, plunged in. Plunged out again, twice as fast. It was scalding: my skin nearly fell off. I looked for a cold water tap. There wasn't one.

'Takes time to get used to' a fellow guest told me later. The springs at Karahayet ooze out of the ground all over the place, boiling up in red mineral spouts, spewing gallons of hot water everywhere. From the springs the locals have channelled their water supplies for washing, cooking, dyeing and as a natural cure-all. Everyone did look remarkably fit. The trees there grew quickly, and the minerals bleached your hair the colour of a ginger-tom. A Canadian guest, having had eczema all his life, called at Karahayet quite by chance while touring round Turkey on a bicycle. After four days, his problem had left him. 'No longer Monsieur le Crapot!' he said.

Karahayet is spared the razmataz of Pamukkale, being just a bit further off the tourist trail: it caters more for the Turk than foreign tourists, and to my mind, was very much better. It was inexpensive, had no frills, the food was consistently good, and a nice village atmosphere. It was quiet at night: there were no discos, no traffic, no nightclubs. I liked it.

We stayed at Karahayet for four days, which improved Ahmed Paşa's condition visibly. The rest invigorated him, lush grazing added sparkle to his eyes. The only thing he objected to was having to drink hot water. It was the very devil trying to find cold water in that place.

I made him stand in the hot springs, which took a lot of patience. But after a tug of wills, I had him four square. He did an impromptu piaffe as hot sharp bubbles prickled and tickled him in an especially pleasurable equine way. Did wonders for his feet. Loosened his shoes too.

Early in the morning on the fifth day, I fed him a good breakfast, ready to leave by eight o'clock. I had no specific venue in mind. Thought to carry on much the same way as we had arrived – a bit of a hit and miss affair. That was what I liked about it. Should hate to have some organised affair, robbing the whole thing of surprise.

Orhan's father gave me directions for the farrier in Denizli, pointed out a cross-country route that would save us having to go along the main road. At eight o'clock I paid my bills, left a present for Orhan, said goodbye and we were wafted out of Karahayet on a high.

Ahmed Paşa was intrigued with his new role in life and felt much better after expunging a large body of worms. He was becoming prone to bouts of over-confidence and apt to wrestle with his rider and incommodious baggage; he was not always easy to control.

That morning he was in a particularly fresh mood, sniffed the air martially as we waltzed out of Karahayet towards the sharp drop down to Denizli plain. I could see the town in the distance and reckoned it a mere two hours ride. Easy going across flat farmland, three hundred feet or so lower down.

He pulled on, comfortable had it not been so energetic. We went tripping forward somewhere in advance of a walk, not quite a trot, making ground rapidly, in an uncontrolled sort of way. As we approached the crest of the descent, his impulsion increased. I eased him back on the reins. He checked his stride for exactly the length of time I hauled him back. Just as we hit the brink of the slope, he broke into a sharp jog, tucked his head between his knees, yanked me out of the saddle. The saddlebags flapped and pinched adding the spur. We took off.

Ground flashed past beneath in a whirr of dusty green. Wind roared in my ears. I remember being jostled in angry pain, a white mane in my eyes, dust flying, the sharp rattle of hooves clattering over rock, being hit in the face by my own hands. Lost my stirrups, slid to one side, trapped my leg under a saddlebag just as he jumped a rock, dived and flipped me over onto my back. Carted diagonally, upside down, with the reins round the horse's ears, going full pelt over sheet rock downhill. My head was full of crunching noises. I kept biting my tongue. He suddenly jabbed, bounding to a halt, hurling me over his shoulder like a rag doll in a long airborne somersault, pitching me into a spiky little bush, completely winded, unable to breathe.

Bruised, gasping for air I saw him striding towards a mare, the saddlebags grovelling in the dirt under his belly. He roared his love into the dust. I made a fumbling attempt to stop him but it was pointless. It was spring, he was a stallion, she willing and I couldn't breathe. I can't account for that mare and have no idea who owns her. When her time comes, her foal will have built-in underslung saddlebags.

It took me an hour to catch my frenzied horse under the growing heat of the sun. Had he not been so restricted in his movements by the bags round his feet he would have gone a lot further. Hoarse and battered, I righted the whole issue, pulling the saddle from round his heaving loins. I rehung the baggage as he continued his bellowing at his new girl.

Our departure had to be swift enough to leave the mare behind, not so swift to leave me behind. I mounted, which took another half an hour. Once on, we tore off at breakneck speed until he calmed to a difficult trot, shaking the mare off and she broke away to graze. He looked over his shoulder once or twice, shouted something at her. Sounded more a note of conquest than anything subtle.

Heaving a sigh of relief at having off-loaded that problem, I composed myself for a less troublesome ride to Denizli, when an irritating rattle struck up in the saddlebags, nettling my already short-fused senses. I groped about for the source of this noise, but couldn't find it. With each step of the horse, it jiggled. I pretended to ignore it, telling myself it would go away. I whistled, sang, then shouted. Everything tin in there joined in metal clankable concert against me. I cursed the man who invented saddlebags and things tin, pulled the horse to a halt, tore the saddlebags from their moorings, threw them to the ground and kicked them all over Denizli plain. Boiling hot, swearing at the top of my voice, beside myself with fury, I saw my audience of three, standing in a row sharing one long grin between them, underlined by Ahmed Paşa's slow, protracted fart.

How we arrived on the main road five miles short of Denizli was another of the day's insoluble mysteries. Preoccupied with exacting some form of revenge on the saddlebags, I paid no attention to the lorries that came snarling sneezing past us. And, Ahmed Paşa caught up in a world of his own, we moved into Denizli without further incident.

Denizli is a sprawling place, on a crossroads between the western route to Izmir modern culture, and the eastern route to the mountains a culture more slow. It's in transition, somewhere between cart horse and motor vehicle. Filled with the clatter and bang of commerce, buzzing markets and a web of back streets down one of which we steered our way to the farrier. This brought us out unexpectedly in the middle of the town, which revealed another trick from Ahmed Paşa's stock of kaleidoscopic surprises. Each time he caught sight of his own reflection in a shop window, he flung a menacing challenge at this shadowy now-you-see-him-now-you-don't impostor copying his every move. Arching his neck, curling his nostrils, he would canter sideways, while I clung onto the reins to prevent him crashing angrily through plate glass windows onto the terrorised shoppers within. This lethal charade repeated itself until, bored with his opponent's failure to rise to his threats, he switched his attention to the plentiful street horses, yelling his lungs out at all of them, turning a quiet part of the town into a snorting circus, as horribly-insulted ponies champed on their bits in response.

We finally nosed out the farrier, a bun-faced unshaven man, slumped in a chair, clutching a bottle of raki. He had no trade. He had set up shop in a squalid corner of town where it was impossible to hold a horse still. I thought to forget the whole business, have the horse shod elsewhere. The question was, where?

In the absence of any immediate alternative, I asked bun-face to do it. He dragged himself to his feet, and with his assistant – an uncommonly good-looking fellow, reeking of drink and garlic – set about the crappiest piece of farriery I have ever seen. His mate all but turned the horse upside down. People pressed in around in that already airless place, Ahmed Paşa had a nasty attack of the horrors sending the farrier scuttling back against a wall with bloodied knuckles. He mouthed a silent scream, grudgingly took up his tools again and badly fitted four new shoes.

Ahmed Paşa's feet were now in better shape despite all that. His shoes no longer rattled and the farrier hadn't lamed him. I paid the bill, which was 2,800 lira: about £2.

When I asked the best way out of town the crowd all pointed in different directions. We left on a compass bearing, heading for the mountains. Leaving the town, I stopped in a straggling street market to buy some barley and fruit, neither of us having had anything to eat since we had set out that morning. As I made my selection from the wheelbarrow, Ahmed Paşa, following my example, did the same, nuzzling a stack of oranges until he burst one, sending the rest scattering all over the market floor.

I wasn't in the mood for this latest development but had only myself to blame for actually walking into a market with a horse I had encouraged to eat oranges. What with this and that, I had wandered in with an empty head, and was paying for the consequences. I crawled round on hands and knees retrieving the rolling fruit. The proprietor, who until then managed to contain his wrath, broke into a high fury when Ahmed Paşa drooled gooey orange juice over him, dropping dollops of half chewed pith down the fellow's neck. I paid: I paid dearly.

Denizli had been a strain. Costly in every single respect. Drained, I looked for the first bolthole for our night's lodging. When we came to a path leading to a muddy clearing, that was it. We weren't going to budge. I tethered Ahmed Paşa, took all the kit off, dropped it down beside a tree. Fed him his barley, gave him another orange and collapsed into a tangle of uncomfortable roots.

Hungry, angry, lonely and tired I watched shafts of evening sunlight on distant hills. As if by sorcery, the village idiot chanced by, taking the opportunity to try the goofy tourist for a light touch and a photograph. I closed my eyes, praying for his swift demise. He remained. Came towards me, prodded me, asked me to take a photograph of him. There, then, in the plume of darkness, he implored me. Something about him set my very soul on edge. I bore him hard feelings, wished him ill. He sat there, bleary eyed, bunched four foot away, demanding.

Why didn't he just clear off? Couldn't he see I was knackered? Not up to doing a thing, let alone take snaps of a nutter in the dark. I tried to explain. I was short with him. Rude even. But the more he insisted.

41

Beaten, I gave up, packed Ahmed Paşa, led him away cursing from the idiot's torrid insisting.

Nursing a bruised spirit, we set out once more on the road at night. Two miles on, we were taken in by Kemal Başkaya in a village at the foot of the mountains. As I lay on my mattress, warm, no longer hungry, with my horse stabled, I knew the village idiot had been a phantom of my own tired imaginings sent by some kind spirit to chivvy me to the bed where I lay.

Refreshed after a good night's sleep at Kemal's house, we set out across the granite mountains. It was a steady climb, on a track winding through beautiful snow-crested peaks. Every two hours or so, we would find a source of water. Either a trough and spring, or some clear elfin pool. The mountains rose tall, sacred, silent. Choughs curled in the middle air, buzzards quartered and mewed. I wondered about finding our way to Aphrodisiac, city of Aphrodite, away to our right. But the lonely track led us on through the high places. Far behind, white and tiny in the dazzle of the sun, I could see Pamukkale and the great mountains we had crossed.

Huge flocks of goats stripped every bit of grazing up there. I had no food for Ahmed Paşa, so walked, to save his energy. A long walk. We passed a lonely encampment where a man, his wife and child sat huddled from the winds in the awning of a huge black tent, eyeing us in silence as we walked by. Rocks stretched above, chasms fell beside us.

In twilight we walked into Tavaş, a grubby little town in the mountains where I was given a night's stabling for the horse and a hotel bed for me. My room was interesting from an entomological point of view. A wide variety of colourful insects shared my bed. In the ripped hair mattress, many-legged things crawled in itchy profusion among the scurfy grime of the countless unwashed bodies who had slept there before me. The sheets, concealing bugs beneath, were an even sticky grey, marvellous in uniformity of filth. The lavatory – a real Turkish bog – shared the same function as a wash basin. But my grime paled beside the appalling filth in which Ahmed Paşa found himself. It would have killed an English horse. He, however, thoroughly enjoyed it, rolling about in it in high delight. Both of us, in stark contrast to our surroundings, were fed prodigious quantities of the very best. And as became true to each place we stayed in afterwards, someone was always appointed to look after us. Usually a young lad, who would go right out of his way to get us anything we needed.

Tavaş was hardly a pretty town. In fact, it looked as though it had just been bombed. A lot of Turkish towns do, or look as though they are undergoing a long siege. But the people are wonderfully kind the minute you cross their doors, and we were both taken into their lives with a candour that was breath-taking.

We got lice in Tavaş, the pair of us. Ahmed Paşa picked up a bevy of ticks too; he gave them to me. They are odd things, you never feel them getting on and must have an anaesthetised bite. Only after they have gorged themselves on you for a few days do you become conscious of them. Swollen, grey, foul: full of blood. The first time I found a few round my waist, my flesh crept. I got used to them: lice too. It was just another part of rough living.

We spent two weeks wandering around those mountains on the way to the sea. Meandering along on little tracks, watering here, being fed there. Spring gathered apace, the weather warmed and birds sang loud in the air over our heads.

From the ruggedness of the mountains, we wandered onto a plateau where domed wells replaced the pools and springs of the land behind. And the devil winked at us from deep dark wells in the ground. Great sweep wells then replaced the domes, and of these Ahmed Paşa had a psychotic terror. They were huge things, like ballista, with two great shafts of wood, overbalanced on a fulcrum. A container on a long chain attached to the end swung down into the well, and could be pulled up easily on the overbalance. Whenever he saw one of these Ahmed Paşa would leave a hundred yard margin between it and us: we never did get to taste the water from them, having to go thirsty when there were literally dozens of these things all round us.

It was good to walk through the high plateau, through the groves of holm oak, to hear the cuckoo, see little foxes run through flowing almond-groves and hoopoes sweep up from the grass. We stayed in villages in backwater hamlets, where pretty two-storied galleried houses stood banked high up above well-tended crops and fat animals. We stayed in villages wretched in every respect, where people suffered from callouses, open sores and swollen limbs. In some places the land was generous and plentiful. In others mean and hard. Each was reflected in the villages, the people and their animals.

One night, staying in a dark hovel in the company of two women, sitting in the glow of the fire I saw their arms deeply grooved by gnarled flesh, and I wondered if they had known leprosy.

Always the people were kind: always they refused payment and I had to pay by stealth, leaving money in blankets, or shoes to be found long after we were gone. The people accepted life with resignation: for the greater part, they were undynamic in what they did. They had a tendency to react in predictable ways, laughing at exactly the same things, coming up with the same suggestions. They all wore a common uniform. The men: dirty trousers, jackets and flat caps: the women, big baggy colourful trousers, headscarves and cardigans: there was never any variation. There was no room in their lives for eccentricity. But they had winning ways and humour. They were without violence, and inquisitive in a narrow, ignorant way. And ignorance when met head-on is frightening in its brutish refusal to want to understand, comprehend. Many of the people I met could read, though I never saw books. Musical instruments were rare. The men were to be found always in the çay shops, playing backgammon, or some numbers game I never got the hang of. They often mistook me at first for a German, many of them having worked in Germany as guset workers, returning home richer, more bitter men.

Women ran everything, getting on with the realities of life, although it is a male dominated society. The women always made the real decisions (the men would never admit that). I found the women more reliably informed than the men, much easier to deal with, less suspicious and, as it seems to me the world over, far more intelligent.

A lasting impression of the village people in Turkey would be that, for all their faults, which perhaps were the result of their own short-sightedness, quite apart from any political interference, they were genuine, honest and loveable. They met life as they found it, had no aspirations over and above what they expected to find. They had a very real charm and an unquestioned willingness to help, which was something I was to reflect on, admire them for, when later, I met people with many times their resources yet who were unprepared to share even the shadows that were cast in their gardens.

The village Turks lived without sanitation such as we know it in the west and without running water, electricity or any of the luxuries we take for granted. If they washed, they did so in public, so to speak, in the hearth around which the family gathered, where the cooking was done. They wove kelims and carpets of traditional design – a stark contrast to the grey hard lives they chiselled out for themselves. I was there in the spring – I can only guess how hard it must have been in those villages in the winter. They were tough, enduring people, always well mannered. I had heard stories of brutality in Turkey, of violence and bandits. I never saw it. I expect it was confined to towns. I never sought trouble, and I found none.

My relationship with Ahmed Paşa grew too. I spent all day and everyday with him. Riding, walking, sitting and talking to him. We built a little life together up there on those ranges. We depended on one another, seeing in each other symbols of security, someone both of us knew in all this unknown territory around us. Inevitably, I grew to love him, feeling him as much a part of me as my own limbs. I would catch myself gazing at him. Found myself wishing to be in his company to the exclusion of all others. In return, he paid me the reward of allowing me to do anything with him. No one else could.

I don't know if he loved me, how can you tell? But if animals feel things in the same way, and I think they do, they love you in relation to their trust in you directly. Xenophon said that a spiritual relationship builds up between a horse and his rider. I have no reason to doubt him.

5

A Few Sleepless Nights

(8 April: Mugla)
I lay on my back on a square of warm marble gazing into the dome and its perforated honeycomb windows. The bubbles fizzed, popping and soothing. I could hear hot water running from antiquated taps in the ante-chamber adjoining the circular part of the building where I lay. The masseur stirred some soapy warm water, massaged my feet and legs. It was self-indulgent and I loved it. It was a long time since I'd been scrubbed, but he scrubbed me again and again: must have thought I needed it. He showed me two ticks he found in my back. Just like the seven I had found on Ahmed Paşa. Wish he could have had a Turkish bath too.

We arrived on the high ground well above the coast in darkness. A warm seaweed breeze came up from the shore. Couldn't see where the shore ended and the water began, whether the coastline was rocky or offered good grazing. The moon hung above us like a pearl.

We reached Akyaka village at ten thirty, having left Ula at six that morning. It had been one hell of a ride. We had followed the road, and had come down a never-ending zigzag in the dark with no lights, and lorries howling up and down. Now we found ourselves in the sweet scent of orange blossom in this warm place. Ahmed Paşa spent the night in a bungalow with a long sea view: it was rather chic. An improbable stable for a horse, it had been the only offer, its owners accepting the night's occupant as perfectly natural. I put down a few rush mats on the concrete floor for a bed, but he ate them. The last I saw of him that night was looking out of a window to sea with a reflective air, like some old salt eyeing the briny, dreaming up tales to tell over a tot of rum on the boat next day.

Akyaka was a pretty village, full of extraordinarily designed houses, which were white, with red pantile roofs, natural wood verandas and balconies, finished off in an eccentric flourish with an Oriental flavour, the most arresting designs I had seen in Turkey. Each house had a walled garden heaving with flowers thick with scents, the over layer with citrus, a heady bouquet.

I had planned to pass straight on through, but the contrast with the interior was so great I was tempted to stay. It had a more sophisticated feel to it than anywhere else I had been. The sleepiness of the village in the morning sunlight slowed me down. I wrote a few postcards as Ahmed Paşa grazed a daisy-matted verge. While sitting in the post office, I met an English woman who lived there and who introduced herself as Chrissy Adham. She offered grazing for Ahmed Paşa, invited me to a bite of breakfast and so I stayed, glad I did.

She led us down through the village to a small wooded valley, behind an olive grove, along an overgrown path to her cottage, sitting pretty beneath a stand of blue gums, on the edge of a small river. The air was filled with the chatter of sparrows and the watery gargle of frogs. There she lived, all alone, waiting for Selim. He was her husband, of royal descent, who had been working out of the country for fifteen months. Every day, without fail, he would telephone her, and every day, in the post office she awaited his call. The devotion they had for each other was almost childlike: but it was complete and loyal. She must have found it hard. But if she did, she never said so. She was resilient, self-composed.

Chrissy mixed at arm's length with the local people, and had some charming friends who were her intellectual foils. The villagers regarded her with a mixture of surprise and diffidence: surprised that their local Paşa had married a foreigner, diffident in that she was therefore the local grand lady, so to speak.

Her neighbour, an astonishingly ignorant man, set himself up as a chaperone, meanly eyeing her every move, and on my arrival, wanted to know straightaway where I proposed to sleep. She took his rudeness in good faith, telling him plainly that I was just a stranger passing through, that I was staying in a pansyon, and that it was as good for her as it was for me to talk in our own language. But he was a suspicious man, and he hung around.

Chrissy knew a lot about Akyaka, the place the people, the history, the strange micro-climate, the castle of Barbarossa. She knew the gossip too, and she told me about Çesme.

Çesme was a good looking bloke, about twenty-seven years old, and a Kurd. He picked up lonely tourist girls, telling them he was a Cossak. They loved his dark smooth ways, romantic looks, his persuasive charms. He was just a small time gigolo. One day, he met a divorced German girl, talked her into setting him up in business in Marmaris. She was in a vulnerable frame of mind. Being older than him she was flattered by the attentions of this handsome young man seeking his way in the world, lacking only the means.

She agreed to part with 40 million lira – which was nearly £40,000 – for a carpet business, on the understanding it would be a joint venture. The kelims and carpets would be sold in Germany, profits accruing in Marmaris would be split fifty-fifty. People begged her not to do it, not with Çesme. He was rotten, they said, shallow. She ignored them. He had given her a new zest for life, a new outlook and an exciting new business. She fell headlong for her beautiful Cossak lover.

Çesme knew nothing about the carpet business. But he knew Michel, a local lad who had earned himself a reputation for honesty, hard work and a good knowledge of the rug trade. Michel knew the wholesalers, the villagers, where to buy the carpets, at what price and the whole of the marketing chain. What was more important, the wholesalers knew and trusted him. They had never heard of Çesme. It wasn't long before they heard he had the cash. Çesme coaxed Michel away from his job, offering him a share in the new shop. With money hard to come by in Turkey and being attracted by the challenge of setting up a fresh business, Michel saw the opportunity, agreed, and Çesme took him on.

Among his other weaknesses, Çesme was also arrogant. He treated Michel abominably. He made him do everything: paint the shop, clean his shoes, make the tea. Çesme loved it, lorded it over him. When the shop was ready, Çesme told Michel to go and buy the rugs, and he handed over the cash; it made him feel big to handle large sums of money. Michel said he would send back the rugs as he bought them, so the shop could open ready for the tourists in the summer.

He went off east and, good as his word, the rugs arrived. So did the bills. Michel bought 40 million lira's worth of rugs on credit and disappeared with the money. Michel the nice guy.

Then there was Fatima. Like all Turkish girls, her marriage was arranged for her. Just before her wedding she fell for a man from the east, another Kurd, who worked in the timber business. But an arranged betrothal is not so swiftly undone and she married the man her parents had chosen. A few months after the wedding, he found her in the woods with her lover. He shot and killed him.

The judge was a local man, and gave him a lenient sentence: after all, everyone knows Kurds are no good, and after what he'd done the man had it coming to him. Fatima left her husband. She walks around Akyaka now. Chrissy says she's different to the other women and likes her. Fatima was in love and unlike so many Turkish women she knows exactly what that means, and it will never peter out, fade. She had had her own way.

Ahmed Paşa's few days of rest were quickly over. Our stay was at an end. Chrissy had added a different complexion to our adventure, filling in the holes in my own views of the people, of the country. Perhaps it was simply because it came from a woman's point of view and was therefore broader. We men are usually a bit dumb about the way we see things, not as cute as women. Still, better not say too much.

We had a farewell breakfast with her and she gave fresh cut oats to Ahmed Paşa and fresh cut bread to me. And English marmalade – that was something else: that and a cup of instant coffee was a breakfast I shall never forget.

I left my green canvas saddlebags with her and bought a pair of traditional embroidered Turkish saddlebags from a chum of hers in Marmaris. They had a rigid leather panel on the reverse side, and dropped straight down over the saddle without having to be tied. They didn't interfere at all with the horse's movement, were easier to carry, and what's more, they looked magnificent on Ahmed Paşa.

He had cleared a four-foot gate that morning, in pursuit of a flashy young mare, who turned out to be no more than a purulent old camel browsing around in the hedge. His amorous advances were becoming very enthusiastic but the thwarting of his designs never dampened his ardour. He renewed his efforts to secure himself a romance at any cost, in exactly the same way as a lusty young man from Liverpool might feel on a first trip to Majorca in a place full of not-so-bashful young girls, bent on a memorable holiday fling.

It was in this light that Ahmed Paşa viewed any quadruped that strayed within range of his long-sighted eyes. It made riding him an easy business since he, ever the optimist, imagined that round the very next corner his longings would be met in full. There was never any need to carry a stick, to kick him on, encourage him to walk faster. He was spurred on by the propulsion of his own pink willy.

Having retrieved him from his camel chase, I saddled him, said goodbye to Chrissy and we made our way along the southern coastline to Ören. We passed no buildings, no houses, no people, no traffic. It was an Arcadian morning's ride along the shoreline under a blue cotton-wool clouded sky, with the sea gliding back and forth on the white limestone shore. Grass, lucerne and barley sprung emerald green on tight neat terraces. Everything that bore a flower burst into colour. Cuckoopint grew in shaded thicket, groundsel, herb Robert, wood sorrel, tall fragmites, erasmus pink and purple, yellow melilot, flax and mallow: there was sage, thyme, coltsfoot, vetches, bacon-and-egg – then dandelions, goatsbeard and others I couldn't name: a floral paradise untouched by chemical and profiting from its absence.

When we stopped at a pool to drink, I watched the little green turtles graze the weeds, roll and tumble in the water as frogs sat motionless on stones. The cushioned land around was feathered in a quiet harmony. Surely this is how God meant it to be?

This footpath must have remained unchanged since the start of time. Had St Paul walked on this spot, seen the coast lovely like this? Was he too moved by the scent of wild flowers and the windblown pine? Did Persian kings tread this route, were their hearts softened by this scene, or did it cause them to desire it as their own?

Strange that these crumbling little 'pattika' were the arteries of empire, or civilisation once upon a time. These vague, unsignposted tracks were the means whereby an envoy might travel from Damascus to Rome, just as people might use them as routes to market – like drovers' roads. As human traffic came and went seeking destiny or fortune, the little turtles grazed the pond weed and the wind blew warm through the wild flowers and grasses, just the same. We moved on.

As we walked, clouds started to thicken and a light drizzle fell. But now I was walking with Ahmed Paşa, and had covered the saddle with the ground sheet. The rain was light, just enough to keep the bees off from the hundreds of hives that lined the track. None of the hives had supers, which surprised me. I couldn't see how they extracted the honey.

We walked into a small village. Some people appeared, cut Ahmed Paşa green oats and barley, which he fell on like an elephant, scoffing great mouthfuls. I was given buns, also like an elephant. As we left I picked up one of the children, put him in the saddle and walked away with him. He jumped off a little later and hid behind his fingers. 'Teşekkür ederim' ('Thank you very much') I just heard him say, peeping at me with little black eyes and runny nose, and he turned scooting home.

The villagers told me the track ended after an hour's walk, then a further seven kilometres would see us in Oren. The path wound on, climbing high above the shoreline and soon we were on cliff tops amongst pine, watching sheets of rain marching in veiled regiments towards us across the surface of the sea. The track ended abruptly in a wall of rock. We scrambled up past it, going through the pine hugging the coast. If we stayed on the coast we would be bound to find Oren. It couldn't be much further. Twenty kilometres later, in growing darkness we were still struggling in rough steep rocks. Everywhere paths led off in indistinguishable direction. We were hampered by a terrible crossing on a cliff face where a scanty path swung round the side of the rock to a foot wide in the middle. On our left the fall was two hundred feet to the sea. On our right, rock vaulted up like organ pipes. Rain had now begun to fall in earnest, globs of water rolling back and forward across the rim of my hat.

Ahmed Paşa looked cold, miserable with his forelock stuck wetly to his forehead. He nuzzled me in fear or cold or hunger I don't know. I took the saddlebags off to stop them rubbing against the cliff face and throwing him off balance, casting him into the sea.

With an orange in my hand in the pouring rain I led him onto the path, praying that he wouldn't refuse half way, since horses have a tendency to step back on a refusal. We couldn't afford an inch there, let alone a pace. I walked as quickly as I dared and he followed me across in his iron shoes. I gave him his orange on the far side realising as I did that I had been shouting at the top of my voice in the pelting rain, that I was shaking like a frightened bird. It drained me of my energy. I looked in vain for a cave or shelter, and he nuzzled me again. We went to a desolate little cottage where a mad old woman came screeching out at us, driving us away.

The coastline was no longer passable, and we struck inland. The black of night fell like a net with the rain, wretchedly we floundered around in short thick scrub. It was there I saw we had not been following paths at all, but water courses. Below us, I could just make out a road. Somehow we got down to it to find it sodden clay.

We waded along it, falling, squelching with trapped feet. At nine o'clock, I knocked on the door of a poor little cottage. They took us in. Ahmed Paşa had a dry stable, oats and saman, but the poor boy coughed all night.

I was utterly exhausted and found it difficult to speak. But unlike so many of the villagers I had met, this family had a share of brains. Once they saw I didn't understand a lot of their language, they didn't shout at me as though it were volume I lacked, not understanding. Quietly I ate hot spinachy soup, eggs and honey. The mother and daughter were a handsome pair, and when I expressed interest in the rug on the loom, the daughter showed me the knots they use, tried to explain with simple words and gesture how they arrive at the design they wove with no pattern to follow. It was a colourful, striking piece of work exaggerated by the plain surroundings.

The house had two rooms: the living room, where we ate squatting in front of the fire, and a bedroom behind, which I shared with the old grandfather. He had chosen for himself an unusual ensemble, wearing a donkey jacket over a pullover through which the grey hairs of his chest had grown and matted, a flat cap, and a pair of pyjama trousers which had lost their cord, for which he fumbled all the time, angrily brushing offers of help.

I slept damply, hearing Ahmed Paşa cough even though I had given him his first dose of penicillin. Grandfather woke me from time to time with a loud tuneful fart.

In the morning I was roused by the mother and father gobbing into the fireplace, narrowly missing the fry-up. It was an unattractive chorus. No one washed and I noticed the mother's hair was thick with scurf. The price of poverty: nowhere to wash when you need to most.

The fry-up was last night's left-overs, and very good it was too. They were a nice family, and I liked them. They had saved us from the filthiest of nights. I left lira in Ahmed Paşa's trough, and we made our way on in morning sunshine. We climbed a gritty slope and all but fell into a Lycaen tomb that had been exposed on a cliff top. Then finally, hundreds of feet below us lay Oren, crouched in a fertile plain bounded by a long sweeping bay.

Our route down was on the cliff face. Of all our mountain crossings, this was the worst. Slabs of rock lay slanting across the narrow goat track zigzagging down. It dropped over loose scree, narrowed to inches and fell in awkward sloping steps. I led Ahmed Paşa down that dreadful cliff, all the way doubting the wisdom of the descent. It was no place for a horse in shod feet and was bad enough for me in leather. I lost count how many times he stood on the very brink of a sharp stone which. had it turned would have sent him tumbling. He held me once on the reins when I slipped. Slowly and quietly we walked down, resting on the wider parts. Only once did he stumble and I caught his nose in my left hand, hoicking him onto his balance as I did so and the sweat ran out of my every pore.

It took us four hours to reach the shore. Looking back on the cliff, it seemed impossible we had come down it. On the water front, I found a pansyon, tethered Ahmed Paşa in an olive grove, found him some grub. No one believed me when I told them where we had come from and my heart ached with pride – this courageous horse grazing blithely out there, looking strong, self assured, this stallion by the sea.

16 April
You go dirty or you go clean. You don't let all your kit go dirty. You wear the same thing for five or six days until you get the chance to wash, then put your clean clothes on, wash the ones you've been wearing. You wear your leather chaps and leather jerkin to keep the trail dirt off. You take every opportunity to shave and wash your clothes. A good wash takes

the same time as a good graze: maybe three hours. So you wash your stuff, hang it on branches to dry, then move on, and you never walk past good grazing.

I sat drinking tea with Seuket Barbaros. He kept me supplied with cut oats and barley. Ripped me off at first, but then it stopped and he asked for less. We sat round a marble capitol they used as a table. It was huge with sculpted deep relief in floral designs, and ram's heads knocked faceless by the fanatic Selçuk Turks when they swept through with the first armies of Islam. I asked him about buying another horse for Chumpie, my girlfriend who was coming to join me from England. He told me to try Ören. I walked there later, it was about two kilometres from the sea.

I saw horses tethered out in the plain. But they were very small: there were donkeys too. I watched a woman beat a peg into the ground with a stone, tethering a heifer, who threw her head about and pulled the peg out. The woman shouted at her, beat the peg in again. The heifer pulled it out. The woman threw the stone at the heifer who ran off high kicking: she'd won. I saw a chicken call her chicks about her as she watched a green-eyed black cat in the wild flowers beneath some olives, swatting butterflies that flirted crazily in the low air. Beyond, the sea rolled a clear turquoise on bleached stone.

Ören was another grubby bit-of-a-place with fascinating ruins, pretty arches, columns lying about like pik-a-stik, capitols used as work benches and a Genoese wall backing some filthy garage.

I didn't see any horses. Back at the pansyon, I collected Ahmed Paşa and went for a long slow canter up the beach. I was the only tourist again. I thought we'd push on the following day to Bodrum.

In the evening I watched the sun fall into the sea. There were four cats nearby, sitting on a wall, eyeing fishing boats out in the bay. When the boats turned for home, the cats dropped down lightly off the wall, waiting at the water's edge. The fishermen threw them a small squid. They had a taste for squid, those cats.

We left Ören at 7 in the morning passing some vast earthworks where men were making as much mess and noise as they could. Engines screamed, machines gouged out huge mouthfuls of earth, gabbed them into other machines which spat them out in raw polyp-shaped dollops. Lorries roared, steel pipes were hauled up and down. They seemed to be making earth pyramids with something dreadful inside. A nasty concrete channel led suspiciously into the clear sea. Doubtless they'll find some horrific effluent to fill it with.

In stark contrast the coastline further along was wonderful. We stopped for lunch in a three house village, in a bay, where a French yacht was moored. A boat rowed ashore. Two men came towards me.

'Est-ce qu'il est agréable?' they asked, enquiring about my trip.

'Ça depend de votre cheval.' I replied: lousy French, but they got the gist.

That night after a long walk, we arrived in the dark in Karaova, staying with another family of weavers, moving on next day to Bodrum.

We rested at midday in an oak wood where the grazing was good. I watched women planting tobacco. Matthias Alexander would have approved of the way women bend in Turkey, from the hips, with good straight backs: they all do. An old ox that pulled the cart with the transplants chewed her cud with her eyes closed, switching flies off her flanks. The air was still and hot, and horse flies buzzed erratic circles round us, biting. I rolled over a stone. Two slim copper-coloured snakes lying coiled in a reptilian embrace moved languidly away: I turned over another and a battalion of black ants swept out. I sat on an immoveable stone sharing biscuits and oranges with my friend. His cough had gone: I gave him the last shot of penicillin that morning.

We arrived in Bodrum at five-thirty. It was noisy, active and traffic-ridden. I wasn't sure if it was the sort of place I wanted to stay in. But I was tired, Ahmed Paşa was yawning, walking like a drunk, and that's how we fell into Mustafa Bardak's pansyon. They were all surprised how much Ahmed Paşa could eat: Ahmed Paşa could eat the whole world.

I had a quick look round Bodrum later. There were a lot of English voices, people spending money like water. A chilling contrast to the poverty of the mountains. I didn't feel as if I belonged there, with those gaudily dressed people all having fun in that way: felt more comfortable with Ahmed Paşa in his stable.

I went back to Mustafa Bardak's place and climbed into bed early. As my head hit the pillow, I heard the first revolving dog. It yapped the same dim-witted three beat monotone as the last night prowler way back in Yukarişkoy. I lay there for a moment wondering if it was the same one, been shadowing us all that way.

It couldn't go on all night again, surely? I was dead beat. I'd sleep through it. The yap faded. Just as before, back it came, louder. I tossed and turned in my bed, trying not to let it get me. But it had me: it ate pieces out of my silence like a beetle chewing leaves. I stuffed bog paper in my ears. The sound penetrated. I dismembered that dog, hanged it, shot it, tore its paws off and on it yapped. I dreamed myself a dogless land, tumbled into the soft white arms of sleep as a contra-rotating dog struck up in higher pitch. An incensing three beat chorus, now in double time, working in opposite directions rubbed itself into my sleeplessness, like a wire brush on a wound.

Set on murder, I dressed, made my way to the front door, groped about in the darkness. The door was locked. I couldn't get out. I returned to my room, shoved more bog paper in my ears, tied a jersey round my head, crawled into the eiderdown depths of my sleeping bag. I re-emerged a minute later suffocating, gasping for air, driven to the edge of bootless dementia. I hated those dogs with a passion; dropped imaginary breeze blocks on them, hurled dream stones, boulders, grenades at them. Still they went on.

All night they revolved. Never broke off once. Was I the only person in Bodrum lying awake torn from sleep by these demonic things? Or was every other English tourist on his bed, eyes open, cursing like me? Couldn't we gang up, fix these dogs once and for all? The sun rose, the muezzin blared his head off, all the cockerels in Islam screeched in the dawn, every donkey in Ionia brayed in the brave new day, tearing away the last vestiges of a long prayed for sleep. Left me racked in misery, exhausted and nauseous. Lead booted, I rose at seven to feed Ahmed Paşa who looked as though he had suffered the same fate as me.

I swore vengeance. Revenge. We left Mustafa Bardak's place at nine, went hunting the streets for them. Not a sign of them: not a whimper. They skulked in black holes, set for the next night's misery.

We walked on through the town. It was pretty, with white flat-roofed houses and raised corners. Markets were being set up and there was a smell of fresh ground coffee. Stopping at a street baker I bought myself a huge sweet white loaf and Ahmed Paşa stole one. We were going to find a place to stay if it killed us, where there were no dogs, no mosques, no cockerels. We were going to stay there until all our sleep had been made up and then refreshed, we would journey on. Ahmed Paşa agreed.

At ten-thirty we found the very spot. A homely unpretentious pansyon in a grassy clover-rich sward a mile out of the village, where no minaret, kennel or hen house marred the site. I decided we would swim, relax, have a peaceful time, then sleep lazily in the afternoon sun. While I put the saddlery into my room, Ahmed Paşa rolled around in the clover. I put on my empire-builders preparing for a day of indolence. When I went outside Ahmed Paşa was still rolling around in the clover. Why was he rolling around in the clover? Because he'd got colic.

That damn bread! Don't know how many times I told him no good comes of theft. I had no medicines for colic so gave him a dose of Ifanca James' diarrhoea compound, which he thoroughly enjoyed. It did nothing for his colic. I gave him some more. Nothing. I took him to the village, bought a litre of olive oil, poured that down him. He screwed his eyes up in piggy delight, continued with his problem.

A niggling suspicion that it was all a sham took hold of me. He was just doing it to get attention, be offered a few of life's more unusual delicacies. For five long hours in the sun I fiddled about with Ahmed Paşa and his colic. Up and down to the sea, in and out of the water, buckets of olive oil. Finally, the fit passed, cast out like a devil only to enter me in a wave of stupefying exhaustion.

I went to bed early that night, barely able to keep my eyes open. I dozed for about half an hour, roused by a pair of lovers, whose impassioned cries, thumping bedstead, heaving thighs, groans, huffs, puffs sweated their grinding lust round every wall in the place. Why did they have to do it in this pansyon? Why didn't they go to Mustafa Bardak's pansyon, do it there, with the revolving dog, and his whirling dervishes of dogdom? Which, I asked myself, did I hate more? I concluded that if it came to a contest, I'd go for the contra-rotating dogs every time.

In the middle of the night I left my room with my sleeping bag, and went to join Ahmed Paşa in the clover. Lay down in the dewy grass, looked up at the silvery sickle moon and stars, as Ahmed Paşa sniffed

Village races in Anatolia

Ahmed Paşa

Ahmed Paşa just after I'd bought him at Çal. He wasn't in the best condition

Yukarişkoy çaylevi after the first night's gallop from the mill

First camp out with Ahmed Paşa

Karahayet village, outside Pamukkale

School children in the village of Denizli

The girl who brought a large ginger cat for Ahmed Paşa's dinner

I wound up sharing a bed with the old man in this picture: these people had very little in those days

An arcadian ride along the southern coastline to Bodrum – all this has since been developed, and ruined

I dumped my English saddlebags and bought these colourful and far better Turkish *heyber* in Marmaris

Both Ahmed Paşa and I were fed and watered by kind people along the way – their hospitality was overwhelming

The cliff we slithered down at Ören

The remains of the little Council Chamber at Iassos

The horses were billeted out under separate trees while Chumpie sets up evening camp not far from Didyma

Chumpie crossing the lower Büyük Menderes – the ancient River Meander – on Şimşek

me, piddled, got up, lay down, yawned, nickered and farted and I spent the rest of the night looking up at the silvery sickle moon and stars until a cockerel crowed clanging in the dawn. Drenched in dew, delirious for lack of sleep, I staggered back to the pansyon where the landlord eyed me contemptuously, as if it was me who had been solely responsible for the amorous carousal which had robbed him of sleep too. He poured a cup of coffee in my lap, slammed his door and went back to bed. The lovers came out as I slouched there unable to compose a single thought. They looked fresh as daisies, skipped out like two young lovers.

Two nights with no sleep.

I pulled myself together, went to Bodrum by buy Ahmed Paşa some grain and worming compound. Called in at the Mylasa Hotel, where I had booked a room from England a few months before. It was too difficult to stay with a horse, so I went just for a social call.

I fell into conversation with a tall, slim Englishman who lived in Bodrum. He had fine sandy hair, pale blue eyes and a distant, far away manner, like a man who had lived on his wits all his life, and knew himself well. He had lived in Greece for sixteen years, having been a skipper on a boat, then ran a bar in Athens. He talked about the smuggling along the Albanian coastline, and the cigarettes the American freighters used to bring in, stored in bonded warehouses, picked up by packet vessels. Small fast craft would take off the contraband from these boats at rendezvous out at sea, run the cigarettes into Albanian and Italian drop-off points.

'Every now and then there would be a sinker,' he said, lighting up. 'Just about all the smokes around these parts get smuggled in that way. Everyone who has a boat here knows that. When the boats conk out, they pull them into Corfu, patch them up. They pay the custom blokes their bit and everybody keeps quiet. There was this crazy English guy who used to come into the bar with thousands of dollars. Skipper on one of these boats. He'd come in, spend all his money, then go out again for another haul. One day, he came in dead drunk, asked me how much to buy the bar. I told him fifteen thou'. He put the dough on the table. I gave him the key and walked out. God knows what happened to the paperwork. Him and his mates drank the place dry, sold the lease for a few hundred dollars, went back out to sea. He was just a crazy guy.' I liked that Englishman.

I was asked out to dinner that night by the Penny's, who own the Mylasa. They were engaging, good to be with. He's got a nice-no-bullshit-Australian way. I expect they thought me silly as a sheep. I was senseless with lack of sleep. I remember a Turkish lady there who knew about the book Grenville Collins had given me, *The Fusus*, by Ibn Arabi. He had a house in Bodrum somewhere. I rode to it next day although no one told me where it was. I went straight to it. Knew it was his the minute I saw it: could see him there, part of it. They call him 'Kerim' – it's an Arabic word, although found in Turkish too: it means 'bountiful'. Shows what they think of him.

Don't remember going home to the pansyon that night, but I was so tired I lay awake for hours.

We left our pansyon after three sleepless nights. I didn't have the energy to explore Bodrum. I couldn't be bothered to find out about Herodotus, the father of history, or Artemisia who had married her brother and built the Mausolea, one of the seven wonders of the world. There was something about the Knights of Malta, and the Knights of Rhodes and Suleiman the Magnificent, but Ahmed Paşa needed new shoes, so that was that.

I found the 'nalbant' – the blacksmith – in a back street. He was ancient. Wondered if he was Herodotus. Don't remember anyone saying anything about Herodotus being a *nalbant*, so he can't have been. He fitted a good set of shoes though, even if he wasn't Herodotus. He asked me for £1.75 for the lot. When I offered him a £5 instead, he called me a madman.

'How much did the horse cost?' he asked – I knew more Turkish.

I told him.

'Stupid tourist,' he said 'could have gone all the way round Turkey on a bus ten times for that.'

He was right.

'Güle-güle' he said, and we pushed off.

The ride up the coastline was another pastoral dream but we didn't go far though. We were far too knackered. I slept under the stars where we stopped, waking for nothing for a full twelve hours.

The following day, I aimed to get within striking distance of Iassos, which I reckoned to make in three days. When I asked people on the way, they said it was impossible to cross the estuary at Güllük. It was wide, had strong currents. There was a fishing weir, the water was four metres deep, two kilometres across. The alternative was to go via Milas, which meant travelling inland again where it would be hot and we would have to go along the main road. It would take four days to get to Iassos that way. I didn't want to go into another town. They were a strain. I liked the open country where there was good grazing, you didn't get ripped off, and there were usually no dogs or muezzins.

I cross-examined them tightly about the River Dalyan – the fishing weir at Güllük, my crossing point for Iassos. Sounded hopeless, dangerous. Perhaps it was silly to attempt. I spun a coin and we went to Güllük.

We arrived in the afternoon and saw the river at once: it was broad. We dropped down through an olive grove to a clearing above the estuary. It didn't look good. I could see the current. The water in the middle moved fast. We went on again, dropped down to the water's edge and stopped where men were mending nets, stripping leaves off reeds. They were surprised to see us. I asked about the crossing: 'Yok' they said – no. To go back would mean having to retrace steps.

'How deep is the water?'

'Four metres.'

'How far is it to the other side?'

'Two kilometres.'

Then a man pointed right out to sea, to a sand spur. I could see it. A long way out. It stretched across the estuary for about four hundred yards, disappeared, then rose again on the far side. Must be the way. One long swim. I turned Ahmed Paşa up through the olives, along the coast until we were opposite the spur then dropped down over the rock to the muddy shore.

Ahmed Paşa knew what I wanted, and kept casting glances across the water, snorting, turning cramped little circles. It looked a long way.

Was the bottom muddy? How fast was the current? How wide the blue strip where the water was deepest? It had to be nearly a mile. A long way to ask a horse to swim, especially a loaded horse.

We turned a few more circles in the mud then took a run at it. We went straight down. Ahmed Paşa lost his breath. We turned, went back to the shore. We'd missed the sand bar. I couldn't see it close to the water. We went further along. I saw the men pointing, went further along again. They held up their hands. That was it.

Ahmed Paşa looked across the water, thrashed in with his feet, pawing like a bull. Suddenly his mind was firm: I never touched him. He hit that water with the velocity of a train. Ears flat, nostrils wide, he tore holes in that sea, ripping through waves. Arab blood pounded in his veins and deeper, deeper we went. Water rose up his flanks, over the saddle, over his shoulders and I felt his feet leave the sand. He sunk a little, then pulled a powerful stroke. 'Good boy! Brave Boy!'

My legs were dragged back by the pull of the water. Saddlebags floated like water wings. We caught the midstream current and it took us out a hundred yards. All the time that horse swum in a single minded effort to get to the other side. On and on he fought. Thought we were losing ground, going back. Heard him catch his breath. 'You beautiful bastard!'

I felt his feet touch sand and we inched in. The water level fell; half walking, half swimming, snarling at the water and we crossed the Dalyan. I heard the men cheering away behind us. We hadn't finished. In front the land was a swamp. In preference, we turned out to sea again to make the crossing to the point, then up over the rocks. The waves beat us back. He knew what to do. Felt it. I gave him the reins. He turned a long slow circle, cut up to the left, gave himself room and we hit that swamp at a gallop. He bucked, fought, floundered, slithered, sunk to his belly – God knows how treacherous that stuff was – struggled through, put his feet on hard ground on the far side. Then the flies hit us.

Tiny, fast-moving black flies – millions of them. In an instant my face was covered and a cloud of them landed on Ahmed Paşa. The minute you brushed them off, they settled again. They bit sharp stinging bites and drove Ahmed Paşa frantic. He bolted, stumbling as he did, then regained his footing, dashed on and the flies disappeared, just as suddenly, leaving us raw with their stings.

I rubbed my face with hoof oil. Brushed Ahmed Paşa vigorously with a dandy brush before going on again. It was a mercy he'd been so plastered in mud, since they hadn't attacked his underbelly at all.

We followed a water course arriving onto a broad flat plain with low fleshy plants. It had a primordial feel, eerie, silent. The air thickened, sickly hot and still. There wasn't a sound. No birds. No crickets. Nothing called out in song. It was a sinister place with a small deserted village in a gully, looked as though it had been abandoned rapidly, leaving galvanised tin bowls by empty houses, piles of wood stacked against walls. Not a soul there. Yet it gave me the creepy, unmistakeable feeling of being watched and I kept glancing over my shoulder. Ahmed Paşa shied at rocks and bushes. A haunting landscape which felt as if it had been cursed.

We moved away quickly following the track round a low hill down to an English-like landscape with rolling meadows, tall parkland trees. We passed, arriving in a friendly little village on the other side of a sweeping bay. I asked for a place to graze the horse and some villagers pointed to a promontory of land to which I led him. Walked up through the olives, tethered Ahmed Paşa in the grass, stood back to look. He grazed among the columns of the fallen temple of Iassos: we had made it in a day.

It was a beautiful place, with a small theatre or council chamber, the smallest in Caria. All around fluted columns rose slender in the long grass. Byzantine arches spanned the eastern part of the Temple, while on the crest, a great rambling fortress crumbled, sprawling into the olives.

I loved Iassos and found a calm there which I had not known before. An untroubled hush breathed about the place and we rested for two days until the spell had passed. It will ever stand out in my mind for its feel, its pastel colours and how I watched Ahmed Paşa graze amongst the columns in the grass that day.

We walked away in a dream from Iassos, the stone, the temple and the sea. We passed through the tall pines on a ridge behind, and stopped in a wood, near Kazikli. I found two little tortoises and introduced them to each other, thinking it a chancy business to find a mate, if you're a tortoise in Turkey. They didn't want to know and parted in a big hurry in opposite directions.

I rode on through the village which took us high up on a hill, overlooking Kabuki, our next stop, where I decided we would stay while

I found another horse for Chumpie. We walked down the mountain to the village where Musa, the owner, of the one-and-only beach pansyon, came out to greet us and took us in.

6

Şimşek

Ahmed Paşa took up residence outside the gent's bogs. It was shaded by olives, protected from the wind by the restaurant and an old Greek church, and had a splendid view of the coastline. There he remained on a long tether, being accorded all the courtesy of a hotel guest, waited upon with breakfast, lunch, tea and dinner, and exercised lightly in the mornings. In this way, he developed rather the air of a retired gentleman of distinguished service record, and similarly, was apt at times to be haughty and wholly unreasonable in his demands.

Akbuk was a pretty place, small and traditional, shorn of frills, perched on the water's edge in a lovely crescent-shaped bay. Behind the simple hotel olive groves marched away into rugged hills and through these every day, Ahmed Paşa and I would amble and he would reminisce about his wartime exploits against a savage enemy, vanquished in heady days before I was born.

The local residents were friendly, acutely interested in how much I had paid for Ahmed Paşa, and again made me feel as if I had fallen for the oldest trick in the book. They soon learned his name, and, finding mine unpronounceable, called me Ahmed Paşa too, which led to confusion. When I said that my girl was going to join us and that I proposed to buy another horse, the story came back that one of us was going to be put to stud, and the other wanted to buy a woman in Milas. It made both of us look like a pair of dirty old men, and tarnished my image of Ahmed Paşa as an irreproachable ageing brigadier.

Our stay in Akbuk turned into a summery break. We swam and wandered about under the dazzling blue sky, exploring the coastline while on our morning and afternoon constitutionals. During our swims – which Ahmed Paşa enjoyed every bit as much as I – I discovered quite by chance that the sea is an exceedingly good medium in which to work a horse, since all their movements are slowed down by the action of the water. You have time to examine them closely, see just how the horse is moving. It is also the perfect place for de-ticking a horse since he will not kick in the water, and you can tweak off bugs with no risk of being knocked toothless. The sea then acts as a general panacea – Panacea was the local goddess of healing in classical times – and antiseptic. That, and a good roll in the sand, gives you an admirable piece of medication largely performed by the patient himself.

I visited the nearby village of Didim – the Didyma of the Greeks. It has a grand and beautiful temple dedicated to Apollo, twin brother of Artemis. Although the ruins were truly magnificent, the whole thing was spoiled by over-commercialisation, which robbed it of its charm. Great buses droned in and out of the village belching diesel through the fluted columns. Hundreds of people gawped about, then sat down to a communal trough, swilled the local ink, stuffed themselves with very un-Turkish kebabs, then zoomed off again, hotly replaced by another ten bus loads, hassled by the trinket men. I didn't stay, but much to my delight, managed to buy a transliteration of The Holy Koran.

On our return to Kabuki in the minibus, we were taken on a tortuous route through vast construction sites. I saw a developer mark out another hundred acres of olives for grubbing up. They're spoiling that coastline with a dogged determination which is terrifying: killing the goose that lays the golden egg. The buildings are nasty, shoddily built, crammed shoulder to shoulder without thought of appearance. With every new brick laid, they speedily remove any reason for wishing to go there.

I found I had a constantly changing view of Turkey. On the one hand, I warmed to its friendliness and people, its strange austerity, scenery, scents and melange of culture. Then I hated the profligate manner in which it is being ruined. There are plans for five villages to be built round Akbuk, and the whole place is served with an indeterminate quantity of subterranean water. The sewage problem alone from the 2,500 houses they plan hardly bears thinking about, since it will be stored underground, which is where the water is also. The easiest alternative which will present itself no doubt, is the sea.

I looked in the neighbourhood for horses and drew a blank, finally making a trip to Söke to try there – which reminded me of Denizli for no reason other than my personal dislike of towns.

The interesting thing about having something definite to do in a foreign town is that you are taken to places you would never visit otherwise. I was hauled round the backest backend of Söke, over open drains, mountains of rubbish, through piddle-ridden backstreets and scores of black, fly infested shacks in search of this new horse. I sat in smoke-filled eye-smarting çay shops drinking sweet tea and tiny cups of thick black coffee waiting for some vendor who would finally bring along some poor, tired old horse, fit for nothing except a long, long rest.

I was adopted by Ali, a man of sixty-eight, who had fathered eleven children – from a number of different wives, he added with a wink. He taught me the Turkish words for all female pudenda which, unhappily, I have now forgotten: otherwise, I'd go and shout them at everybody in Knighton.

We went wandering around Söke together, he rambling on in conversation I was beginning to grasp. I liked him, my square-faced, cloth capped and self-appointed assistant who had a wicked sense of humour, and a good nose for a large tip. We were joined by one of Ali's friends, a nice fellow, improbably called Johnny, who told us we were wasting our time in Söke, that he knew two horses in a village nearby that might well be the answer.

There was something believable about Johnny, so we all piled into a bus, rolled out of Söke, while Ali tested me on my knowledge of female parts. Johnny helped in this instructive game, adding a few words of his own which made Ali weep with laughter, and demolished the other occupants of the bus. I was always surprised at the jungle telegraph in Turkey, and so on our arrival we had a reception committee waiting, fully informed as to my needs and recently extended vocabulary.

In the çay shop, in front of another picture of Kemal Ataturk, we all guzzled the statutory gallon of sweet tea. This accomplished, and all the village niceties and politics out of the way, we went tin kicking down a dirt street. We were shown into a neat courtyard, where three gaily painted carts heralded the presence of a proud horseman. He turned out to be an old man, with white hair and no teeth, wearing a fez, pyjama bottoms and a woolly blazer with glossy brass buttons. He cut a quirky dash of an altogether unconventional sort. He questioned me closely on my needs. On discovering that I wanted a horse for my hanim – woman – he gave me a look which made me feel like something unpleasant on a carpet. He was taken aback. There followed a lot of chat and he said the horse he had in his yard would be too big for a hanim, and why didn't we go on the bus like real tourists?

However, not wishing to deprive himself of ready foreign currency, he changed his tune with a hefty nudge from Ali, and showed me a handsome white stallion. He was not unlike Ahmed Paşa; only about eighty years his senior. This creature was a draught horse for his carts. He showed me his dependability by rolling underneath him, shouting one of the words I had just learned which collapsed the hangers-on into hysterics.

Obviously the message I got was that if the horse failed to react to the thought of what the old man expressed, he was a very calm kind of horse. Still, the old boy wasn't that keen on selling him, being rather fond of him, and I imagined they must have grown up together.

Tea was brought by another chap, and we all sat beneath a tree in a semi circle like a bunch of Red Indians having a pow-wow. It led to a lot of head scratching, and a lot of direct questions from Ali about my bank balance. After further probing from Johnny, the old man revealed that he might be prepared to sell the horse's son, who lived in another place, a few streets away. We got up to go, and Ali gave me a wink and tapped the side of his nose: 'this-is-the-horse' sort of tap.

We marched through the village streets, a growing crowd tagging along, interested to see what new word I would be taught, or use. We reached a pair of rickety wooden doors peeling a faded blue in the glare of the sun, and the old man shouted. The door was opened, we were all told to stand back, and a very bright strawberry roan-cum-grey stallion popped out. He was the best horse I had seen for a long time. An odd colour, and in the sunlight he even inclined to pink, with grey overtones and dark points. He was probably a Barb by ancestry, with Arab thrown in from his father. As I stood back admiring him, Ali handed me a fistful of cardamom seeds to chew, and said, 'Genk' meaning young.

The horse was about four or five years old. The old man winkled a lad out of the crowd, told him to sit on him, which he did, displaying an easy grace and really natural seat. They threw a bridle of a sort on, and they shot out of sight. The old man bawled his head off, saying the tourist wanted to see the horse not watch him disappear.

He came back. The horse had certainly been ridden, was no stranger to a mounted horseman, but easy to see all he had ever done was go everywhere at full pelt. He probably knew nothing about standing still, or walking, trotting or generally behaving himself at anything other than full gallop. They whirled around in the street and the lad slid off.

It was my turn. This was a horse, although only 14.1 hands, but definitely horse not a pony. He had a horse's mind, a horse's strength, and the slipperiness of a box of rats. When I got on him, he was all over the place, only just controllable, and when he ran, he raised his head above the bit tossing it around like a flag in a hurricane. I felt he could be trained, and as I fell off, decided I liked him, despite the snags.

Ali did the rest. He didn't wait for my assent or bother about what price I could or could not afford. He put my hand together with the old man's, and shaking them, said that I agreed to pay 400,000 lira (£365).

'Çok güzel' ('Excellent') he said, and I had bought another horse. There was no barter, no fight, no hassle. Dazed, I nodded in agreement, gawping open-mouthed at the old man, whose jaw also dropped, and remained open, shaking. Ali immediately started talking about a new name for my horse. I'm sure I could have bought him for less. It all seemed so easy I didn't care. All that remained was to pay the old man, which meant another trip to Söke, Johnny agreeing to walk the horse to town, where we would conclude the deal.

The name Ali suggested for the horse in a whisper I said out loud, which made him gag me, causing Johnny to duck, pretending he had nothing to do with anyone there. A few other names were suggested, all of which turned out to be not the sort of thing one could shout and get away with, and we finally settled on Şimşek. Pronounced Shimshaik. It means lightening in Turkish: a little prosaic after the other suggestions, but I liked the ring it had. In Söke, I cashed my travellers' cheques, paid the old man and we all had another round of tea while waiting for Johnny.

The problem of how to get the horse back to Akbuk was resolved by the ever-resourceful Ali, who had a friend rather the worse for a mid-morning raki drinking session and who had a totally un-roadworthy truck. Ali shrugged off my concern about the safety of the vehicle with an expressive, throw-away unarguable gesture.

Johnny arrived with Şimşek whom he frog-marched straight up a short flight of steps, turned him and jumped him into the back of Ali's mate's sawn-off bit of a van, and that was that. I've never seen a horse loaded from such an alarming position into such dangerous transport so speedily, with so little hassle. We have a lot to learn in Britain about the absence of fuss, which is perhaps both a good and a bad thing. Ali then suggested that I give them all a large tip, which I did. They waved goodbye as I climbed into the seatless van with Şimşek slithering around in the back. They said they might come to Akbuk to have a look at my hanim, told me to forget about the receipt because the horse was the receipt, the old man couldn't write, and anyway, nobody had a pen.

We roared off to Akbuk, arriving an uncomfortable hour later, Şimşek showing not a shred of concern about leaving his friends or that he was about to carry an English artist up the western coastline of Turkey. On arrival I jumped him out onto a pile of earth, paid Ali's mate, waved goodbye, then took Şimşek to a bit of ground near the sewage inspection lid, which was to be his patch – at least for the time being.

Obviously I couldn't keep the horses together as a pair of stallions. It would have been easier to have bought geldings, or mares, but there aren't any geldings in Turkey – at least not at my sort of money – and no one likes to part with a mare.

Ahmed Paşa gave me a full scale bollicking when I saw him, for having been away all day. He didn't stop moaning until I appeased him with oranges and chocolaty bribes. But he wasn't fully satisfied until I had gone into long rambling explanations, of which he finally bored, and with a sigh he yawned, and ended my monologue with one of his slow protracted farts.

I had now doubled my problems. I had to exercise the horses daily which would entail a lot of toing and froing, since, by keeping them apart, it meant I would be involved in hours of lugging about, having to carry my saddle from one to another.

That is precisely what happened. I seemed to spend all day and every day carrying my saddle from one end of Kabuki to the other, by night I was totally exhausted from the exertions. Added to which, the grazing arrangements were extremely inconvenient, there being no water nearby. So as well as my saddle, all the grooming kit and dry feed, I was forced to carry large quantities of water.

One of the chief snags I had discovered about Turkey was an astonishing paucity of stout pails. The entire country suffered from an absence of containers of any sort. The only buckets I came across had been poor things with crappy zinc handles that ripped off the minute you filled the things up. I found myself carrying water in a curious hotchpotch of containers that were always impossible to carry, and always leaked. So, should some philanthropist feel obliged to offer gifts to Turkey, I humbly submit that buckets would not go amiss.

I hadn't yet told Ahmed Paşa about Sims and kept wondering if he'd twigged or not. Neither did I intend telling him until I had fathomed out some way of introducing them without being killed in the process. An opportunity arose, in an oblique way.

One morning, I had a fight with Ahmed Paşa. It concerned his proprietorial rights over the gent's bog. The whole thing had been brewing for a few days, suddenly coming to a head when, because he regarded it as his spot, he had refused anyone entry. On this particular day, he refused me too: point blank.

To be caught short is one thing, but then to have to wrestle with a horse in order to relieve yourself is quite another. I began to feel for all the chaps who had had to make alternative arrangements, which had no doubt been inconvenient, to say the least. However, I shouted at him, to which he took deep offence and started a scrap which cost me the loss of a patch of skin on my knuckles. He ran off from his tether, went giggling round Akbuk, with me in angry pursuit. When I caught him, I gave him a belt: I regretted that. At least, he made me regret it because it practically broke my fist, tore a patch of skin off that hand, and he laid a boot into me which stopped me breathing for what seemed like half an hour. We became sworn enemies.

We were enemies for days, with me having to eat humble pie and feed him oranges at arm's length until he regained some of his former composure. While he was cooling off, I took Şimşek for a long ride, finding him a thoroughly nice horse, although extremely strong. I had guessed correctly that he had done everything at a gallop and training him to calm down was not easy. However, on the principle that the sea had sorted out Ahmed Paşa, I took Şimşek to the water's edge. After a few minutes refusal, he was swimming too, sloshing around in the clear blue sea beneath the pines.

That evening I decided that I would introduce the horses to one another next day, and take full advantage of Ahmed Paşa's beef against me, which would, I felt make him a lot less possessive of me, and less likely to do any lasting damage to Şimşek. It obviously had to be done sooner rather than later, since I was bored of carrying everything around, and Chumpie would be arriving soon. I had also found a grassy patch which was big enough for the two of them.

I decided to do the introductions well out of the village in amongst the olives, out of sight. The whole thing filled me with apprehension: I knew that stallions can get very savage. As I was eating a supper of Ayrhan (a kind of yoghurt), grilled fish, and cigarra börek (a sort of cheese-filled brandy snap without the brandy) I gazed up into the sky, wondering if I would be alive the next night, and saw an upside-down poodle fart a koala bear in the heavens – wonderful shapes, the black clouds of evening.

The following day, Ahmed Paşa was still nursing his grievance against me, so the moment was propitious. The opportunity had arisen.

Ahmed Paşa lacked affection for me that morning, so I was sure he would be less troublesome. It was he who concerned me most, since, as the bigger and older horse, I could foresee a very ugly scene developing with him and Şimşek tearing each other's throats out and me mangled on the rocks, eaten by ants. Neither did I want any of the Turks to know of my dilemma. I imagined they would be likely to favour a good fight, earn a few lira by way of a well-placed bet. So, before it was too hot, I rode Ahmed Paşa up under the olives a good way out of the village and tethered him on a short line. I hobbled him fore and aft just for good measure, then went to fetch Şimşek. Saddled him, rode him up to Ahmed Paşa who I knew would hear us coming. I hoped he would shout and forewarn Şimşek. Well he didn't, he kept silent. Nevertheless, I hoped to have the advantage over him by riding this new horse, whom I was sure would act demurely. He didn't.

The little bugger all but poked the old gent's eye out, jumped about, snorted, flailed the air thrashing with his hind feet all at once. Hurled himself in the air, went over vertical, I fell off, then he twisted, fell on his side, sprung up and made another broadside into the poor old brigadier, who behaved in an exemplary way, maintaining his distance with equanimity, curious that one of the younger generation should find something to be so audible about. The whole thing was over in seconds, and they both broke away to graze. No one was injured, no one's throat had been torn out, and I wasn't a pulp on a rock, being eaten by ants. I realised I had over reacted to the whole business and made a volcano out of a wormcast. That was the closest they ever got to each other. From then on, they lived together, apart.

They grazed for the rest of the day in that peaceful setting amongst the rocks, olives, the cicadas, darting lizards and columns of ants. In the evening, I walked them down one at a time to the shore and their patch of new grazing. When I took Ahmed Paşa down, Şimşek raised merry hell. When I went up to get him, Ahmed Paşa went berserk in turn. I had two horses at either end of the village, screaming their heads off, only to quieten down when I appeared with the other.

In this way, they became the very best of enemies, eyeing each other, circling about like a pair of Sumo wrestlers, but they never actually came to blows. They couldn't live together, and they couldn't live apart.

After three more days, Sims was behaving himself far better, walking well and beginning to respond to instruction with great heart. I think he learned a lot from just watching Ahmed Paşa – by no means the soul of equine manners – but he was a sight more level headed. Of the two, Şimşek was the more intelligent, but I dared not say that to Ahmed Paşa for fear of reprisal. Yet Şimşek would persist in jiggling around, and never really got the hang of standing still for mounting, often treating the whole thing with an absence of seriousness that was exceedingly trying. Ahmed Paşa meanwhile waxed fatter, enjoying his grazing and loafing around by the sea. Riding him after Şimşek was like driving a very old and stately Rolls, smooth, solid and quiet as against an unpredictable hot-rod with wild acceleration and no brakes.

For a week or more we waited for Chumpie to arrive and both horses benefited from the general pampering, good diet, grooming and de-ticking. There was one grim incident when children started pelting them with stones. They only needed telling that it was unkind, together with a bribe not to do it, and they came to heel.

I swum the horses as much as I could since salt in their coats kept flies off, and added lustre and shine. They looked terribly funny swimming in that clear water, just launching off into doggy-paddle. I kept expecting them to do another stroke, sidestroke, breaststroke or crawl or something. And they pulled their top lip up over their teeth when they swam which gave them a cartoonish air. But they genuinely loved it, and never hesitated to go in the sea and slosh around under the warm sun.

On the last evening before Chumpie arrived we were all very excited and went to bed early. The children – the stone throwers – came peeping in on the horses at feed time, just to say, 'Iyi akşamlar'. Good evening. Very sweet really.

7

A Turkish Telephone

Both horses behaved abominably on the morning of Chumpie's arrival. They managed to get at the barley and oats I had so carefully hidden and gorged themselves into a state of silliness that was demonic.

Şimşek had taken to donkeys with a passion, irrespective of gender. He was mooning over a diminutive little she-ass nearby, not much larger than a goat: although I must confess, she was a she, and very pretty. He raced around yelling himself into a frenzy about this quiet little creature who grazed on, oblivious to his frantic love-cries. I daren't have Chumpie's horse behaving like this on her arrival: she'd think I'd gone bonkers, bought her a mad horse. Hardly likely to set the venture off to a good start.

Ahmed Paşa joined in the yelling and the little she-ass approached, winding them up with a provocative wiggle and smouldering look, like a stripper down to her nothings in a bar of hopefuls. Their agitation grew so intense that very shortly a group of onlookers came to see what all the fuss was about.

Mercifully, the donkey's owner appeared, amused to find his animal had caused mine so much heartache. He led her away. She teetered off, blowing the horses a kiss which drove them completely wild, running about, snorting, yowling with their willies out until she disappeared, leaving them both quivering like jellies, pawing the dust. Equine erotica subsided, and things went back to normal.

Since it was still early, I thought to telephone Chumpie in the Mylasa in Bodrum, where I knew her to be. Telephoning in Turkey is never easy, since the public system is based on a slot machine principle, operated by jetons – small brass coins, sold only in obscure and incongruous places. I didn't have any. Decided to give the one and only telephone in Akbuk a whirl.

It was in a dirty shack, serving principally as a post office. It was where all the locals gathered to get communally bored. Inside there were four grubby plastic chairs, a desk littered with uncollected mail and a slob of a post-master who sat, fat and unshaven, behind the desk, smoking and uninterested. He cast vague rheumy looks about. His attendant played with the telephone keyboard, from which a solitary dust-coated wire hung, connecting Akbuk to the rest of the world. A transistor radio blared in a corner beside an oaf I'd previously seen lugging himself about the village.

When I gave the attendant the number for Bodrum, he copied it incorrectly. I corrected it, and he wrote it down wrong again. Someone else put it right. Then he stuffed dirty cotton wool down the receiver for no immediately obvious reason. Nothing happened.

After a few minutes the telephone rang. No one moved. It rang again. The post-master nodded slowly breathing out thick nostrils of smoke. Someone fiddled with the switchboard, lost the line. I thought it would be quicker to walk to Bodrum, certainly ride. Someone tried the number I had given. I waited. Behind the post-master a 1977 calendar hung on a rusty nail. I anticipated a further ten year delay.

Two hours later, after a lot of hassle, miraculously, the connection was made. I spoke to Chumpie through the cotton wool. All I understood was she would arrive sometime that day.

In the meantime, I went off to buy more grain, and at two-thirty, Musa came down to me at the horses, and in pidgin Turkish for my better understanding, said, 'Siz hanim.' Chumpie had arrived.

8

Şimşek, Chumpie and the Unjumpable Tree

'Hello,' she said, 'your nose is peeling.'

She was sketching under shade on the water's edge. 'And it's cold.'

The weather had changed that morning. Rain clouds gathered on the horizon and a cool wind was pitching in from the east. Chumpie looked like something out of a Ryder Haggard adventure story. She was wearing a long split skirt, a broad-brimmed felt hat, faded blue shirt, a green jersey and fawn windcheater. The whole was rounded off by a pair of old riding boots. She looked classically English-colonial, in an unconventional way. Like the wife of a 1920s tea planter nearly-gone-native, just arrived in town after six years in the bush.

She's comely, has clear features, comes from distinguished stock. Chumpie – a nick-name she was given at school – is a dedicated artist. She sketches and paints non-stop. The trip was to be for her a painting expedition to the remoter parts of Western Turkey, accessible only by horse. I had my reservations, since I had experienced already how long it took to get from one place to another and what a performance it was parking one horse, let alone two. That, and all the unforeseen: I felt our problems had now begun in earnest. With four of us, we had quadrupled our difficulties and furthermore, I expected we all wanted to do different things.

Well?' she said, 'can't you speak? Where's my horse?'

I was apprehensive of introducing Chumpie to Şimşek. I was not at all sure what he would do. I had told her that he was a nice little fellow, but omitted to say that he was a knave. I expected him to grace us with one of his larks, put on some appalling performance just to have me lose face. Especially after his antics earlier.

I put Chumpie's baggage away, happy to see she had not brought some huge pile of clobber. I showed her the way down to the horses, through the village, past the cows, lucerne, old fig tree, the shop, my friends in the post office, past the mosque to a walled grassy spot where the horses were grazing on long tethers. Boats nodded up and down in the sea. There was a smell of fish from nets drying out.

She looked at the horses coolly.

'Ahmed Paşa?' she said, 'he's a flea bitten grey.'

That's smart horse parlance. She has an artist's eye: wouldn't be content to call him white, as I had. She observes colour carefully. She remarked on his dark muzzle, deep brown eyes, and his knobbly knees.

'He looks like Asterix's horse' she concluded. I felt hurt. It was a tart remark.

'Beautiful, but definitely Asterix.' That eased it. Then she turned her attention to Şimşek, who was taking an interest in what was going on, just about to complain, feeling left out. Something else was going on in his mind, but there was no guessing what it was. She walked around him. They eyed one another darkly: gazed, taking in each other's points. She was being more generous than Şimşek, nodding her approval. He, on the other hand was considering something altogether more arcane. I could see it in his eye; Had a rascally look: not malicious, not an ounce of malice in Şimşek, but he was solid with mischief, and that, he made no attempt to hide.

'He's got a big head,' she said finally. 'But he's very pretty. He's four or five perhaps, and a Barb. I love his colour: very unusual. He's a kind of strawberry grey – almost unpaintable.'

She approved. Whenever something is turned into a painted image, for Chumpie, it means its good. It might even be very good. She's not big on superlatives, doesn't throw adjectives around.

Şimşek regarded her for a few more minutes, I imagine trying to guess how much she weighed. Then he tossed his head in the air, turned his backside on her, and with a swish of his tail, got on with his grazing, just to show he didn't give a hoot what she thought anyway.

The saddle Chumpie had brought was a second-hand hunting saddle, recently restuffed by Martin Lee in Cirencester, and it fitted Şimşek to perfection. I had a spare head collar bridle, bit, reins and had bought another long tether rope when I bought Şimşek.

Chumpie had left the buying of saddlebags until she came to Turkey since there were good ones to be had at a fraction of the cost of English makes, and I wouldn't wish the experiences I had with mine on anyone.

In the late afternoon, we went on a long ride around the coastline through the pines, to an old Lycaen Tomb on the headland. The horses behaved well, but it became clear quickly that we could not ride side by side since they kept threatening each other with broken noses and thick lips. Ahmed Paşa was insistent on his role as boss of the whole outfit, so we had to ride along in tandem. It caused further problems because Şimşek walked faster than Ahmed Paşa and Chumpie had to spiral off on several occasions to keep away from his back end. On top of this, the analogy of Don Quixote and Sancho Panza wasn't a bad one.

That evening, we went to Söke and bought a pair of rough jute bags for £3, more grain for the horses and coffee for roadside brew-ups.

Back in Akbuk, Chumpie sewed up the bags to fit Şimşek. I cleaned and oiled the tack with saddlesoap Chumpie had brought out. I had finished mine off in the mountains and had been using Nivea. You could buy it anywhere. Saddlesoap was unheard of. Nivea had other values too. It acted as a mild fly repellent. I wiped tiny smudges into the corners of Ahmed Paşa's eyes, when he wasn't wearing his fly band. Nivea darkened the leather, but didn't seem to affect the stitching: it was a good stand-by. Nevertheless, I preferred to use saddlesoap. It has better penetrating qualities, and my saddle had become dry from constant exposure to bright sunlight. I had kept my kit in good condition, never neglecting to clean or mend it.

We rode a dummy run the next day, to a curry-scented island about ten kilometres from Akbuk, tethered the horses to trees, in the plentiful grass and clover there. Chumpie painted while I brewed up coffee. Everything went fine: boded well for the departure of the expeditionary forces the following day. The horses were munching away, Chumpie was scribbling all over a big piece of paper. Then a cloud-burst, dropped most of the Mediterranean on us: icy cold. It was a freezing ride back to Akbuk – such a contrast to the downy warm weather of the past few weeks.

I found shelter for the horses, towelled them off, but Chumpie fell victim to a cold which hit her with a fury. She went back to her room with her soggy drawings. I sat down and talked to Ali, who'd come to have a look at her, see what he thought. He still wore the same clothes he had on last time: shirt done up to the top, tatty old flannel suit, cap and clumpy shoes. Had three day's growth on his chin. He was in good spirits.

He chatted in a friendly way, and when he saw that I was serious about taking my hanim along with me on this daft venture, said it was bound to fail. Wasn't she already sick? Why didn't we forget the whole thing, go by bus, not risk problems and bandits, and have a much more comfortable time? Besides, he could see clear as day I had no idea what I was doing, not a clue with horses. Chuck it in! Anyway, I had paid far too much for the little horse, he said. If I had left it to him he would never have dealt with such a dishonest old man. He could have bought two good horses for the price I'd paid for one bad one. He nearly suffocated at his own joke. Then added wistfully, that maybe it didn't matter, because the old man had given him 100,000 lira for his pains. Incidentally, he added, if I or any of my friends wanted anything else from Söke at the highest possible price, then I could rely on him to fix it. Howling with laughter, he caught the bus home: I liked that old rogue. Funny thing is, if I did want another horse in Söke, I would go to him.

In the morning, Chumpie was sniffling with her cold, the horses in fighting form, the weather more indulgent we had a farewell breakfast with Musa, his friend Ibrahim, wife, children and hotel staff. Everybody posed for photographs, they gave us food for our journey and wished us luck.

Chumpie then saddled up and mounted Şimşek, who gave everything a close inspection, sniffing her belongings warily like customs men looking for contraband. She looked good on him. He gave the impression of being ready for whatever was required. She definitely looked like something out of the 'twenties, perched up there on that young stallion with her felt hat, knapsack, saddlebags and bedroll. Şimşek looked the part too in his smart new saddle and tack, skeleton knee-pads – which gave him a racy, Lambourn air – brown head collar bridle, and blue cavalry halter rope. I was proud of them both.

Ahmed Paşa was equally well dressed, now wearing his new kneepads, clean leather map cases and polished saddle. Having gained weight and condition he looked a very stylish expedition leader indeed.

I paid Musa for our lodgings, all his help, and the frightful inconvenience we must have been to the village. He charged me £100. They all came out to wave us goodbye. 'Güle-güle!' And we clattered away.

Ahmed Paşa had revealed a new side to his character in the past few days and as we rode along the coastline to Didyma I found him more difficult and erratic than ever before. Either he was taking his role as leader of the party with burdensome responsibility, putting on a very formal show of it or else was developing an equine trait which can be difficult to deal with.

I knew by now that travelling horses behave in a different way to stabled horses, since, having no home to go to, you, the rider, represent the only security he has, so he becomes close and malleable. That's if there's only one horse. Now, because of this new horse, Ahmed Paşa was showing signs of leadership which he had had no cause to show before.

As leading horse, his duty was to warn the herd – that is Şimşek – of any hazards ahead, which he did, with relish. Any leading horse will do this. Stabled horses are more subtle about it: the whole thing only becomes really apparent in travelling horses. The leading horse communicates in a visible and exaggerated over-reaction. From the moment we set out on the ride north, Ahmed Paşa turned into a monster to handle. He shied violently at rocks, tree stumps, leaves and mostly, at walking stones – tortoises.

Behind, Chumpie and Şimşek jogged along quietly, spiralling off every now and then, while Ahmed Paşa cavorted off sideways in double-speed half-passes at anything he suspected of being potentially hostile.

It was a long ride to Didyma. The afternoon ride on the open hot plain was airless and fly-ridden. Chumpie was handling Şimşek well, which took skill, since he was a very strong young horse, and I was impressed with his performance since he had not done anything openly dreadful. He had followed behind faithfully, if noisily. I planned to camp somewhere on the far side of Didyma for the night, not to make too long a day of it. Thirty kilometres or so were quite enough for both Chumpie and Şimşek on their first day's ride.

As we approached Didyma, Şimşek proved that he had not yet fully recovered from his infatuation with donkeys and roared his head off at every tethered ass in the place. Chumpie had a hard time holding him, and as I turned once, I saw them gallivanting off, Şimşek's eyes rolling, toward a placid donkey who, suddenly finding itself the object of his hottest desires, answered in a fit of impassioned braying. Şimşek responded. Chumpie grappled hold of him, pulled him away and narrowly missed being party to a rape. They broke away, once again joining Ahmed Paşa's Circus To The North.

The combined antics of the horses made any attempt to stop in Didyma impossible, although Chumpie wanted to see the Temple of Apollo, having come three thousand miles to do so. We passed it on the wrong side, totally obscured from view by a high stone wall, desperately trying to control the horses, who had worked themselves into full cry.

'That was Didyma,' I said to her. 'Now we're going to Milet.' As we came sideways out of a back street in a whirr of dust and hooves, I heard her say, 'Going to Milet? Or past it?' I caught the note of sarcasm in her voice, aimed, I felt, more at Şimşek than me. The road out of Didyma dropped down onto what in Greek and Roman times had been a sea bed.

We started looking for somewhere to spend the night straightaway, which is never easy, and we were forced to carry on for quite a few miles in the late afternoon. We could see Milet in the distance raised above the surrounding plain: too far for us to make for. We had to settle for something closer. We found ourselves in a built-up area, which is the worst possible place to be with horses, because not only do the people fail to understand what you need, but even if they did, they couldn't supply it.

We pushed on, Chumpie and Şimşek showing signs of fatigue, until we arrived at a camp site whose proprietor was cagey about letting us in. Discovering he had no other campers, we paid in advance, plus a bit for grazing, and were shown to a filthy billet, with a squalid bunged-up lavatory and disgusting sleeping quarters. Chumpie was in no mood to be choosy. Besides, we didn't have any alternative, so agreed to make the best of it.

The horses however had good grazing, with lots of deep-rooting herbs, and a generous topping of star grass and wild lucerne. While I tethered them, Chumpie sorted out what could be done to make our accommodation more bearable, and decided to abandon it altogether in favour of a windswept lean-to. In there she turned a table on its side against the wind, and rolled her sleeping bag down alongside. She was in no state to go on, was hacking with a cough and settled down more-or-less straightaway. We watched the sun set across the water and the moon rise huge and cratered. We had a light snack of bread and tomatoes and, as we brewed some coffee, Şimşek created a diverting pantomime that started innocently enough, but lured him on into a strange affliction which remained with him thereafter.

I had tethered him on a long line to a telegraph pole, which for reasons known only to him, he was attempting to climb. Try as I might to stop him, he persevered in this pointless endeavour, tearing holes in his chest as he did. I swapped his tether to a tree. He did the same thing.

'We'll have to find him an un-jumpable tree' Chumpie shouted, and went off to look. A few minutes later, she found a near-prostrate fig tree quite close to our shack, so I moved Şimşek, and he was unable to jump up, climb over or in any way vault this tethering post. From that night on, whenever we parked, we had to go to considerable lengths to find a suitable recumbent, un-jumpable tree, to save Şimşek from his own extraordinary and exhausting eccentricities. Ahmed Paşa, in the meantime, annoyed that he had missed out on all the fun and attention, broke into a woeful tirade, furious he could no longer see Şimşek and set up such a battery of shrieking that a group of villagers turned up to see what the trouble was.

I had to move him too. I found a place where he could see Şimşek, was as much out of the wind as possible, could see us, had plenty of grazing and water. In amongst the gardens, shrubs and landscaping, none of that was easy. We just settled down for the night, when Şimşek started yelping. It sounded as though he had been stung. I could find nothing on him, and as I walked away, he did it again, but I saw that time. He was sniffing his own flanks, and squealed each time he did. It was a peculiar action, and I was beginning to realise that Şimşek was altogether a rather peculiar horse. What he did, of course, should have given me a clue as to what was stirring around in his dirty little mind, but it didn't. I stopped him with the application of a handful of soap.

I returned to the shelter and Chumpie had crawled coughing into her sleeping bag on the hard concrete floor, with her numnah, her mattress, her saddle, her pillow.

The moon hung a soft yellow over the dark sea: the wind whipped up the breakers on the shore and the waves rolled a tangled rough music all night. Mosquitoes whined round us, leaves rustled in trees and none of us slept a wink. We were up the following morning at dawn and brewed coffee. I fed the horses a barley feed, and sat down shivering to a breakfast of stale bread. The sun gathered in light and power, and we mounted, made our way to Milet. The ride took us through rich farmland where crops of sorghum, barley and wheat were rising tall and green under the spring sun.

As we approached Milet, the old sea bed stretched away flat and wide, to the great mountain range of Samsun Daǧlari lying like a sleeping giant east to west. It had been visible from as far back as Akbuk, looked every bit as imposing all the way. We grazed the horses en route, then arrived at Milet at midday. Milet or Miletos or Balat as it is known locally is an ancient Greek city, one of its claims was to be the first Greek city to coin money, owing to its position as a trading centre on the sea. A number of its citizens were directly responsible for contributing to the foundations of Western philosophy, men such as Thales and Anaximenes: and Hakateos is generally supposed to have been the first man to have produced a geographical map.

Of the city itself there are wide-scattered remains including a vast Roman theatre in very good repair, which seated twenty-five thousand. I found it astounding that such large audiences could be counted on in those times and reflected that a theatre today would be so lucky to get five hundred sales in one go. Perhaps these great amphitheatres are better compared to football stadiums, with the same kind of appeal, while in the little theatres, such as Iassos, the really high-brow stuff went on.

We stayed in Milet for three hours looking at the ruins. While Chumpie painted, I tended to the horses, switching their plentiful grazing there. They were constantly squaring up to one another, standing at the end of their tethers mouthing threats, pawing the ground like a couple of overfed gladiators anxious to do the other one a mischief.

Since it wasn't too hot, I thought we'd move on in the afternoon, and skirt the shoreline to Davutlar. We could spend the night in Karine, which didn't look that far on the map. Maybe a three hour ride. Unfortunately, it meant missing out Priene, which was a pity, since I'd heard it was well worth a visit.

Priene had been a sister town to Milet and, like her, once occupied a position on the sea. Now it stands well inland. Like so many of these classical sites, it has a fascinating history. Round Priene, Persephone, Goddess of Spring, while out picking wild flowers had been seduced by Hades, kidnapped and taken to his Kingdom of the Dead, where he made her his wife and queen. Demeter, Persephone's mother, searched in vain for her beloved daughter and in her despair cursed the earth, forbidding trees and flowers to blossom or fruit. Since all life on earth was threatened by this, Hades was compelled to release Persephone for nine months of the year. But she had to remain with him for the remaining three, thus symbolising winter, and her release the annual rebirth of nature, Spring. She'd been out for a month or more by the time we got there. But, for all the colour and magic of classical myths, we couldn't hang around and set out for Karine.

We were still riding at nine o'clock that night. The map was wrongly charted. Karine was much further than we had supposed. The riding had been hard and in the twilight, we had been attacked by mosquitoes. The only water had been brackish. There were no villages, no food and nowhere to stay. Chumpie had fought Şimşek who persisted in his donkey-loving-dance every time he saw an ass, and Ahmed Paşa had behaved abominably. Something was aggravating the horses terribly, and for the first time, Ahmed Paşa turned on me.

Şimşek wouldn't let Chumpie lead him, and she became frightened of his actions towards her. I couldn't see it. We pushed on doggedly for Karine in darkness, and, having arrived at another fishing weir a man told us there was nothing at Karine, certainly, no water. We turned back, collapsing into a pine wood. Fortunately, the horses had good grazing, and we were able to get water from a poor little house nearby.

We were all exhausted. Chumpie had a raging temperature, and I felt responsible for everybody having such a nasty time. But I was puzzled by the horses: I couldn't understand why they were behaving so oddly.

We stayed there under the jagged Samsun Daġlari, unmolested by insects. Chumpie slept at least a little. The horses lay flat out. I lay awake listening to someone drive around way above us in a bulldozer all night and caught the distant bay of the ever-revolving dog.

The dawn hurried us out of our sleeping bags since we had parked quite close to a large number of bee hives, and had to be up and away before the bees. We were all covered in citronella, which is a wonderful insect repellent, but, being a beekeeper myself, I knew it was a swarm attractant for bees. It may be the only thing I know. But I learned it well, by experience.

We left our campsite at the crack of dawn, beating the bees to it. We retraced our footsteps back to Karine to skirt the coastline to Davutlar. In the daylight, it looked quite different but every bit as hard. Limestone rock crumbled high above us on our right, and to the left, the sea shone like mercury. Instead of mosquitoes we had horseflies. Big black glistening horse-flies, delivering savage bites, making the horses wince and rear.

It was a ghastly ride. At Karine we were confronted with a cliff face beyond the capability of even Ahmed Paşa. The footpath marked on the map was exactly what it said: a footpath for men, not horses. The whole thing was a wasted journey. We would have to go back, find another route over the mountains. Disappointed, we turned our little foursome round again and headed along the track inland. The same gruelling crossing again, for the fourth time.

Chumpie went through all the wrestling with Şimşek all over again while he rolled his eyes at every donkey in Doganbey and Atburgazi, where we stopped for some water. I dismounted from Ahmed Paşa, bought some bread for us and a soft drink while he guzzled gallons of water, which was his way of drinking – once a day. I offered him water all day, but he would only drink once.

I had understood it to be bad practice for a horse and to be discouraged. But in a land where water is at a premium, to be able to manage on one watering a day is a very real advantage. I let him, and he thrived on it.

By four o'clock that afternoon, we were in Priene. A hand-painted signpost which read 'Pansiyon' with the 'N' back-to-front took us up to

Hassan's place. It was a white concrete house with a wide view of the plain and Gullubache, the village.

Hassan, the proprietor, was a delightful, completely drunk landlord with a captivating smile and no teeth. He called me his brother, showed us a room which had been painted quite recently, in which there were six mattresses and two rusty iron beds, and that was it. When I asked him how much it was to stay there, he said he didn't know, hadn't thought about it, and would we like tea or raki? He also had good grazing. At last we had fallen on our feet. There was a tap outside for washing, lemon trees, shrubs, figs and an out-of-control vine which tumbled in lavish profusion over the entire building. The roof was full of holes, but Hassan pointed out that since it wasn't raining, it didn't matter. Chumpie said she was uneasy about the two snakes who kept half falling through one of the holes in the roof onto what was to be our bed. Hassan said they never did fall, he liked them and had watched them for hours. Were we sure we didn't want any raki?

The house occupied a position away from the centre of Gullabache with the acropolis above. I could buy oats for the horses in the village, a good meal for Chumpie and me. Altogether it was an opportune find, since Hassan also knew a path across the mountains to Davutlar. What's more, he knew the local blacksmith. It was relaxing being at Priene with such a congenial landlord and we all four benefited from the three days we spent there.

In the evening we walked round the ruins and the remarkable site the Greeks had chosen. When the sea had risen to the foot of the town it must have been lovely indeed. We walked down to Gullubache, sat drinking tea beneath the Byzantine water cascade. It was calm, balmy even. We looked forward to a good night's sleep and turned in early.

I heard Hassan coming back from a raki drinking session at midnight. He was cannoning round the kitchen with saucepans on his feet. Then a drum struck up and a miserable sounding sing-song, which continued all night. It was the beginning of Ramadan.

Whether Hassan was celebrating the advent of Ramadan, I rather doubted, but between them, I lay awake listening to Chumpie cough, Hassan fall about in the kitchen, the drum, the sing-song, and every other racket that happened to fill the ether with itself, and wondered if ever I would sleep again. In the morning Hassan asked me if I had heard the drum. I said I had. I asked him if he had heard the man who came in at midnight with buckets on his feet and dance about in the kitchen. He said he hadn't. But, he said, if I heard him again, I was to tell him, and he would cut his ears off. He said he hadn't been able to sleep because he had drunk too much raki. Sometimes, he said, he couldn't sleep because he smoked too many cigarettes. Anyway, he didn't plan on doing anything that day so he was going to sleep under the lemons.

While Chumpie went off to make friends with the natives, I jiggled the horses' grazing around and was moved to a condition of apoplexy by Ahmed Paşa who resolutely refused to cross a four inch trickle of water to graze on the opposite side. I tried every trick I knew to get him to put his foot over this piddling little ditch and he did his toughest best to remain fixedly on the other side, where there was no grass. Having had enough of his pig-headedness I was considering whether to kill him, when a chum of Hassan's turned up promising to show me the footpath over the mountain. He said it had to be done then because he wanted to have a sleep later.

I looked at Ahmed Paşa, thought I would leave him where he was and let him sort out his own wretched grazing. I was livid but he was unimpressed with the horn of plenty I was offering. I made one last attempt to pull him toward the overgrown Byzantine hanging garden with the long delicious grass in the shade where there weren't any flies. I yanked sharply on his head collar which I know is wrong but did it anyway. Then I hit him. He reared. I shouted. He shied. I lost my temper. So did he. He bolted, catching my legs in the tether rope, dragging me a short distance along the rough track. I threw the rope off, tied him where he stood, whereupon he blithely stepped across the trickle, browsed about as though nothing had happened. Just then I could have killed him.

Hassan's friend watched all this patiently and as soon as everything appeared to be settled, he said, 'Haydi gel!' ('Come on!') and off we went, up this tortuous path towards the acropolis. It was a long way up. A very aching climb. He treated it like a race. He was at least seventeen years my junior and when we arrived at the top, my vision blurred and I thought I was dying.

He pointed out the path to Guzelçami which led on to Davutlar. It looked very rough indeed, and an old shepherd on the top said it would be madness to go to Davutlar that way. Go by the road, he said.

Then my guide took me around the enormous acropolis, which had a view so commanding that at once it became perfectly clear why it had been sited there. From a strategic point of view it was quite impregnable. We then started the descent of the cliff on a zigzagging path, inches wide. Why was he doing this to me? We rushed back to the pansy on, where I arrived pouring with sweat. He proudly announced we had done it in two hours, ten minutes. The last tourist took three hours: and a further two days to recover. The last tourist, he added, gave him three thousand lira.

The blacksmith came at six thirty and was the best I met in Turkey. Ahmed Paşa needed a complete new set and was a brute to hold. The shoeing performance lasted for three quarters of an hour, and I wound up with a nail in each leg and indeed still have the scars. We had a delicious meal with some villagers, who were curious about Chumpie, which made a change from the endless enquiries about the cost of the horses. They seemed to find it hard to grasp that she actually chose to travel in this way when there were perfectly good buses. I think, at the time, Chumpie did too.

Diary Entry: 11 May
Set out from Priene at six this morning. Cool. Both horses going well. We found the mountain pass Hassan told us about and rode high above the plain. Stopped for a three hour lunch break overlooking the coast on the northern side. Ahmed Paşa lay flat out underneath a huge old conker tree. Şimşek lay down under a bush. Chumpie sketched. Afternoon ride to Davutlar, then to the sea where we found grazing and a pansyon with a shower and bathroom, which was wildly exciting. Events for the day: Stallions very racy, chased three mares.

Everybody was much refreshed after a night's sleep, and we made good headway along the shoreline. We set out late in the morning but it was cool moving along the beach toward Kuşadasi. The horses were enjoying being near the water again, and just after skirting a rocky outcrop, Şimşek gave Chumpie a dunking. It was deliberate. He took her further out into the water than I had walked in front with Ahmed Paşa, and being that much shorter was a good bit closer to the surface. Just as a good swell approached, he sat down. All her paintings, all her paper, her clothes, everything she wore were drenched. It was very funny. Chumpie didn't understand. Şimşek was delighted. Chumpie was bolshie for two hours after that.

We had to stop to dry out all her stuff, which gave me an opportunity to de-tick and swim both horses. In the mountains behind, they had picked up a lot of fast-moving, blood-sucking flies, that attach themselves to any shady part of a horse, particularly right beneath the tail. They were quite impossible to kill and even if you squashed them between thumb and forefinger, they would fly away, land on some other poor beast. They were foul things. We called them by their Latin name, 'arsehole flies'. Both horses had their quota of ticks too.

I learned another technique of de-ticking Ahmed Paşa, who was more prone to them than Şimşek. I found that by roping the off-side hind then walking round to the other side, gently lifting the off-side hind with the rope, holding it over his back, but carefully so it didn't bite into him, you could then de-tick the horse from the nearside. He couldn't kick, since one leg is off the ground. If he toppled, you simply dropped the rope. It worked rather well. I was also able to apply nail varnish remover to ticks that were well bedded in, and they pull off in minutes following the application. Chumpie brought the stuff with her; it was very effective. All that, and a roll in the sand, and the horses were bugles.

Our arrival in Kuşadasi brought us into contact with a lot of traffic, which we were unprepared for, although we had met trucks crabbing towards us in a shroud of diesel fumes. Here it was worse. There were a lot of tourists, and it became obvious that we would have to leave as quickly as possible since, if we stayed, we ran the danger of the horses running amok in amongst the crowds, who undoubtedly would submit large accounts for damages. A stallion is a tricky beast at the best of times, but two stallions, both too big for their boots in a town full of tourists all of whom wanted to stroke them, was little short of madness.

We found ourselves a bolt-hole up behind the town and left before dawn the following day.

Even then the night had not been without its problems, since Ahmed Paşa had been released from his tether by some idiot, and found the nearest mare. Şimşek had had to be found an un-jumpable tree and had squealed himself dumb when Ahmed Paşa disappeared. But we did learn something of interest, which was to save us trouble: there were loose horses at Ephesus. Had we not known that we would have ridden straight into Ephesus, and into trouble. Neither of us wanted to stay in Kuşadasi. It had a brassy cosmopolitan air. When you have been living with a horse for a while, the commercialisation feels shallow, silly. You're better off with the horse, and everyone else, better off without you.

We rode through the silent streets as the sun rose. There was no one around. We passed the great caravanserai, now a snazzy hotel, past the harbour then out along the coast road, cutting off again onto tracks, paths, heading north. We were aiming for Pamuçak, from where we could easily visit Ephesus and Selçuk. As we rose above the shore, a cool wind caught us, and we saw the little village down in the sweep of the bay. A short day's ride. It gave me time to reflect on the trip.

Travelling with horses heightens your senses. You arrive and depart at a pace men have moved at for centuries, which Crusader and adventurer would have recognised. You get bitten by the same bugs that would have bitten them, your horse shies at the same rock maybe theirs would have shied at, or tenses at a mare, as theirs' might. He stumbles and you spill off, just as they would have, and you get scratches that refuse to heal and you keep hitting them again and again. You get rope-burned hands, and get preoccupied by the things that would have preoccupied them: the grazing, the water, whether it's brackish or drinkable, and you eye mountains for accessible paths, ways across. You look at rivers for fording places, long beaches for ease of riding. You have little idea of what is round the next corner, but unlike being in a car, you have time to think about what is likely to be there. You worry about your billet for the night, where you will camp, whether anyone will see. Intelligence of your surroundings, you gather swiftly.

When you approach a village or town, you look at it closely, for high points, low points, the nature of the place and usually, you sum it up right first time. In a car, it comes and goes, and you never even feel it.

As night falls you find your grazing, water and food for your horse. Then, you feed yourself and lastly when you tie your horse at night, you trust you have tied him securely.

9

Guardian of the Mountain

'Whoso relieves himself here shall suffer the wrath of Hecate' is a stern warning, considering Hecate was the dreadful three-headed monster deity of the underworld: sender of phantoms, ghouls, ghosts, sprites and the eerie haunter of crossroads. To a man for whom Hecate was in all probability real, such a caution would be enough to send him off to piddle elsewhere.

Graffito like that brings a city to life. That was cut in the stone, near the arched gateway in front of the library at Ephesus some two thousand years ago. Not in English. It's a telling remark. Easy to picture the scene of the man fed up with people fouling his doorway after a night on the local vinegary wine. Wonder if he hung a lamp over it so it could be read in the dark? It shows he expected a lot of people to be able to read. And concern perhaps for keeping things up to scratch: this was a sea port, busy and prosperous.

The name Mithridates is cut in a great stone. Somehow, for me that lifted him out of the pages of a history book and placed him there, real, tangible. This king of Pontus was welcomed by the Ephesians as a conqueror who freed them – temporarily – from the Romans in 88BC, and butchered all Italian inhabitants irrespective of age or gender.

Ephesus was a place of pilgrimage where Artemis, Apollo's sister, had her temple, one of the seven wonders of the world: the others are the Pyramids of Egypt, The Colossus of Rhodes, The Statue of Zeus at Olympia, the Hanging Gardens of Babylon, the Lighthouse at Alexandria and the Mausoleum at Halicarnassos (Bodrum).

Artemis (Diana) was Goddess of the Ephesians. She represented fertility and oddly, chastity. She was protector of the animal kingdom, having her origins in a mixture of Diana and Chimera. She conferred a special honour on the city, and was held in high regard. The city was dressed in statues of her, rather than of Roman Emperors, even when they were the overlords.

Ephesus had great names associated with it: King Croesus (he of the riches), Mithridates, Alexander, Julius Caesar, Mark Anthony, Cleopatra, St John the Divine, Mary Mother of Jesus and St Paul of Tarsus. St Paul had caused a bit of a stir in Ephesus when he was there. He'd upset the local silversmiths with his talk, costing them their trade. It's rather like imagining the Moonies putting Sheffield stainless steel workers out of a job on account of some strange new fangled ideology no one had ever heard of. He was run out of town: hardly surprising. Unlike the Moonies, he had something to say: Ephesus went Christian. St John, author of Revelations is generally supposed to have died there. There is doubt about it. Mary, Mother of Jesus, was taken to Ephesus by John, Jesus' friend, and she died there too. It's debated.

Ephesus is a fascinating place: the largest archaeological site in the world. It's been restored in part, making it more comprehensible to common gawpers like me. We saw the loose horses too.

It had been leggy work wandering around, so we hitched back to Pamuçak and got a lift on a tractor. The driver stopped on the way, jumped off, picked some lilies which he gave to me to give to Chumpie, sitting beside me. We'd left the horses beneath some gum trees, having pulled up into a closed beach camp-site, run by a man in a string vest and wearing pyjama bottoms. Pyjama bottoms were pretty trendy in Turkey.

We had dinner in one of the shenzi dukas on the beach. It was very good. Ramshackle beach huts are always good, they never offend: they fit in well somehow with the landscape. It was disappointing to hear that the whole area is to be developed, the marsh drained, two or three villages thrown up, the birds deprived of their breeding and feeding grounds: the very things that make it worth visiting, all thrown away.

There had been a lot of explosions going on round the headland in the direction which we were to travel. It was quarrying work for the new road linking Pamutçak to Claros, our next destination. We planned to ride straight over the mountain, so needed no road. In any event, we'd be well away from the new road. From the map, it looked like a two hour ride. We left the camp site at six in the morning, rode along the beach towards the headland and met the estuary of the Kuçuk Menderes about three quarters of the way along.

The river itself was very narrow, but it was boggy, fast flowing and deep. Having crossed the Dalyan with Ahmed Paşa, I knew to go right out to sea to cross the river mouth rather than attempt the shorter, trickier crossing. By making an arc out to sea, it was a little over two hundred yards, easy enough on Ahmed Paşa given his height advantage.

On the other side I turned to watch Chumpie and Şimşek. She was nervous about it. Hadn't swum the horses as I had, wasn't sure what Şimşek might do – he'd been behaving oddly with her again. She followed a long line straight out, which was right, then turned in half way, just a little too sharply, and found the bottom further down than they both expected. That was her second dunking.

It was too early to hang about drying, so she rode soggily on until we found a spot where she could spread her belongings all over Turkey again. We rode on to a village on the shoreline, behind which the mountain stretched up and around the point to Notion (pronounced Notium) and Claros. There was no road. A local fisherman showed us the beginnings of a path, which we followed. It was eight thirty in the morning: time enough for a quick dry out for Chumpie before going on. It didn't look more than an hour's ride.

We arrived eight hours later. Although we followed the fisherman's directions, the path hadn't been used for a long time. We went up a steep incline, which brought us out into a scrubby plateau. The path disappeared. All round was a mass of jagged little rocks, dense holly-like shrubs. I took a compass bearing and, leading Ahmed Paşa, went weaving off through the scrub. Chumpie had also dismounted, but said she didn't trust Şimşek when she led him. I couldn't understand why. I went down, losing sight of her in the bushes, met a dead end, and shouted to her to turn back. She didn't answer. In the noise of the wind, I thought perhaps she hadn't heard me anyway.

I retraced my steps, floundered around in the bushes, all the time calling for her. It took an hour to find my way back to the plateau. There was no sign of Chumpie. I took the kit off Ahmed Paşa, tethered him and let him graze, and called Chumpie again and again. Then I heard the explosion.

We were right above the dynamite. We had met what we aimed to avoid. I could smell cordite, split rock, fright. I thought all the things you can at a moment like that. I called again and heard Şimşek whinny somewhere above me, up in a tangle of bushes. It sounded like pain. I stumbled over rock, ran, falling, tripping, and saw Chumpie. She wasn't right. Ran up to her. She was frightened, cut and bruised.

Şimşek had attacked her. She'd heard me call, had been unable to answer, fighting off Şimşek. He'd pushed her over, knelt on her repeatedly. She hadn't heard the explosion.

Both stallions had been scenting off her, sent their passions racing. It explained everything. All the signals had been there but, not being female, I hadn't, couldn't see them.

Şimşek badly frightened her. But we still had to get down off the mountain, couldn't ride on that stuff. To her lasting credit, Chumpie swallowed her fear, led him down, mounted him when we got to level ground.

We camped beneath olives that night on the shore, near Notion. Şimşek was tethered to an un-jumpable tree, Ahmed Paşa to a well head. We were near Claros, known once for its Oracles. Before the Trojan War, the Sybil Herophile made her predictions from there, forewarning the fall of Troy.

The Oracles of Claros survived well into Christian times before the settlement submerged into mud. Notion was a larger port, and Colophon, further inland was famous for its horses and peculiarity in using dogs in war. Little remains of these places now.

It took several days to reach Izmir. We camped out every night beneath the stars, while the horses grazed beside us. During the day, we sought shade from the strong sunlight, away from pestering flies. One day we sheltered in green thicket under a stand of withy and stayed there while willow seed blew in the air around us.

One night we camped just outside a little village, on a river bank. All the villagers visited us. They brought tea, bread, yoghurt and barley for the horses. They were fascinated by Chumpie: couldn't understand why the tourists travelled in this way.

I left *The Fusus*, by Muhyiddin Ibn'Arabi on the river bank there, and my Holy Koran: forgive me Grenville, they had become too difficult to carry. We left little piles of coins in the grass wherever we stayed, whether it was a night camp, or just a place we pulled up in during the day. In my books that morning I left a 5,000 lira note for the villagers of Develiköyu, who had been so kind. I have often wondered who found it: whether it was the poor old woman who brought us milk, or the daughter who brought us radishes and yoghurt, or one of the little children who stood by and stared.

We followed the river up towards Izmir aiming to ride through the town, rather than skirt it. I know the hinterland of these Turkish towns to be never ending. Although riding through was a terrible alternative, it was something we could accomplish in a day, rather than three or four days in suburbia.

The ride up was varied, starting off in a broad river valley, past a new dam, through high rocks, through forestry, onto open moorland, finally winding up in the town rubbish dump. We rode through a gunnery range, along tracks, through a weird eerie deserted factory, like something straight out of the War of the Worlds.

We never met a fence, which was the great beauty of riding through Turkey, and neither were the people proprietorial, but always met us with a smile. By and large we stuck to farm tracks, weaving in and out of fields, skirting field margins, fording streams, little torrents in our path. On the few occasions we found ourselves on a main road, all vehicles hooted. Whether it was to get a reaction from the horses or from sheer bonhomie I cannot tell, but it was always terrifying. Lorries all had triple air horns and came careering at us never leaving a margin of safety. I don't think it was malicious, more a question of being unable to see the consequences.

The weather became a deal hotter and we rode early in the morning from six until ten, then again in the afternoon, from four until dark. It made for slower progress, but saved the horses. Flies were a constant ordeal since we'd finished our citronella, had nothing as effective, being suspicious of chemical compounds which are always expensive and nearly always useless. Without a close reference map, we guided ourselves along with the old compass allowing for its inaccuracy, which I checked against the north star, and knew vaguely the margin of error.

On 23 May, we rode into Izmir, and found nowhere to stay. Both of us were tired, both filthy, the horses hungry. The next day we knew would be a fearsome ride straight through the centre of the city. A little like riding round Hyde Park Corner in peak traffic with everyone hooting from cars with no brakes and no silencers, on two strong and very fit stallions, who hadn't had a day's schooling in their lives. The insanity of it beat its fists against my better judgement but there was no other way. Izmir was in our path, and through it we had to go.

We searched in vain for somewhere to stay, when an old man, wearing a shabby uniform and military cap, called over to us in French. He was riding a glossy little stallion: he was the first mounted horseman we had seen.

'Suivez-moi!' he shouted, and he had us following. He trotted off, leading us back in the direction from which we had come, then up into the mountain, outside Boca, south Izmir. He told us he was the Guardian of the Mountain and knew a place for us for the night. The track was rugged and he rode quickly, explaining in his broken French that he had not eaten since sunrise because it was Ramadan and was anxious to be round the mountain swiftly, before eating with his friend.

Near the top, he pointed to a little plateau which was protected from the wind by a ridge of high ground behind with a view right over Izmir. You couldn't hear a thing from the city. The place was thick in rich grass, shaded by olives. A heavenly spot.

'C'est bon ici, mais faites attention aux petits animaux qui vivent sous terre.' ('It's good here, but be careful of the little animals who live in the ground') he said and lobbed a stone against a tree, telling us about a spring nearby, how we should recognise it from the tree which was the same variety as the one he pointed out.

'C'est un très vieil arbre – peut-être mille ans.' ('It's a very old tree, perhaps a thousand years.')

Then he rode away and as he did he waved and shouted, 'Dormez bien et ecoutez bien pour le bul-bul, c'est très agréable.' ('Sleep well and listen out for the bul-bul, it is very pretty.')

We waved goodnight, grateful to him, all four of us. We never did discover what 'les petits animaux qui vivent sous terre' were, but they might have been sylphs that haunted those trees with a hush, perfuming the air with the scent of grass and olive leaves.

The sun dropped into a pool of crimson light. The city lay before us, silent. We found the spring, just as the old man said beneath the ancient tree. I took the horses to drink, one at a time, then returned them to crop the grass. Chumpie and I washed and drank there too. It might have been Holy, for the enchantment of that place. I spun a coin into the water, grateful to have drunk there.

A shepherd boy sat down with us in the last light of the sun as his sheep grazed a little way away, their bells jingling a tinselly melody. He left us to ourselves.

The sky deepened from blue to a glossy blue-black and the lights of the town lay scattered like a handful of diamonds cast at random on black velvet. Over to the right the great range of Kemal Paşa Dağlari fused with the darkening sky and stars shone jewel-like and coloured. I lay back on my bedroll, watched the horses quietly grazing in the darkness and Chumpie, lying beneath the trees. Stars shone through the moving leaves and a nightingale sang all night – the bul-bul. The very earth seemed to sleep calm, like the night before a battle. And Pallas Athene '... *held the night long lingering in the west and in the east at ocean's stream, she kept Dawn waiting by her golden throne and would not let her yoke the nimble steeds who bring us light, Lampus and Phaethon, the colts that draw the chariot of day....*'

10

The Betrayal

'*And sitting down by the green well, I'll pause and sadly think –
'Twas here he bowed his glossy neck when last I saw him drink ...*'

The Arab's Farewell to his Horse. C. E. S. Norton.

We left a ring of coins in the grass, and rode down to Izmir as the sun rose. We had no map of the town: it was to be another hit and miss affair, relying on the compass to see us safely through.

From our olive grove we had been able to see right across the city to the plains beyond – our destination. It looked about ten miles: not a difficult ride. But in reality, we knew we should have to weave through the streets and roads, through traffic, cross the river on some beastly bridge, go through crowds on hard tarmac roads – an appalling prospect.

We emerged first into the southern suburbs and made our way swiftly, before the heavy traffic began. The roads were like mirrors to walk on for the horses, whose iron hooves were polished from the grassy crossings in the mountains. It was bad enough trying to stand on a flat surface, but we found ourselves near the Velvet Fortress, where the town twists into a series of hills, in a network of passages and streets.

I turned to see Chumpie cut across a side street trying to find a gritty patch for Şimşek, watched him slip, lose his footing, hind legs splayed underneath 'He's going..!' I heard, then he righted himself, sprang to a firmer foothold, and I don't know how they got across.

By eight o'clock the traffic had built up into a fast-moving aggressive fug. The air was rancid with the stench of petrol and diesel fumes. Buses roared past, lorries howled down on us, pushing us sideways, totally ignoring us, clattering dustbins and litter that swirled in front, terrifying the horses. They shied at motorcycles, watched children who wheeled about us on bicycles. Ahmed Paşa started his lethal horse-in-the-window charade, and I had to tug him free from broadside offensives at his reflection. We found ourselves in crowds, then suddenly on a frantic dual carriageway, with traffic racing past, leaving us no room at all.

I turned off down a back street which led towards the docks through a factory landscape where men were tearing down buildings on one side, throwing them up on another, where earth-moving machines screeched, chewed up crumbling steel, riddled mouthfuls of concrete, spitting them into contorted sores, gouged up by another machine and dropped into groaning trucks.

We rode over a bridge under which oozed a river purple with pollution, spewing a putrid black pus into the sea. We wound through a scrap yard, then a harbour along a sea wall where we asked the quickest route out of the town only to be sent bolting back by a train looming down on us on hidden tracks.

Some men pointed to a dual carriageway. Traffic moved at a speed along it. 'There is no other way!' they said, 'you must go two kilometres along it, then you will find a small road.' They held up the traffic for us as we crossed onto the right side, and in tandem once more, with vehicles racing past us, we rode along. A cliff stood above us to the right, and on the left, the port of Izmir.

As we walked I felt Ahmed Paşa was inches away from a full-blooded bolt. I caught sight of a vast yellow earth-moving machine roaring up behind, overtaken by cars on either side. Ahmed Paşa was watching something else. I saw it, just as he sprung – a water duct on the road. He suddenly plunged into a wild half-pass, shot out into traffic which was moving at fifty miles an hour. I seized him in panic, and remember how my own voice sounded slow and distorted. I glimpsed the yellow machine, heard a shriek from Şimşek, thought I heard a crunch of bones, tasted blood in my mouth, bolted into a gap in the rock, ran into a compound and Chumpie joined us. Şimşek had followed Ahmed Paşa's bolt into the traffic, but incredibly, neither of us had been hit.

Being on a horse in traffic is a terrible experience. I remember feeling sick, wanting to be anywhere but there. Why didn't the people in the cars try to move over? Why did they have to drive right on top of us? It was by the grace of God alone we hadn't been hit. And yet, I knew what madness it was to do what we were doing. But what was the alternative?

The sun burned us, the horses sweated, flies bothered us and we choked in diesel fumes. We wound up in squalid back streets, in busy crowded markets and in a straight nine hour ride, we pulled in under a fig tree, the horses exhausted and terrified by the sheer hardness of the ride.

It must have ranked as one of the world's worst rides. I would scale mountains, ford rivers, swim estuaries, cross swamps, anything to avoid having to ride through Izmir again.

We were in the back end of town, in a field bordered by trees with only a scratch of grazing. A well beside a hovel contained the carcasses of two dead sheep. We all needed food and water, and we still had the major routes of Izmir to contend with, although we had cleared the city itself. None of us felt like budging. Chumpie suggested a truck. A truck! Why hadn't she suggested a truck when we were in Boca? Why now when we were nearly all dead? Why hadn't I? Ten minutes later, I secured, through the wonderful grapevine of the ever-present çay shop, the use of two exceedingly dilapidated vans.

I knew Şimşek would travel but was less sure about Ahmed Paşa. We scraped up all the money we had between us, which left us penniless, and it was Friday. Tough. Şimşek was loaded from a pile of earth into his van, and I rode Ahmed Paşa up the same pile into the back of his. They were open-topped pick-ups, and so we roped the horses in. Standard practice in Turkey. There's no such thing as a dinky little horse-box.

The vans raced each other out of Izmir, swaying around without a thought for the horses. We implored the drivers not to drive so fast, but they wouldn't listen. I began to wonder if it was safer riding the horses after all. We sped out of the suburbs, and in the late afternoon, jumped the horses out onto a bank, and that was that.

We camped under the stars again in a long grassy field above the sea. The stars shone brilliantly and we were chirruped to sleep by a thousand cicadas. The horses gorged themselves on the grass, and the sea slapped away on bleached stone. Heaven to heaven, by way of hell. Safe.

Chumpie's five weeks in Turkey were up: she had only bargained on being there for that time. She started talking about leaving.

It meant for me, having to chose between the horses. Should I sell

Şimşek, go on with Ahmed Paşa, who had become so difficult to handle? He'd been stumbling lately. Was it a sign of something more serious? Or just the hard riding in Izmir? Or should I sell him, go on with the younger horse? Yet Ahmed Paşa was so much a part of me. Such a different horse from the one I had bought in Çal. He looked magnificent. Yet he could be such a brute. And Şimşek? A funny little chap with a great big heart, and the most willing horse I have ever known. Perhaps someone could join me from England. I thought of Athene English. She could ride one or the other with me back to England. I decided I would ring her.

Then I heard that it was illegal to take horses from Turkey to Greece, so sooner or later, I would have to sell them both. Something I dreaded: I like my animals, get attached to them. Find parting with them very hard. We moved up the coastline, staying in Yenifoa for a day. It was a nice old town, with lovely buildings, thankfully, being restored. It had an unhurried air, a place at peace with itself, disinterested in the gloss of the twentieth century.

The people were chatty, friendly. When I explained to the owner of the restaurant I had no money on me, he fed us anyway, told us to pay when the banks opened. He wouldn't take my watch I offered for surety. Maybe it's a rotten watch. Someone caught a little shark out in the bay, brought it in under his boat. We all squeezed round to look at it. Then he cut it free, and it swam slowly back out to sea.

We stayed in a pansyon and it was strange to sleep under a ceiling again. It felt stuffy, claustrophobic. Both of us were fond of the open air, and apart from the odd bug, had no trouble with insects, snakes, rabid dogs. We always chose our campsites carefully, out of view, well away from roads. Chumpie would only drink the water up in the mountains. But I drank the same stuff as the horses, and they looked all right on it.

We followed the coastline along on an ancient paved track for miles and miles. It took us through a Ruhr valley look-alike, then up to Aliaga, on to Myrina, where we pulled in for the night in an olive grove. We had tried to find Gryneion and failed.

It was late and quiet. I tied the horses on their lines by the water's margin and they grazed young fragmites. I gave them their barley and oats. I went to sleep quickly that evening, but was woken by something in the air. Half awake, I thought I was in a room full of dressing gowns hanging around the walls. When I focused properly, I saw they were not dressing gowns, but trees, and the ceiling, the stars.

The air was sad. A burden lay on me I couldn't describe. I looked for the horses, saw them lying down near the water. Chumpie was asleep in the grass beside me. There was nothing there, just us, the frogs, the horses and the moon. I felt caught in a whorl of anguish and grief. Our time was up, something said. In my heart I knew it, dare not say. Ten days later, I sold the horses.

Şimşek went first. Chumpie cried where she stood watching him walk away. The last I saw of Ahmed Paşa he was walking off behind a wall. He never knew what was happening. I know he didn't: thought we would be back for him, later. Şimşek knew: I saw it in his eyes and he broke me, like a reed.

God bless them, my horses, my friends. And if anything we ever did was of any benefit to them at all, I hope that for the two or three months that we were with them, they acted, behaved, shouted, snorted as stallions should. They were patted, photographed, fed well and looked to properly and I pray that in that fleeting time, Ahmed Paşa felt all his ancestry. That in some way, however small, I did him proud as he did me. That night I wept into my pillow.

When it's time for me to go, they can bury me with my saddle and I'll go to Trapalanda, where all horses go, and I'll find Ahmed Paşa there because I know he'll wait for me. And I'll put my saddle on him, and ride him back to those mountains near Çal. We'll share the raisins again, and he can graze by the stream while I sleep in the sun. I loved that horse with all my heart.

Transition

We caught the ferry to Lésvos and from there to Kavalla. Chumpie went west to Thessaloniki in a wrenched wordless parting; it felt like being broken up in little bits. I went east to Alexandropolis, full of feelings of loss, recriminations. What had I done?

I couldn't bear thinking about Ahmed Paşa: kept wondering where he was, how he was. I knew he'd be wondering about me; it was just second nature. Lost without him, lonely without Chumpie, I wasn't up to much at all. I never got to Alexandroplios but went to a taverna in Lagos and fell asleep in the afternoon.

When I woke, didn't know where I was. Couldn't think where I'd tethered the horses, or where Chumpie had gone. Couldn't remember riding through that strange watery landscape. It only lasted a few minutes of course, then it all came rolling back. I'd broken the ride – didn't seem to be any other way. Tough. Never set out to win any prizes.

I pulled myself together and went to Ktima Litsas, where I had been seven years before.

11

Greece: Ktima Litsas

'Yassou!'

The retsina was sharp and tangy. There was a lot of noise, coloured lights hung up in trees. The village square was full of people. Tinny music played loudly in the tavernas, the distinctive noise of bazouki, its rising and falling rhythm. Smoke from grilled souvlakia wafted in the air, and the clatter of kitchen pans. A waiter hurried over to our table with a basket of bread, huge sliced tomatoes swimming in olive oil, feta cheese sprinkled with oregano. I cut a slice of bread, chewed it.

'Stin-i-yassas!' ('Good health!')

The night was black and cool, everyone wore thin cotton clothing.

There was a lot of excitement, a lot of eating. Greece had just won the semi-finals of International Basketball.

It was good to see Rex and Penny again. I met them years before while I'd been working in northern Greece, and had riding lessons in their outdoor school at Ktima Litsas. It must have the best view of any arena in the world – all across the bay of Thessaloniki to Mount Olympus, all the way east to China. It's just below Panorama.

'I suppose you're going to stay a few months and dump a horse on us, just like all the others,' Rex said.

'What others?'

'All the others who come wandering through here on horses. Like Aydin: he rode up from Syria on an Arab mare called Farrah, who was a direct descendant of the mare of the Prophet, and he brought his dog, Christopher Columbus. He rode on to Spain, left Farrah there, flew to America, rode two horses across the States and back, flew to Spain, picked up Farrah and Christopher Columbus, rode back to Syria. Some time ago now. He was rich. Took him four years. There was Philippe, who rode down from France: he wasn't rich. Then there was Patrice and his girlfriend who rode from France, through here, down on into Turkey the opposite way to you: had their Appaloosa killed by a truck. The last one to come through was a French saddler called Jacques. He came on two little horses, went back via Bulgaria, Romania, Czechoslovakia, Hungary and Poland.'

'Cor, makes me feel like a real amateur.'

'You are.' Nice to see Penny hadn't changed. She's got the knack of being brutally frank yet nice with it somehow. It's a real talent. She can put you in your place with one well aimed word.

I liked these two enormously. A good looking English couple, they had come to Greece about twelve years before and took on a rundown riding school, turning it into the best. They had thirty-six horses. I remembered some of them from my first visit, I remembered Thalice, a lovely thoroughbred stallion who belonged to Taki Litsas, owner of the farm. There was Carmen, an Arab mare who'd been party to a cracked femur for me in 1979, Pindarus, Penny's horse and boss of all horses, and of course Akis, Rex's classic black gelding.

I remembered Penny's Skiros ponies she was busy saving from extinction. Some people maintain the breed was used by Alexander on his campaigns, being tough and resilient, and if you look at the old friezes it's easy to see why. They bear a striking resemblance. The Skiros ponies were good in the riding school too. Penny put children on them to learn, because they were dependable and bomb proof.

The waiter shoved a plate of souvlakia in front of me.

'Perissótero retsina parakalo!' More retsina please.

We dug into our meals. Penny prodded a salad about. 'Where did you sell your Turkish horses?'

'On the way up to Canakkale, in Ayvalik. At least we sold them on the sea. I've never known an unhappier day. It was terrible. Just not knowing where they've gone, and there's such terrible cruelty in Turkey. Then, as you know Chumpie went back to England, and I came here because if anyone knows where to find a horse, you do.'

'We'll find you something,' she went on, 'but they're scarce in Greece now. About four or five thousand horses a year have been exported to Italy for meat. It was illegal to export healthy horses, so they used to poke their eyes out, or break their legs or something. All that was stopped by the International League for the Protection of Horses, but there is still dreadful cruelty. The place is all but devoid of horses, compared to what it was like. Our blacksmith said there used to be forty horses in his village just five years ago, there's only one now.'

'You need a common village horse, or an Araby sort of a thing,' Rex said.

'Yes I do.'

'Well I haven't got one.'

And we drank the rest of the retsina.

'Yassas.'

I was put to bed in the tack room later that night.

'We don't want you in the house,' Penny said. 'You're probably fleasy. You can kip in there with all the saddles, and don't give them any of your lice.'

I had a quick look round before turning in. I remembered Ktima Litsas as a great rambling old farmhouse with a string of outbuildings and stables all hidden beneath an avenue of aging pines.

Taki Litsas lived in the far end of the house – a bit late to go and see him. It all had such a peaceful air, with horses out in the corrals in the dark, some stabled, one or two on long tethers. It was nice to see them all looking so well fed and content: a contrast to the undernourished head-shy horses in Turkey.

Many of them had been rescued by Rex and Penny from frightful hardship, where their owners had imported them for show jumping, then got bored, and abandoned them. Or they hadn't been able to handle them, and had tried to break their spirits through cruelty. These two took them over, not only saving them from terrible lives, but turning them into thoroughly good horses into the bargain. They had an enviable skill with their livestock, and everyone who went there to ride knew it.

Back in the tack room, I curled up on the bed. The air was thick with the smell of leather. I slept for a while, to be woken by Penny's dog vomiting on me, followed by a joint chorus of guinea fowl just going broody, who screeched in dawn far too early.

Penny gave riding lessons at nine-thirty the following morning, and after having helped to feed the horses with Angelici – a good looking

Greek girl with strong classic features and Amazon-like figure – I went off to talk to Taki. An old friend, I found him up to his eyes in new schemes for his farm, busy setting up an organic farmer's cooperative. He voiced his concern about farming in Greece since, having joined the EEC, the country was in the throes of accelerated agricultural production, in danger of throwing sound farming practices to the wind, in favour of mass food output. He went on to say that there was very little livestock about nowadays – it just didn't fit in with the EEC support system and, like Penny, he thought it might not be easy to locate a good horse.

'You remember when you were here in 1979, we drove round Northern Greece looking at farms, and how much farmers depended on animal power? Well, all that has gone. The agricultural bank has lent money to farmers and they have had to buy sophisticated machinery just to keep pace. Sure, the country looks neat and tidy, but I wonder what the long term effect is? The snag with mass production is that apart from anything else, ingenious little homespun businesses get thrown out of the window, and everyone gets on the bandwagon. Still, after Chernobyl, some people feel very responsible for the land, want to do the best by it, as opposed to squeeze the most from it. I hope we fall into that category here. We diversify: I think I'd go mad if I didn't. We produce kiwi fruit, wheat, olive oil, chrysanthemums, exotic plants, shrubs, cut flowers and of course, the horses form an important part of the farm economy.' I've always found Taki about six paces in front of everyone else – he keeps the best retsina for miles too.

That morning I met English, German, Greek and American people who all came to the school for lessons. I met Karen for the first time, an American who had married an influential Greek businessman. Karen was to give me immeasurable help with my paperwork for exporting a horse, and I also met Sandy, a Greek-American, who had lately undergone a traumatic experience with her dog, Chlöe. Chlöe was not a bad dog. 'Actually, she's quite cute,' Sandy would say in that inimitable American way. She was fond of her, took her everywhere. Being mindful of her wishes to sniff everything, she bought an extending retractable lead, which would enable Chlöe to wander off at will, saving her the tiresome business of having to visit every tree with her. They were both pleased with this latest discovery.

One day, Sandy went to Thessaloniki with Chlöe, went to see a friend who lived on the first floor of a block of flats. In the lobby, Sandy met her chum, and they chatted, waiting for the lift. Chlöe wandered off to the other side of the foyer.

The lift arrived and, still chatting, Sandy and her friend got in, pressed the button, and up they went. Chlöe suddenly found herself in a deserted foyer hurtling towards a pair of closed steel doors.

An old lady walked in just in time to see a small dog shinning up the lift doors, and remain at the top for several seconds, rotating. To her horror, Sandy realised at once what had happened, and pressed the descend button, and down she went.

The sight of the dog walking backwards down the lift doors and greeting the occupant warmly, so overwhelmed the old lady, she had to be taken home. Sandy threw the extending lead away.

Sandy was engaging at the best of times, and had a chestnut mare called Tsikalla whom she rode from time to time. She amused us all with her good dry wit. She had been following closely the basketball finals, and it was in her company that a group of us sat on the lawn watching the finals on television, and witnessed Greece win after a thoroughly vivid game, turning a noisy night in the tavernas into a whoopee of major proportions. The delight was endemic, cars drove around honking and hooting, Sandy went crackers and the whole of Thessaloniki was gripped by a fever of celebration for three days solid.

Of their English friends, Bob and Anna were frequently at the farm, owning a huge Irish ex-show jumper called Romany, whom they adored. He was a handsome horse and had been dragged from the jaws of death by Rex and Penny, and these two could do anything with him. It's absolutely true that animals respond to sheer kindness. When they bought him, he'd been a cowering skeleton, wholly unpredictable. Horses are incredibly sensitive animals, and like computers, they don't forget. Bob and Anna showered him with kindness, and when I met him, he was a kind bonny horse, with the gentle manners of a giant. They never hit him: I never saw anyone hit a horse there, and it was one of the reasons the horses were all so reliable – but they were not without spirit.

Bob was a ship's surveyor, a bearded man with a calm, laid back disposition, and clear blue eyes. He had an instant grasp of mechanical things and had rebuilt a 1956 BMW 500cc motorcycle while in Greece, on which I would slip off with him for a beer in the evenings, when all the others were riding.

Everyone helped out at the farm on the day of the gymkhana, when a score of children turned up to compete in the games. Each adult was allocated a 'brat' by Penny, with strict instructions 'not to let the little bugger win twice,' so that everyone would go home clutching a prize. We had egg-and-spoon-on-ponies races, grand mere's foot-steps, musical ponies, dressing up, tugs-of-war. All manner of things that the parents enjoyed as much as the children in the pine-shaded sunlight of the cake and retsina-swigging afternoon. All the children went home with rosettes, little prizes, medallions, flushed and excited, tired and proud.

At last there was news of a horse for sale. It was a mare, and property of the local knackerman, who, whenever he had a horse that was too good to send off for meat, would ring the farm, tell them what he'd got. This time, it was a white mare of 14.2 hands, who was supposedly eight years old. 'That'll mean she's fifteen,' said Penny. But we went to see her all the same.

It was odd to see Greek orthodox priests as we drove through Thessaloniki on the way to the knackerman: I'd forgotten all about priests. Kept expecting to hear muezzins, see mosques.

We pulled up in a back street near the railway station, in the junk yard end of town. Made our way through a pile of rubble and polythene tunnels, met the man. He led us into his stable, where three horses stood dying. He pointed out the white mare in a dark part of the building, adding he wanted 70,000 drachmae for her – about £325. For some reason, I couldn't begin to get interested, even though the alternative for her was grim. I just didn't have that feeling which tells you when something is for you.

We left and went instead up to the mountains through the hill villages to Leviathan. It was beautiful weather, neither too hot nor too cold, and as we drove we scanned the hillsides and villages for horses.

We stopped in Lavation, just outside a kaffenia, where men were playing cards. Pigeons cooed softly in trees and an old man was snoozing on a chair in the shade in the square.

Penny asked about horses, and we were directed up through a back street to a farm she knew, having heard about a horse for sale there some time before. In the farmyard Penny called out, and a man answered. She told him what we were there for, and he took us off to his stable. They talked for some time without my understanding. Penny translated for me.

'He's got a good line in patter this one' she said, trying to smother a laugh. 'I'll translate. He's got a couple of horses, he says, and one of them will be just right.' With that, a very bright little grey gelding popped out of the stable into the sunshine on the grassy bank outside.

'This is the one,' Penny grinned. 'This bloke says it's the best horse in the world. This pony can read and write, knows his alphabet backwards, can add and subtract, he's as good looking as you are (he was talking to Penny), and you won't find a better horse, not even in the next world. And,' she went on, 'he says if you buy him, you'll be friends with this bloke afterwards.'

'Cor, sounds marvellous. How much?'

'He says he will give him to you for 150,000 drax. A bit over £650. Well over double his worth. The bloke says he can't reduce the price because it's such a good horse, and tomorrow it'll be 200,000 drax.'

The pony had a very sunny disposition, but at that price and only 14 hands, it was a bit steep. I asked about the other horse.

'She's a bit cheaper,' Penny continued translating, 'but she's just run into a tree and has got a broken shoulder.'

She had: it was a pity. She was a lovely little creature of just I 5 hands.

'What do you think, Penny?'

'I think he's a crook and his horse is too and if you buy him he'll run back home after a week.' So that was that, we returned to Ktima Litsas, fed the horses, played 'Don't fence me in' on the record player, went to a taverna and ate a lot of vegetables.

I looked at one or two horses in the area after that, but as Rex said, they really were scarce and I might be better advised to go to Yugoslavia and buy one there. The snag with that plan was that I should miss out on riding through Greece, which I wanted to do. Then we heard about a filly for sale up in the mountains at Goumenitsa.

Once again, she was the property of the local knackerman in that area. He had owned her for two years, during which time she had been tethered constantly in a stable. Rex, Penny and I went to see, and found her, thin, wormy and lice-ridden. She was jet black, about 14·3 hands and young, perhaps three or four years old, with unshod, overgrown feet. It was clear she had been handled quietly, being a very nice calm little creature, with an anxious look in her eye. Penny and Rex liked her straightaway, saying that a few weeks would sort her out nicely. We could break her in at the farm and in a month I could be on the road, having sorted out all the paperwork in the meantime. I liked her too, but felt that her age and absence of experience weighed against her.

'I can't go to England on a horse with Turkish slippers who is only a baby and doesn't know what's what.'

'Course you can,' Rex said. 'Train her as you go. Besides, she's a black mare, and you had a white stallion, so it fits.'

He was right really, but I still couldn't make up my mind.

'What sort of a pony is she anyway?'

'Well I think she's a local breed,' Rex went on, 'with a dash of thoroughbred in her from the improvement stallions they used here some time ago.'

'Yes,' said Penny, 'that means when she runs away you'll never catch her.'

We all got into the car, and drove back to Ktima Litsas. On the way Penny told me she thought I was an idiot if I didn't buy that mare. When I said I thought she thought I was an idiot anyway, she said she did. Sometimes I wonder why I like Penny.

Back at the farm a new development arose while I was thinking about the black filly. It concerned a true desert Arab, called Azarax, who had come to Greece from Iran, having been imported by a man called Hubert, and the story was a strange one.

Hubert was Dutch, and a dedicated horseman. He was once well heeled and had worked in a highly paid job in Iran as an engineer. He became increasingly bored with his job and more and more involved with horses, finding the Iranian breeds fascinating. He had been helping out at the Shah's bloodstock stables and bought two wild desert Arabs, of which Azarax was one. He named him: it means Son of Fire.

He loved these horses, and having been trained in the old school, his skill was recognised, and he started to teach riding in Tehran. He trained riders in a very tightly controlled regimen which went over and above the mere training of a rider on a horse. It included a philosophy of life whose demands were as rigorous as his training techniques. He believed that complete discipline could be learned from riding, and overall, he saw his methods as being crucial to the entire development of the mind and body.

When the Shah was deposed, Hubert was thrown into prison for no real reason, later found to be 'clean' but was asked to leave the country. He did, taking his two stallions with him. He eventually made his way to Greece, where after several attempts to set up business on his own, he was forced to take on a business partner. Then he lost one of his stallions to the colic.

By now, he was seriously short of money and had only Azarax who was greatly prized for his speed and beauty. He was a strange horse, with great presence. He acted like no other horse and was known to be unpredictable and savage. Only Hubert and a student he had taken under his wing, Thanassis, could handle him. Gradually, Hubert became more and more isolated, withdrawing from the world, losing interest in money and commercial challenge, becoming further dedicated to improving his work.

Very few people could stand it for long, finding him distant and too demanding. They wanted to play with horses, not be controlled like one. Yet Hubert retained his integrity and conviction in what he did. Thanassis had strength of character to go along with him. He was the only one who did. The spartan and singular discipline Hubert demanded suited him.

Gradually, Hubert just faded away, eaten by cancer of the liver. Although people spoke highly of him, he died practically friendless, and broke. The only assets he had were his papers, and Azarax, whom he had promised to Thanassis. Owing to the way in which he had been involved in business, his assets were seized, including Azarax. But Thanassis was resourceful, had presence of mind and cash enough to offer a price for Azarax, whom he got, then promptly shaved off his mane: this was a mark of respect for his late owner.

He was heart-broken at the loss of his unusual friend and gifted instructor, and when I met him, found it hard to draw him out on the subject. He loved the horse, and the reason I became involved was because he had his call-up papers for the army – there is conscription in Greece – and felt he couldn't keep Azarax. Rex suggested that I borrow the horse from him, ride to England, then after his three years of army service, return Azarax to Thanassis. It was a possibility. I assured him that Azarax would be given a good home. I would have loved the horse, almost for his romance alone.

But Azarax had a terrible reputation. Rex had looked after him once and found him a real liability. Tino, a German lad staying there, said he had never known a madder horse, and had seen him kick down a solid steel door. He was in livery at the time in a riding club near the sea, and they were all terrified of him.

I spoke to Thanassis on the telephone, met him and went to see the horse. Incredibly, he was the image of Ahmed Paşa, although he had boxier feet and was more grey. He was the same type. He certainly had presence and was very savage. I couldn't help feeling that he was little more than a half tamed wild horse, which, I suppose he was. But one thing was staringly obvious to me: Azarax was meant for Thanassis, and Thanassis alone. There was something between them, I told Thanassis. He didn't need telling twice. He still has Azarax.

Next day, I went back to Goumenitsa and bought the little black filly. When I asked her name, I thought they said Mavro, which means Black. No, they had said Maro, which is short for Maria. I wasn't sure if I wanted to call her Maria, and cast about for some classic Greek name. While drawing money from the bank for her, I asked the girl cashier what she thought I ought to call my new little filly.

'You can call her the same name as me,' she answered brightly.

'Oh? And what's that?'

'Maria.'

12

Maria

'His horse, who never in that sort
had handled been before,
what thing upon his back had got
did wonder more and more.'

The Diverting History of John Gilpin, William Cowper

Maria (or Maro) arrived at the farm in a flat-bed steel floored cement truck, but owing to her unshod feet, the experience had not proved to be traumatic. She looked desperately thin alongside the horses on the farm and went directly into the quarantine stables, along with all her lice: she was the itchiest horse. She was nervous, and knew nothing, but was as sweet a tempered a pony as you would be likely to meet. I wondered what she made of it all in her green young heart.

The weather changed almost the minute she arrived; it became hot and the midday sky was a dead level white.

Penny stepped in to break her and on the second day, we put a saddle on Maria and a bit in her mouth – just for two minutes. Penny had a true understanding of horses and could see the minute it had gone far enough: that is to say, not far enough to frighten the horse, but far enough for them to understand. She was very patient, and went to great lengths. When I wanted to put the saddle on again in the afternoon, just for two minutes, Penny said I did so at the expense of undoing everything she did.

'Go away and drink some beer,' she said, 'Leave it to me. You couldn't run a bath let alone break a horse.'

So I left it to Penny. On the third day, she took one of her light girl students called Vanessa who leaned across the saddle, again, just for two minutes to accustom the horse to pressure on her spine. Vanessa was the first to ride Maria and during the day, Penny let me walk around

117

the farm leading her. She told me to walk on walls, on logs, or anything higher than the pony so she became accustomed to me being above her. 'On no account try to get on. You're a fat slob, you'll ruin everything.'

Meanwhile Rex attended to her feet, cutting off bit by bit, until she was standing properly on her toes. She looked quite different then. Within several days she was carrying herself properly. He formulated a ration which brought her along steadily, putting her on a lucerne hay diet to start with, then, like the other horses who were in work, she was given grain and molasses with a calcium supplement from which she benefited visibly, being still young. She began to look good in no time. He wormed her, gave me fungicidal powders, and Penny gave me anti-louse shampoos for her. I still wound up inheriting most of her bugs, who transferred deftly at bath time: of that, I'm certain. On her seventh day, I took her for her first ride away from the farm up alone into the mountains and she behaved beautifully. That's when I appreciated what Penny had done with her. She had a bright, interested, forward-going step and when we reached a grassy patch, I dismounted, putting her on a long tether underneath trees beside a stream, just two miles from Ktima Litsas. It took me straight back to Çal and the first day's grazing with Ahmed Paşa. It brought a lump to my throat too.

I sorted out the kit to suit her better, although everything fitted remarkably well. I decided to buy a hammock for myself in preference to sleeping on the ground and save myself the nightly business of ferreting bugs out of my sleeping bag. So one morning I left Maria on a long tether, went off with Penny to town to buy a hammock. When we returned, Maria had gone. I found her tether rope in the grass: no one had seen her go.

The hunt was on to find her. Rex drove round the area, Tino and his girlfriend rode all over the hills I had ridden with her the day before. I searched the farm buildings, the field, everywhere. There was no sign. Rex returned and telephoned the police: I had lost my 'Mavro alogo' – black horse – and as he said it, I became really concerned. Five hours later, we still hadn't found her. I walked the whole area again, checked the stables once more just in case she'd come back. I combed hedges, looked into deep ravines, wandered through every field as far as the village. It was hot work.

Penny rang the neighbours and Bob and Anna right up in Panorama telling them to keep a look out. I imagined the worst. She'd been found, and sold for meat. She'd fallen under a lorry. She'd slipped down one of the deep banks and had a broken leg. She'd rushed off into the pines in blind panic, and now ran around thirsty and terrified. Exhausted, she lay dying on a hillside.

By 7.30 that night, my deepest concerns had turned into despair. She'd gone: gone with her, all my dreams. I sat in the new hammock and prayed to St Anthony, patron saint of lost articles. Fervently. I even exhorted St Jude to intercede on my behalf.

The throb of a large motorcycle broke the evening's quiet. I recognised the whine of the gearbox, the deep throated engine.

'I think I've found the horse...' Bob said, and before he'd finished the sentence, I was on the back of that bike. He responded instantly to my rush, spinning it on the spot, and we roared out of Ktima Latsas like Bulldog Drummond, in a hail of grit and stones.

We thundered up the hill towards Panorama, wind howling in our ears, with Bob crouching low on the seat, the bike vibrating with the fierce thrust of the pistons, the rugged beat of the exhausts.

About three miles on we slowed down, Bob pointed to a solitary horse, standing not far from the road. For a moment, my heart sank. It looked too good for Maria: too classy. We stopped, I walked towards her, called, and she came running. Bob found her. I could have kissed that fellow!

I've never forgotten the favour he did me that day: whether he was sent by St Anthony or St Jude I haven't got a clue, but it was mighty coincidental. I bought him all he could drink later that night.

Maria walked back quietly down to the farm. A little adventure that put us closer together: I realised how much that smelly little horse was already beginning to mean to me, how much I depended on her. From the nuzzling I got, I think maybe, just maybe, she felt a little the same.

I watched over her carefully in the next few days. I saw her gaze in blank disbelief at walking stones – tortoises – stare wide eyed at sheep, jump when lizards darted in bushes. She became used to sloshing around in streams, had her first set of shoes on, which made her feel very important indeed, impressed with the big new noise she made.

It was a wonderful experience bringing her on like that, and I spent hours upon hours with her, visiting her frequently during the night and then decided to sleep out with her under the trees, try out my new hammock. On the evening of this experiment, I went to a very good taverna on the beach with Taki, returning at about 1.30 in the morning, well fed and completely drunk.

If you are used to sleeping in a hammock and stone cold sober, it's probably an easy thing. If you are not, and drunk, in the dark, it's not. It took me half an hour hiccupping around in blackness setting the thing up, and the night being cool, I brought my sleeping bag which I intended to get into once in my hammock. Maria stood by, on the end of her tether under the trees while I fell about undressing.

I threw the sleeping bag onto the hammock and tried to get in. Maria, in the meantime, started chewing on something which sounded as though she had a mouthful of marbles, and came over to see what was going on with all this cloth in the darkness, what all the swearing was about. Then a bazouki band started up in a house nearby. I could still hear Maro crunching away on these marbles, and somehow managed to get into my sleeping bag, and onto the hammock.

I lay dead still, exhausted from the effort. It was uncomfortable to a degree. I hadn't tied the thing tight enough so it hung limply in the middle and I was forced to lie with my feet uppermost. I couldn't be bothered to do anything about it.

Maria came over to have a closer look, finding the end supports conveniently placed for scratching her bum on. Whatever she was chewing sounded as though it was removing all her teeth then she wiggled her backside violently against the hammock support, inches from pitching me out of the thing onto the floor. I slapped her, she moved a little away, pounded away with her chewing, then lay down so suddenly, I thought she had died.

I shuffled out of the hammock, wriggled towards her in my sleeping bag and she jumped up, shook vigorously, and piddled all over my clothes. Peeved, I crawled back to the hammock, which took a quarter of an hour to find, then once again, swung up into it.

This time I was head low with my feet practically vertical above me, annoyed I hadn't taken the opportunity to do anything about the tension on the strings. The hammock eased to one side, which I centred very carefully, since quick movements shoot you straight out face down into the earth beneath. With my feet well above me, I was putting a lot of pressure on the head end, angry because I didn't want to have to get out to right the thing. I don't like late nights, I was both hot and cold at once, had my arms down the sleeping bag scratching at Maria's lice. I lay contorted and uncomfortable, cursing with my eyes dosed, listening to Maria munching stones with a bazouki band blaring.

Suddenly, my stomach was left in mid air as I was catapulted into the roots of the tree behind with tremendous force and held in a half Nelson by the hammock strings, completely snared, winded and brained. Maria took fright and was tearing around on her tether somewhere out in the darkness. Out of the corner of my eye, I saw racing stars collide into one another in swirling branches above.

When I had overcome the shock of the strings breaking, I wrestled the thing off, unzipped the sleeping bag, threw it on the ground and lay down on it, still fighting for breath. I had picked an ant hole.

At five in the morning, with my piddle-ridden clothes, I walked starkers back to the tack room and fell asleep amongst the saddles.

In order to move a horse from one country to another, you need papers: quite a lot of papers. When I bought Maria, Rex had the good sense to tell me to get everything I could, including a form from a periptera – a sort of street kiosk, where you can buy everything from lollipops to stocks and shares. This completed and signed form gave me the officially-recognised right to claim Maria as my own personal property and was proof that I had parted with 100,000 drax (£465), rather than just nicked her. Or so I thought when I bought her.

I was also given a wad of mouldy-looking documents by her owner, including a blue form with an impressive crest heading. Everything was written in Greek and might as well have been written in mirror writing upside down Sanskrit for all I cared. It meant nothing to me. All I knew was that I should have to have a health certificate for Maro and she would have to undergo several tests, of which Coggins was one. (Coggins is a test for equine anaemia.)

Fortunately, Karen – the American girl who had married the local influential businessman – was kind, or daft enough to offer to help. She spoke fluent Greek and saw that I had no chance of securing a toothbrush for myself, let alone the documentation for exporting a horse. With Karen, to whom I am ever indebted, we set out early in the morning to Thessaloniki's Ministry of Agriculture. Karen is a bright, attractive girl, with that breezy self confidence which comes from backing your own judgement and proving yourself right. She had a composed no-messing air about her, which I was sure would stand us a good chance of resolving the whole issue easily. Well, I was wrong.

The first Government office we went to was not easy to find. When we did, we were shown into a room where a pair of benign-looking characters were sitting at desks facing one another. They were benign. They were also utterly clueless. The fatter, older and wiser of the two told us we needed only veterinary papers to export the horse, nothing more. We would get these from the vet, then they would stamp them and I could go to the moon with my horse. It all looked rather more simple than we had anticipated.

Back at the farm, we learned that the vet was coming and when he did he pronounced Maria fit, took a blood sample, said it would take a few days, but it was highly unlikely to be positive. 'So,' he said, 'if you give me the papers, I'll sign them.'

'I haven't got any papers.'

'Didn't the Ministry of Agriculture give them to you this morning?'

'No. They said you would have them.'

'Me? I'm only the vet! I can't be expected to cart a lorry load of paperwork round with me. You need Ministry papers! certificates! export documents, export licences, transit visas and anything else you can think of that's got a picture of a horse on.'

Less happy about being fobbed off so easily, we were back in the Ministry of Agriculture next day, went to the same office, meeting a different, watery sort of a chap who didn't want to get involved. He said he didn't know anything about papers, wasn't prepared to give us any forms, put a rubber stamp on anything. Karen sunk her teeth into this refusal, narrowed her eyes, and made watery man feel pretty uncomfortable. She demanded to know about transit visas, export documents, export licences, and so on.

'Not necessary,' said watery man, and we were joined by one of the men from the day before – the fatter, older and wiser of the two who pronounced that his documents were internationally recognised, that no more was required.

'Not so fast buster...' she said it narrowly: Americans are best left to Americanisms: they're deliciously good at them.

'Where do we get these festering papers, eh?'

Something was mumbled and they shuffled their feet. A bored-looking secretary with a logo on her tee shirt which read 'smile' – came in with a long face and a faded photostat copy of an English horse identification chart.

'Is this it?' Karen spat out 'What a lousy looking thing. I thought at least we'd get something in gold leaf. Why the hell didn't you give us this thing yesterday?'

There was no answer. The men just stood there in silence. Like two little boys who had just been caught piddling on their sister. We then tried the customs office for a licence to be told that licences were issued by another office on the outskirts of Thessaloniki, in the fresh fruit wholesale depot. There, they insisted, we would be given the correct forms. 'I just can't see what the export of a horse has got to do with the import of fresh vegetables,' Karen queried distractedly. We found section 'D' we had been advised to locate where, on entry, we found everyone involved in a full-scale fight. 'Export – horse!' Karen shouted, and there was silence. They all looked up, struck dumb as if by pronouncement of some fearful disease on all of them.

'First, you must go to the Chamber of Commerce in Thessaloniki for the correct paper, then bring it here, and we will sign it.'

'Why haven't you got the correct pieces of paper here anyway?' Karen asked.

They shot looks at one another. No one had ever thought of that. A fellow shrugged his shoulders. Karen kept her cool, which will be ever to her credit, and we returned to Thessaloniki where, with difficulty, we located the Chamber of Commerce.

A thin-lipped little man showed us into an office where a staff of eighteen shared a single telephone on a long cord. Karen explained why we were there.

'How much did the horse cost?' they enquired. Karen told them.

'You'll have to go to Athens, we can't deal with that here.'

'Now just look here you guys.' She said it slowly, in a drawl: it even chilled me: when it comes to screwing the last drop out of a word, the Americans have it on us.

'Now just look here you guys, if one of you doesn't pull his finger out right now there's going to be a big stink.'

There was stunned silence. A supervisor was sent for, chairs were dragged in. We were asked to sit, given cups of coffee. It was generally agreed then, that we shouldn't have to go to Athens, but the whole business could be resolved by a bank. So we went to a bank.

Having visited four banks, Karen had devised how to overthrow the entire Greek civil service and replace them all with automatons. We met a man in an ivory-towered commercial bank with marble everything, who understood. He was the first on our side.

'Where's your pink paper?' he asked. He wasn't on our side.

'What pink paper? Nobody said anything about pink paper.'

'To prove you imported the cash to buy the horse.'

'Oh, yes, I cashed £500 worth of travellers' cheques.'

'That's not the same. You'll have to show that you imported the money.'

It took a long time, cost a fortune in telephone calls, but Karen fixed it, and I imported another 100,000 drax. Maro was now a very expensive horse, and I was going broke fast. But we were excited. It looked like we were nearly there. We nearly were.

'Have you got any other papers?'

I gave the man the mouldy wad, including the blue form, the one with the impressive heading. Karen's face fell.

'What did you do that for?' She struggled the sentence out with as much composure as she could.

I couldn't believe it, but I had given them Maria's call-up papers. In the event of war, or even in the event of the event of war, every able-bodied horse in Greece is eligible for call up to the army, is therefore sub-judice, army property. Maria's blue paper confirmed her as an army registered horse. Maro was a war horse. Little Maro!

The title prevented me from exporting her from Greece as a healthy horse, which is why so many horses were brutally maimed before exporting them as meat. The man turned nasty. Now there was no way in which I could get Maria out of Greece. I saw the whole thing fizzle out before my very eyes. But we hadn't reckoned on the support of the rest of the office staff. They were all on our side. Particularly one man.

'Forget it!' he said to nasty man, 'forget it, let them take the little horse out. We've got tanks in the army now. We don't use horses anymore.'

The man didn't soften. He would put his call through to his superiors in Athens if it killed him. The atmosphere became tense. A faction took hold in the office. Nasty man had a hunted look, chain smoked, sat down heavily behind his desk darting bloodshot unfocussed looks about. He dare not lose face in front of us: dare not appear a brute in front of his colleagues: he was in a jam. You could see it. We sat tight. He was playing for time, inspiration.

The telephone rang. He jumped to his feet. Breathed a pall of smoke down the receiver. Looked strained. He spoke. Karen clapped. Up went a cheer.

'He's fixed it! We've got the licence! He asked if there were restrictions on exporting livestock – not horses!'

Ten minutes later, a very relieved man handed us the export licence. It was valid for twenty-five days. All in all, they gave us export documents for a horse they hadn't seen, from inaccurate papers, bought with cash specially imported for the occasion, to someone whose identity they hadn't bothered to find out, for a horse whose ownership might have been claimed by the military. Everyone was delighted. We left the bank as the doors closed.

All that remained was the Coggins test results, and Italian and Yugoslav permission to transit both countries. The Italian permission came through the next day, Tast Cavalli sent me my International Transport Documents, and my T2. The Coggins results were negative, and we had eight days clear to reach the border. The only hitch was the Yugoslav embassy who told me I wouldn't need a transit visa for entry.

Rex said he was sure that was wrong. After my experience with the Greek authorities I had no reason to suppose the Yugoslavs would be any more brilliant, and I had an uncomfortable feeling Rex was right. But I didn't have any alternatives. 'Anyway,' he said, 'you can ride all the way up no man's land, straight to Siberia.'

I telephoned Rupert Sanders, my solicitor in England who was sorting out all the mess I left behind, and told him of my next destination. He broke the news to me that the Oxford County Council were rather keen for me to go to jail for non payment of a parking fine. Somehow, that all sounded very remote.

'Oh bugger the Oxford County Council!'

He asked if that was an instruction. It wasn't a problem that I really felt like countenancing, I told him. He said he'd tell the Oxford County Council.

Maria was re-shod the day before departure. I shampooed her again, gave her a long day's rest and a good feed. I arranged a last minute barbecue the night before I left, and under the pines that night, Zoe frazzled up a souvlakia, Thanassis came, and Katerina, who'd made a new headcollar bridle for Maro. We all drank and chatted in the warm night air and swirling smoke from the fire. I watched Taki gazing into the flames, twiddling his moustache, dreaming up another way to market his chrysanthemums.

The party faded out at three thirty. I said goodnight and goodbye to everyone, visited Maria, then weaved my way back to the tack room as stars cavorted around like fireflies in the dark. I fell asleep in a retsina-coloured dream as Karen fed pink papers to Maro, Rex reshod Taki, Bob roared around in the sky on his motor bike, Anna swum a river on the moon on Ahmed Paşa, and Rupert stood trouserless in a prison cell ripping up parking fines.

13

You, I love you, Maria

I felt rotten as compost next morning. I didn't want to get up. I especially didn't want to get up and ride Maro to England. Retsina can do horrible things to your head the morning after. I throbbed all over; felt all heavy and grey and porridgy.

I crawled out of bed at 6.15am, fed Maro, and crawled back in again. It was going to be a hot day with thick, still air. I lay there, trying to think of excuses not to have to do it. Got up again at eight, collected Maro and dizzily packed her with all the baggage.

Rex fell out of the house at the same time. He looked pretty rough too. It was far too difficult to speak, so we drank coffee in silence, shook hands and I pushed off, feeling like nothing on earth. I didn't know where I was going to spend the night or anything else about anything: I was completely unable to think. In front of us was 2,500 miles of unknown everything.

I'd looked for Taki but was unable to find him. Walking down through the hot, quiet farmyard I felt lonelier than I had ever felt before. I turned the last corner out of the farm, and Taki arrived in his car. He got out, looked at me with bloodshot eyes, pointed north, kissed me on both cheeks, and said, 'Kallo taxidi Yeremias; kallo taxidi Maro!' (Safe journey Jeremy, safe journey Maro.')

I could have wept.

The sun rose a huge dazzling globe, pouring heat down on the parched land. I felt ghastly. It was blindingly bright as we struggled up toward Panorama, with Mount Hortiatis on our right and the bay of Thessaloniki stretched out behind, mirroring the white level heat of the sky: I could see Mount Olympus in the far distance accenting the ground we had to cover.

Maria was sweating profusely, and panting even though I wasn't riding, but walking with her. It was hotter in the valley as we skirted the roads, going by track over the ridge behind the farm towards Hortiatis. A brute of a place to get out of on a horse. On one side there's a main road with heavy traffic, while the other is cross hatched with deep angular ravines and sharp rugged ground where, unless you know the way well, you find yourself confronted with chasms and drops, forced to look for other routes. Before arriving at the gorges I cut up to the left, thinking to clip the outskirts of Panorama, then go on to Lake Langadhas.

By the time we reached Panorama, Maria was puffing heavily. It was over-heated, but she seemed desperately hot, sweat pouring off her. Somehow too, we had managed to get fouled up in a lot of buildings in the residential area. Having crossed the main road, we were deeper into Panorama than I wanted to be. Maria was stopping frequently to rest and, anxious as I was not to stop there, I waited for her to recover before pushing on. I'd been walking with her, but she was a lot more affected than I was, and I was the one who'd been on the booze. She rested her foot. I felt it. It was very hot. She was pinned up. Damn! The blacksmith must have lamed her. That was a savage blow. I hadn't had trouble with horses' feet ever before, and now this, just after setting out!

I found a grassy patch in the shadow of a house and asked if we could stay there a minute – the little horse wasn't well. A young lad hesitatingly agreed, saying something about his father. I took the saddle and tack off Maro: she was dead lame. She swung her weight over her hind quarters in a painful way – something was very wrong. Unfortunately my knowledge of horse ailments is limited – I've never had a horse go ill on me: I didn't know what this was. Five minutes later, she collapsed. I ran around searching for a telephone, rang Rex. Within the hour he had found us.

'She's not lame,' he said at a single glance, 'azoturia.'

'Who?'

'Azoturia. You've over-corned her. I expect you went and gave her a full day's ration yesterday in preparation for her marathon today. You shouldn't have. Should have cut her rations back. Some horses are more prone to it than others. It's a sickness the old dray horses used to get in England years ago: overfed on a Sunday, then worked hard on a Monday, and down they'd go. It's sometimes inaccurately called Monday-Morning sickness.'

'I've got it too.'

'So've I. Keep her quiet: keep her cool. You'll have to sit it out with her. You'd better come home tonight, I'll take all the kit back. Hard luck, stay with her. She'll be right by eight thirty tonight.'

There's horsemanship!

He took the saddle and all the baggage back down to the farm in the car, said he'd be back to check us out at eight thirty, not to move her before. I stayed with her in the shadows. She moaned and groaned, ears held limply on her head; sweat ran off her, and all around the sun burned angrily.

After an hour, the owner of the building returned, and with one look, told us to get out. I explained the horse was desperately sick. All we asked was a little shade, some shadow. No, he said, get out. It was only shade we wanted: not food, not water, not anything, just not to be in the direct glare of the sun. We had nowhere else to go.

He screamed in petulant rage, and I had all but to carry Maro the twenty yards or so across the road to a tiny triangle of scrub in the full power of the sun. She fell with her head in my lap, and I looked back at the man, still shouting. I knew then what the lad had tried to say – this was his father. What I had seen in the lad's face was a look of fear. This man was a brute. I wasn't angry with him: I pitied him. I pitied him for his propriety and meanness, because if that is the coin of his choosing, that is how he will be paid. I shrugged him off.

I watched the sweat roll off Maria's flanks as the sun beat down on us. Listened to her breath, heavy and uneven and, as I held her head in my hands, nothing else on earth mattered to me, nothing at all but the recovery of this little horse.

I stroked her face, her funny rubbery muzzle, and she slept with flickering half-closed eyes, twitched, whickered, snorted, dreaming important horsey dreams while sleep made its magic cure. When she woke, she was better. I was burned to a frazzle and had paralysing pins and needles.

By eight thirty, she was up and browsing around in the grass, such as there was. Rex arrived, just as he said. 'OK. See you later. Walk her back quietly to the farm, give her some hay and we'll go off for more vegetables in the taverna.'

Again, he set us on our way, this time back towards the farm, and I so admired and respected his skill.

We walked back the way we came, over the little hills to Thermi arriving in darkness, slipping through the shadows to where Maro was always tied. She was given water, a little hay, some straw and a watermelon, which she sucked and slobbered over. After a quick bite in the taverna, I flaked out.

Two days later, at 5.30 in the morning, quietly, I saddled and packed Maria again. Felt better this time. As the sun came up behind Honiatis, Rex came out. He gave me an 'evil eye' from Taki for good luck. 'It's why you made a cock-up of it last time, you never took one of these.' I carried that little thing the rest of the way: I still have it.

At 6.15 we shook hands.

'Go on: piss off,' he said.

You need a lot of confidence to talk like Rex and Penny. No one gives you that, you have to earn it. Or maybe he was sick of the sight of me. Expect he was. Maria and I made the trip again out over the ravines at Thermi. We were up beside Panorama in no time, cutting down past the monastery, then up through a load of prickly gorse-like bushes and we were on our way.

The ground was sprinkled with dozens of dancing butterflies, swallow-tails, blues, commas, brimstones – and horseflies: big ones. We waded over the rough ground on the hillside, over crevices, little gorges, rocks, trees, bushes and Maro sailed through it all, never once looking for home, simply accepting that we were on our way. She knew it: it's strange, but I know she knew.

Then we met fences. Fences! A new thing! I had forgotten all about fences. And the people were all very proprietorial, sour. They seemed self-obsessed somehow, and the sudden advance in materialism hardened them. I wasn't a Mercedes-Benz nor was Maria a Madonna with rubies and together we didn't add up to a row of beans let alone persons of property and worth. They shunned us with sullen looks, unsmiling eyes.

We walked on, forced onto a busy slippery main road, fenced on either side. It heaved with traffic, which Maro had only encountered once before, when walking her back from the sea after a day's swim. Confronted with this howling rush, she did what any full-blooded horse would do: she bolted. I clung on as long as I could, then fell off in the path of a wheezing, hissing cement truck. Maro dragged me down the road, did the splits as she met another lorry coming in the opposite direction. I lost her, caught her again, then she knocked me over under the wheels of a truck, and I spun on my back just as a hoof smashed into the tarmac, grazing my nose. Air brakes rasped, a horn sounded and the lorry was gone.

Back on my feet I clung onto her, both of us shivering. I was bleeding quite badly on my elbows and knees, and I shouted at her, which I instantly regretted. Both of us were badly frightened. I looked for a way out, found a cut in the wire, pulled it apart, and squeezed into a pine plantation on the other side. Incredibly, I found a well, so cleaned up, and both of us had a drink. I vowed to stay off the roads.

We followed the Turkey-trot routine, of field margins and a compass bearing, and in the late afternoon, we pulled up in a shenzi, a noisy, dog-barking taverna. Tucked away round the back, beneath a stand of young acacia trees, was a little night-sized grassy patch which beckoned Maro. We went in, between the people, and she busied herself with the all-important business of filling up a horse. I was proud of my little girl. People brought us treats, asked questions about our trip, how long it would take to reach England – all sorts of things. Then, the proprietor's son, who had been the victim of a bad car accident, with brain damage as its legacy, came over to us in the darkness. He put his hand on her back, and struggled out a question, and I told him her name. He paused, and pointed to me. In English he said slowly and quietly, 'You,' still pointing, 'you, I love you, Maria.' And he was right.

The following day took us into the very heart of lorrydom. There are definitely too many lorries. Try as we might to escape the roar of trucks, we wound up in dead ends, ravines, gulleys, rubbish dumps, forced back onto the road, lorries howling at us – I know nothing more frightening. Somehow, they become inanimate things: driverless, brutish, careless and spiteful. I began to hate them. We arrived in Lake Langadhas in the early afternoon.

While I was staring at a row of storks sitting on a roof, wondering what it is about them that reminded me so much of Latin masters, Maria wandered off. Then I heard her squeal, sounded like World War III had just broken out and she was on her side totally wrapped up in a fishing net. She fought and fought the thing, rapidly exhausting herself and so I unravelled her. It took a lot of doing. Having recovered, I led her to a bit of good grazing on the water's edge, where she trod in a pot of tar, which stuck to her foot. After the fishing net, this latest thing was more than she could stand. She slipped her tether and ran off screaming. That's when I remembered what Penny had said about not catching her. She was right.

Maro shot through the village hot on the road for Ktima Litsas, when I remembered a trick which sometimes works. It's to shout at the horse, then run off in the opposite direction and they'll follow. Maro fell for it, so I caught her, tarry foot and all. It took an hour to scrape all the grit, polythene and rubbish off the foot of that excited and thoroughly wound up little filly.

Looked like it was going to be an adventuresome sort of a place, Lake Langadhas. And indeed it was. Many people came to visit us that afternoon, including a group of English archaeologists, who very kindly changed some money for me, told me about glass beads and ancient types of grain, did the *Guardian* crossword puzzle, said there was nothing much going on in the world, put me right on which day of the week it was, then pushed off with all their shovels, and very nice shovels they were too.

I telephoned Rex, who drove out later to have supper with Maro and me on the shores of the lake. Mara had to come because she bawled her head off if I left her alone.

We were joined by a couple of hitch-hikers in amongst whose straggled possessions Maro and I bedded down for the night, while mosquitoes whined about, droning away six inches from your face, unswattable.

At five in the morning, I woke just in time to see Maro run off again, having once again slipped her head collar toggle which baffled me, since it was tight and needed fingers to undo. Once again, I sprinted after her semi naked, and caught her at the far end of the village, receiving astonished glances from early rising villagers surprised to find a trouserless foreigner wandering about leading an excited young horse. Back at the shoreline, I packed and saddled her while she shuffled, fidgeted, snorted and complained until I mounted and we made our way westward from the lake with the sun rising orange on the water.

We followed field headlands, went through lovely country lush and green like English meadows with tall leafy poplars and aspen on level ground without fence or hedge for miles and miles. Behind us, Hortiatis shrank and we moved up the dry plain toward Kilkis. All the place was filled with the crying shrill of cicadas and crickets, and I even saw tree frogs.

Just a month earlier Maro had had a saddle on for the very first time. Now, just thirty days later, she was on a long journey, fully packed and loaded. She was a good little horse – just a slip of a horse.

We spent the night in Dromos, in the corner of a field, where I managed to buy some trifilly (lucerne hay) for Maro and a salad for myself. The field had been recently harvested and there was a good amount of straw about, so I made myself a mattress, determined to have a soft bed for a change. Sleeping on the ground is always hard and I had abandoned the hammock for being unfriendly.

I piled up a classic quantity of straw, spread the ground sheet on it, put my sleeping bag down, went off to the village, bought a couple of bottles of retsina, and as the sun set and the stars came out I lay down on my soft bed staring up into the sky. I took gulps of retsina, and played 'Don't fence me in' on my mouth organ. Gene Autry sings it. The lyrics are glorious.

Give me land, lots of land and the starry skies above,
Don't fence me in.
Let me ride through the wide open country that I love,
Don't fence me in
Let me be by myself in the evening breeze
Listen to the murmur of the cotton wood trees,
Send me off forever, but I beg you, please
Don't fence me in.
Just turn me loose,
Let me straddle my old saddle beneath a western sky
On my cayoose let me wander over yonder
And see the mountains rise.

I want to ride to the ridge where the west commences,
Gaze at the moon till I lose my senses,
I can't look at hobbles, and can't stand fences,
Just don't fence me in.

It made me all maudlin and lumpy-throated. I drank some more retsina. That made it worse. I played 'Mae Hen Wlad Fy Nadau' and 'Cwm Rhondda', 'The Green Green Grass of Home' and Maro munched trifilly. All alone out there I felt terribly vulnerable suddenly. Not in the sense of being attacked, but in another way – small, insignificant, daft.

How immediate everything seemed! I hadn't given a moment's thought to the larger issues of life for months: didn't even know what the larger issues of life were. Hadn't considered a future, but had just gone on, clodhopping my way relentlessly closer to Oxford nick. I found myself wondering where the nick was in Oxford. Did I really have to go? And wasn't all this whole thing utterly futile, and I was blowing the only buttons I had in the world on this idiotic adventure, and now sitting down half-pissed in some field in the middle of Greece unable to play my mouth organ properly even. I closed my eyes, suddenly awash with recriminations.

Then the earhole and nostril flies launched their first offensives. These were a new species. I knew about the arsehole flies the animals got, picked them off every day. But earhole and nostril flies were new. All night long the little buggers struggled to get up my hooter and down my lugs. Sure, you can shove bog roll in your lugs, but you can't bung up your nose can you?

My soft bed of golden straw turned instead into a torture chamber: sleep in any form was denied. And Maro got up, lay down, piddled, snorted, farted non-stop.

I watched the stars move round in the sky and the sun come up again, tried to count how many night's sleep I had had in five months, and it wasn't many. If travelling with horses is wonderful in every respect, it falls down on the amount of kip you can expect to aggregate in a five month period. I looked across at the plains we had to cross that day in the heat and wondered if Greece was always this hot. I'd restricted travelling from five to eight in the morning, then six until eight at night.

It was just unkind to ask more of any animal in that heat. It knocked my average of thirty kilometres a day down to twenty or so, and that was enough.

While I was packing up, a little pony came to see us. I don't know where he came from. He and Maro sniffed each other's muzzles the way horses do, swapped jokes then he must have said something he shouldn't because Maro gave him the deadliest battery of booting you can imagine. But he took it like a hero, went off pretending not to limp.

Following a burning day's ride we arrived on the river Gallikos, which is shallow and wide, all broken up into little rivulets. The water was clear, cool. Both of us were boiled and dusty. I unsaddled her on the water margin, we both sloshed straight in. She rolled in the stream and I copied her, dropping the lead rein. That was the sixth time Maro took off on a prolonged cross-country race with me as the exhausted runner-up.

I was fed up with all this running away business by now, couldn't imagine why she had to do it. What got into her? No good clouting her for it either. I didn't want her thinking I would belt her every time we were together. She took two hours to catch that time. Played this wearisome 'come-closer-see-if-you-can-get-me' game. When I did finally collar her, we just had to go back to where the big disappearing act had started, pretend nothing happened, and roll in the steam all over again.

We crossed over to the village later where I rang Rex who said he'd bring a party out for the last time, since it was becoming too long a drive. I looked forward to it immensely. Oddly, unlike Turkey, I had little contact with people in Greece. Maro and I were alone most of the time. The people were not inquisitive like the Turks, hadn't stopped me as they had in Turkey. When we passed through villages, we frequently met black looks and a cold shoulder. I began to wonder what we'd done. In one village I was told that since I was English I wasn't welcome. When I told them I wasn't English but Welsh, they said that was all right then, and I could stay. To be with friends who didn't care if I was a Martian was worth looking forward to.

I picked a camp site in a pretty place on a sandy bank, collected fire wood and laid out all my stuff. Maro and I waited for Rex in the dark on a small road a quarter of a mile away. He knew the country well enough to hazard a random meeting place then, at about eleven, I saw headlights swing up in the sky, then drop, and a car came quickly down the road towards us.

Rex brought a gang, and in no time we were round the fire, drinking retsina, chatting. I learned then that Greece was in the grips of the worst heatwave in memory. Reports from Athens estimated some fifteen hundred people had either died or been hospitalised as a result of it. I reckoned Maro and we were next.

Maro lay down with us all and, leaning back on her, Bob took a swig of beer, and said if ever I decided to chuck it in, he'd have Maro. It was astonishing how calm she was, to actually lie down with a group of people around a fire. It was wonderful to see those faces all held glowing in the light, the hollow woolly blackness behind, Rex, Bob, Anna, Roz, Eleni and Maria.

I took Bob's advice the following day and followed the river north, although it took an easterly swing. It meant we'd have water all day long so we walked in it.

We made far better progress that day than any day before, since it was cool wading through the streamlets and Maro sucked away on rich juicy grasses along the river bank, enjoying the sweet feed.

The river narrowed the further north we went, frogs were trapped in dwindling pools, then it petered out leaving us on a broad, baking-dry river bed. A stark contrast between Greece and Turkey showed itself there. Unlike Turkey, the fields round about were vast, wholly given to monocultural cropping. There were hundreds upon hundreds of acres of maize and sunflower, mile after mile. Fields had been relatively small in Turkey, which, not being in the EU was not subject to the support system of the Common Agricultural Policy. This huge-scale cropping gave the plains a bleak feel and vast irrigators sprayed plumes of water in rainbowed rotation.

Large-scale cropping is impressive, but as Taki had said, there is little ingenuity in it: just a question of capital, and an assured price. How much more interesting Turkey had been, how much more varied. If they lacked the machinery of the Greeks, they never lacked for food and never funked hard graft. From an ecological point of view the Turks have it over all of us, being a tough and thrifty race of people. It was strange, but the further away I drew from Turkey, the more I became to admire it.

I met a farmer in a field of sunflower staring at his crop, shaking his head. I understood only in snatches what he said. He'd borrowed a large sum of money from the Agricultural Bank to produce sunflower to extend his old fashioned farm. It looked good on paper, with assured cash returns. But now, in the heat wave, with complete absence of rain, he said that in five more days, he would lose the crop and be ruined. He didn't have an irrigation system. Previously he'd have managed because not then growing sunflower, all his crops would have been harvested at that time of year. Everything would have been in. I wondered how many hundreds of others there were like him. The heatwave went on for another ten days.

That evening, having passed through a village where I bought something for our supper, Maro and I made our way down to a shady valley, to a stand of old oaks. It had a strange elemental feel to it: a sensation of things hiding behind gnarled old trunks: not an uncomfortable feeling, just one that kept you guessing. Maro started to graze while I went off to find some water. On my return, she'd stopped eating, and was looking out into the trees. I thought I had seen another horse there too, or a large animal, but it was very shy.

I caught sight of its back end again later. Then I thought I saw a man move rapidly through the trees with a horse, in silence. I was unsure, because I know twilight can throw peculiar images into your mind and turn bushes into all manner of things. Whatever it was, it alerted Maro, made her restless and she gadded around on the end of her tether quite a few times. Then I thought it must have been a large deer.

I rolled my sleeping bag out on the ground, played my mouth organ, and dozed off, woken at midnight by a car and its three occupants. They came over to me. One of them spoke English with a heavy American brogue.

'We heard there was a strange man with a horse in the trees,' he said.

'Oh, I see, that would explain it,' I answered. 'No wonder Maro has been so edgy.'

He gave me a surprised, quizzical look.

'So there's more of you?'

I didn't understand that question, distracted by the bottle of beer I was handed.

'No, only Maro and me – and this other bloke.'

'What other bloke?'

'The strange man with the horse in the trees.'

'You're the strange man with the horse in the trees!'

'Me? I'm not a strange man with a horse in the trees. I thought you meant this other man.'

'What other man?'

'The geezer with a horse in the trees!'

He shook his head. We weren't getting through to each other somehow. I said I thought maybe I hadn't understood really, but it hardly mattered and wasn't this nice beer?'

They offered me grazing in the village for Maro, dinner for me, and company. They'd also unsettled me enough with talk about this strange man, so I readily accepted their offer, and while two of them drove off with all the baggage I walked up with the American talker and Maro.

We were lavishly entertained by the villagers that night. It was warm and friendly to be with these farming people with whom I shared in common an agricultural background, if nothing else. They were chatty, generous, and asked for the one and only time on my entire trip about Margaret Thatcher's Britain.

However, being wholly ignorant of politics, genetically unable to sustain a speck of interest in it, the conversation mercifully was short-lived. We talked about cows and barley instead, which I think are far more interesting. They were surprised however, when I told them I would have to go to jail for not paying a parking fine, and suggested I just stay in Greece. I did roll it over in my mind

I realised in that village that night that Maro was frightened of the dark. She liked street lights, bazouki music, clatter and bang and big noises. She didn't like being alone in the country in peace and quiet as I did. So she had her way that night.

I bedded her down, rolled out my sleeping bag beside her, drank a last glass of chipero with the farmers – it's a local firewater – lay down, and was plunged into a chipero-induced coma, which left me senseless until dawn. In the morning I asked about the quickest way to Efsoni, the border town with Yugoslavia through which I had to pass with Maro.

'You go back down through the woods you were in last night, then you'll find a track which will take you to within fifteen kilometres of the border.'

'Epharisto parapoli! ('Thank you very much'). And by the way, those old trees – what's their story?'

'Nothing much. They're very old. There is some story of their being haunted by a centaur : you know, those half-horse half-man things of ancient Greece, some people say they have seen them, but it's rubbish really.'

As we passed through the trees, I left a bottle of wine there, and some oats.

We spent the first hour of the morning walking to the Greek frontier post beyond Efsoni, along the dual carriageway. At that time of day there was little traffic, except for the ever-present fast-moving freighters, whose vortex of wind swept grit into our eyes, leaving us in a swirl of fumes and dust.

It had been a long walk up the day before through the plains and hills, through fields of almonds and maize, eaten all the way by flies. Then we'd followed another receding river up to Efsoni, spent the night with an old boy who spoke Turkish, which I understood better than Greek. I was nervous as we approached the border control and passed straight up between the cars, feeling I risked trouble if I queued.

A customs man came out to me, took my papers, told me to wait. Ten minutes later he came out to say my export forms were inaccurate, wrong. However, since I was on foot, and he noticed, it was my birthday, they'd let me through. I couldn't believe it! Simple!

'Kallo taxidi!' they waved, and Maro and I walked into no-man's-land, between the border controls. There's about half a mile of it between the frontiers, and as we walked I could scarcely believe my luck.

I was apprehensive of entering Yugoslavia, having been told strings of dreadful stories of banditry near the main roads. My first objective would be to get quickly away from the big roads, and up into the mountains. It also meant having to learn another language, Serbo Croat or whatever it is they speak, figure out all the currency, and learn quickly the words for oats and dinner.

It was nevertheless uncomfortable walking along on the tarmac, dreading Maro having a horrible attack of the heebie-jeebies, which she was perfectly entitled to do being unfamiliar with dense traffic, and all these howling, mocking people waving their arms and legs around at her.

Once again, at the Yugoslav post, we queue-jumped, quite simply to be away as quickly as possible, and if anyone there objected to it, they never said so. I handed in my passport, gave the man Mara's papers, he glanced at both, put a tick on Mara's, stamped mine, handed them back and said 'Welcome to Yugoslavia.'

That was it. I was in. It was a cinch. Why had everyone made such a blooming great fuss about it? We walked away from the customs point toward Bitola in the distance and started to look for a way off the road, so we could get into the safety of the mountains. There was an equivalent of a 'Hoi!' from behind, 'Doctor's inspection!'

I went back, handed over Mara's papers again, and the waiting began in earnest. My joy was short-lived. The sun burned down hot on the tarmac, traffic started to flow busily. We pulled onto some grass, got kicked off with a 'Dass iss verboten' by a brute, then just hung round, waiting.

A slightly-built, wispy bearded hippy came to talk to us. I was glad of his company. I thought all the hippies had died out and I'm glad they haven't – I always liked them, they're such a peaceful lot. This one – who called himself Gabriel – was quite young, wore a great many beads, with a flower-power shirt and bell bottoms. He talked about a tepee he had in Spain, was now on his way to Greece and having a look about. Puffing on a pin-thin cigarette, he added that he had been spared the appalling ordeal of having a career, worked at anything that came his way, but mostly, he liked to weave. He was much intrigued by Mara, saying he had quite taken to the idea of having a donkey once, but not knowing about them, had stuck to his thumb, as a faster and cheaper way of shinning around.

When I told him the Greeks let me through because it was my birthday, he remarked it was very sharp-eyed of them – which indeed it was, because they celebrate name days, not birthdays in Greece. Then he suggested we get drunk instantly. He disappeared, arriving back a few minutes later with a bottle of vodka, and an observation about how a border control point is an excellent place to get boozed up in. He'd done it lots of times. For one ghastly moment I thought he was about to offer me a joint, but held out one of his pin cigarettes. But I don't smoke.

I enjoyed his rambling chit-chat and he lightened the blow that fell later that morning when the customs men came over to me, saying I couldn't enter Yugoslavia on foot. I never did get to hear the reason. I suspect it was the transit visa business. Gabriel suggested I go to Bitola, take a train. No the guard said, nowhere on foot, not even just down the road.

'You must return to Greece. Perhaps you can take a train from Polycastron to Italy.' That was a bitter pill to swallow. I was glad Gabriel was there. He and his vodka made it more bearable, despite that we had been drinking at that hour of the day. I thanked him, wished him good luck, as he did me, offering me his tepee in Spain if I happen to be riding through. I'll take him up on that one day. I had another gulp of his vodka, shook hands and it's strange how in chance meetings like that, when your knowledge of each other is only fleeting, it's intense too. I was genuinely sorry to say goodbye.

The slog back was hot. The road to Polycastron was long. We arrived at seven that night and I found, with difficulty, a place for Maro to stay with a man called Metrios – 'who loves horses' – amid a group of ageing village ponies, chicken shit and dogs. Maro scoffed mouthfuls of trifilly as children screamed about, bazouki music rattled and banged in tavernas nearby: all the things she likes. Dispirited in a taverna I considered the options. Things were looking bleak. My veterinary papers were just about to expire, the export papers also, and I was nowhere near a frontier I could get out from. I considered the trail across Northern Greece to Corfu, then across to Brindisi, but that meant going south to go north. I watched children wheel about on bicycles in the square, self-conscious promenaders parade up and down, diners stuff themselves with hot greasy meals, olives and feta, drinking ouzos. The sky was black and alight at once with the thrill of a Saturday night when nothing quite gets off the ground. Dogs criss-crossed the streets looking for a scrap, trees slept unmoving draped with coloured lights and someone roared into town on a Massey Ferguson 135.

In the morning I was told there was no train from Polycastron to Italy, that if I wanted to go by train, I should have to go back to Thessaloniki and I would not be allowed to accompany the horse. I couldn't really see the point in travelling without my horse who was on a train I wasn't, in the vague hope of meeting her somewhere in Italy. Too much to go wrong with that plan.

Maria was astonished to find herself back in Ktima Litsas, as indeed was everyone else. I popped her back under the trees where she slobbered over another water melon as though nothing had happened. She had been a wonderful companion and I had never met such a tactile horse before. She was always anxious to be handled and I had become used to her nuzzlings. She was a sweet creature, and I wanted to keep her.

I determined to give it one last try and extended her veterinary documents by a week. This meant it was impossible for me to ride her out of the country. I would either have to fly, ship, freight or rail her out. The first quote I received was for a truck for Italy, via Yugoslavia in which I could travel with her. The price was £900. There was one very simple answer to that – it was too much.

The next quote was a truck to Igoumenitsa on the sea, near Corfu, for £300, but I would have to find an enclosed truck and ferry to Italy – a further £400 or £500.

I was also told that because of my illegal export documents I would have to produce an ATA Camet, whatever that was. Since I am not Greek, nor had any business in Greece other than tourism, I could not be issued with one. The only chance of securing an ATA Camet, was to give the horse to Penny, who had a business, and who would then be registered as her owner, and I could then borrow the horse from her in order to comply with EEC regulations on these peculiar documents, which seemed to serve no other purpose than keep you guessing as to what the next rabbit-in-the-hat would be. By this method, all my other papers would have to be renewed since everything was registered in my name, not Penny's. Having gone through all of that, I was told I wouldn't need an ATA Camet after all, and had been misinformed.

I struggled with documentation, ferry crossings, securing trucks at reduced rates and the whole thing was utterly unintelligible. There seemed to be no way of getting my horse to Italy without calling her a slaughter horse, in which case I risked having her led off the ferry in Brindisi and promptly butchered. It was a hopeless situation and no way out. No one could tell me clearly what papers I needed, where to get them and how to ship a horse. No one.

I spent over £200 on telephone calls, telexes, documentation, stamps, taxis, buses and petrol to be told time and again that I could export her to England, not Italy. When I asked if I could simply get out of a lorry in Italy, the answer was no, I couldn't, because I would be on the driver's papers, and then he would be in trouble. The bureaucratic machinery was such a concerted morass of unintelligible bumf, I could only suppose it to have been devised by one, or a whole committee of half-wits. It was impossible.

I booked my flight to Rome without Maro on 11 August. In the morning, at five thirty, I went to see her for the last time. She watched me walk towards her, and I didn't know where to put my thoughts. Yet I was unafraid for her, as I was afraid for Ahmed Paşa. She was in her home, knew everybody, and everyone loved her, though none as much as I. I patted her, stroked her, ran my hands over her soft muzzle as she stood quite still, listening as she had always done.

I put my face to hers, told her I was leaving, that I would see her again one day and that she was in the safest hands in the land. And I couldn't contain my sorrow, remembered the lad who had said the words I whispered to her again, 'You, I love you, Maria.'

14

Italy

Colonello Federico Franco Caldari is a lovely man, and Gonzales da Mendoza D' Alta Sierra D' Argentina was the reason for our introduction. Gonzales da Mendoza was Colonello Caldari's horse. I had been in Italy seven days before I found one. My search had taken me through Rome and its neighbourhood.

I was bowled over by Rome. I had never been there before and after the kind of place I was used to it felt opulent, dignified, austere. The place dripped in ornament and statue. Down every street and avenue was something to marvel at, delight the eye. The language rang like music too, and I was surprised how much of it I could understand from school room Latin. It evoked classroom memories for me, cobwebbed words, dark images of columns and agora, and a, ab, absque, coram, de, palam, cum, with ex and e and strings of other meaningless jingles they pumped into us at prep school. How they managed to make the study of Latin so boring staggered me when confronted with Rome face-to-face.

The ruins in Turkey had in some way prepared me, but I was still amazed. Maybe that sounds corny. I don't care: it rocked me. I found horses there too. I asked a bloke on the Spanish Steps, and he shrugged his shoulders muttering something about a place called Testaccio Vecchio. I took a bus there.

I could smell horses. So I wandered round Testacchio Vecchio sniffing. Then I found them in a great old courtyard which was all falling apart. They were trotting horses. A couple of fellows were exercising one, round and round an arena. He was white with sweat. Pretty rough on a horse that. If you don't know how to exercise them properly, no amount of torture will make them give their best. They were all huge, thoroughbredish things with long gangly legs. Not the sort of boxy thing I was after.

Sitting in a chic coffee shop with marble floors and silk wall hangings, gilt framed lithographs, circular topped tables and waited on by men in frock coats, overhearing talk of music and art, then rushed six quid for a couple of coffees, I realised I was in the wrong town, and went straight to the station. Got on the first train out, and wound up in Assisi.

It wasn't planned; just happened that way. I booked myself into the first 'camere' I saw directly opposite the station in Santa Maria degli Angeli. I looked out of the window right onto some horses. It didn't take long to find out who owned them. I could see the Great Basilica of Assisi from there too.

That evening, I went up to Assisi, and in the Temple of Minerva – which is a completely preserved Roman building – I lit three candles. One for Ahmed Paşa, one for Şimşek and one for Maro. In the basilica Inferiore, I lit one big candle for all horses, mules, ponies and donkeys who are maltreated or go hungry. If I can light candles for horses anywhere, I can light them in Assisi. It's one of the oldest cities in Italy, home of St Francis, regarded by many as patron saint of animals. Of course, most species have their own patron saint. Hippolytus, for instance, is the patron saint of horses. He was a Roman priest, martyred in 235, when he was 'torn asunder' by two wild horses at the mouth of the Tiber. Some accounts say he was literally torn to pieces, others say he was tied to their tails. Can't quite see how that was done. In any event, seems an odd reason to be their patron saint: I should have thought the very opposite. Still, I don't have a saint's logic. We have a link with him in England in the church of lppolitis in Hertfordshire, where they used to take sick horses to his shrine.

St Francis preached to birds, called all living things his brothers or sisters and when walking 'gadyrd the wormes out of the wayes, by cause they should not be troden with the feet of them that passyd by.' He exhorted men to follow the first commandment of Christ, to love one another. Somehow, I heard echoes in it of a man way back in Turkey, who said, 'Love is a boundless ocean, in which the heavens are a flake of foam. Know that all the wheeling heavens are turned by love: were it not love, the world would be frozen.' (Jalal Din Rumi – Mevlana). To throw these two men together may seem a strange thing to do in the light of their different cultures; but that is all it is.

The town of Assisi is full of intriguing stairways and glorious architecture, built in the soft pink stone of the mountain. In the basilica of St Francis, I counted twelve horses in the murals: maybe there were more. The complexity of the buildings and paintings was bewilderingly lovely, with a strong peaceful presence.

The Umbrian landscape round about was soft, dotted with large shuttered farmhouses shaded by trees. Figs, and even bananas, draped green over grassy gardens. While walking round Santa Maria degli Angeli, Francesco Marchetti – owner of the horses near my *camere* – told me he had located a horse for me. With Febbio, a friend of his, we drove out through the plain below Mount Subasio, past the irrigated sunflowers, maize, vines and tobacco, down an avenue of cypress, into a courtyard where a big old house rambled in peeling pastels, smothered in climbing plants. Its shadow angled sharp across a dusty yard.

A figure of a faded Madonna was cut in a niche in a wall, picked out in the glow of the evening sun. The house was surrounded by stables and corrals, where browsing horses flicked up eddies of dust from their feet.

We were met by a short, heavily-built man smoking a cigarette, nodding his understanding as Francesco explained why we were there. He showed us round to the front of the house, past a collapsed old vine to a corral, where a single, unusually coloured horse watched us approach. He stood quite still, ears pricked, sniffing. 'Strano colore!' ('Strange colour!') Francesco remarked. The man nodded, blowing out a plume of smoke.

'Gonzales.'

We leaned against the corral rails, but the horse didn't approach. He kept his distance. He was kind of pearl grey, with dark points, like a Siamese cat. He had strong feet, a powerful chest, and quarters like a Suffolk Punch. His coat was fine, shiny with a brand mark on his nearside hind in the shape of a double 'S'. He had a thick mane divided on his neck.

He was a Creole or Criollo, imported from Argentina, which explained his Spanish name. A gelding, 15.1 hands, he had worked the pampas in South America as a cow horse. He had been broken from the wild, and to me his colour said it all. I was immediately intrigued, since Creoles were the breed Tschiffeley had ridden on his stupendous ride from Buenos Aires to Washington in 1926. It took him two and a half years, and his horses did the entire trip. He had been greatly impressed by the type, finding them tough, resilient, unlikely to go ill. They had been introduced to South America in 1526.

The foundation stock came from Barbs, Arabs and Andalusians taken there by the Spanish. That alone must have been some feat – all that way, with horses, in galleons. When some Spanish garrisons were overrun by Indians, the horses went wild. They reverted to a natural state, and only the very toughest survived. Natural selection weeded out the poorly-bred and left the survivors with short, thick legs, strong bones and an amazing digestive system. They can go along on anything. One look at Gonzales, and you could see the whole history.

His pearly coat was really rat coloured, feral: even there, in that courtyard, he was well camouflaged. To this he added lightening reactions and wild horse behaviour. He had been imported into Italy a little before, and was the property of Colonello Caldari, in livery at Snr. Vignati's stables. He had a full batch of import documentation, had passed Coggins, Dourine, Mallein, Glanders and a string of other veterinary inspections, a very strong point in his favour. He was the right size, and eight years old.

'Bello cavallo!' ('Nice horse!') said Francesco. 'Voi montare?' ('Do you want to get on?')

The man fetched a saddle. I noticed that Gonzales had three raised vertebrae on his spine, whether from injury or badly fitting saddle I couldn't tell, but they didn't seem to worry him. His bridle was slung over one ear, and bitless. The reins were long and unbuckled. Not an arrangement I knew.

I was legged up into the saddle, grabbed the reins with both hands and Gonzales cavorted about, snorting, kicking and bucking. It took all my energy to stay on. I found him immensely powerful, impossible to control.

'One hand!' Francesco shouted, 'he neck reins!'

That takes getting used to. With his speed, freedom of movement and sharp reactions, I didn't know what would happen next. We confused each other completely. He eyed me over his shoulder, responding with a vigorous whirl on his hind legs. A hard contrast to Ahmed Paşa who reacted twenty minutes after you wanted him to – or twenty minutes before – or to Maro, who responded when she felt like it. This horse responded instantly.

But I fouled it up, didn't know how to get the signals through to him. If I wanted to turn right, he went left. If I wanted to go left, he went right. If I wanted to stop, he bolted, if I wanted to canter, he stopped. He did everything in total reverse. He was as baffling to ride as it would be to drive a fast car whose steering works the wrong way round, through a slalem cambered the wrong angle. You are left unseated for the next bend since you don't know which way it's going to pitch, by which time it's too late.

In spite of my confusion, I liked him. There was something else about him too. Something I have never had words to explain, which neither Ahmed Paşa, nor Şimşek nor Maro had, but which was second nature to this horse. There were questions I wanted to ask.

As I struggled with him, weaving back to his corral through the maize, the light faded and the great bell of Assisi sounded long and sombre, the deep boom giving sound to the setting sun. Come dusk in Umbria, as the light softens and the yellow sun dulls to crimson, a quiet comes to the land. Men stop working, grazing animals still, and a balm breathes into the cooling earth. It doesn't last long: just time enough to relax within it. Then the business of preparing for evening is upon you. The clatter of pots and china, children crying, all the noises that were there before return. Somehow, you are shaken down, not so much re-charged, as re-geared.

As I sat on Gonzales wondering which was right and which was left, the sunflowers rustled in tiny whirrs of wind. I rode back, unsaddled him, and stared at this strange Argentinian horse in Italian twilight, and asked him to come to Wales with me.

Back in Santa Maria degli Angeli, sitting in the square sipping cool white wine with Francesco, we talked about the horse and the 2,800,000 lira they asked for him. £1,300: expensive. The likelihood of finding another horse at a lower price was small.

Next day, I transferred the cash, Gonzales underwent further tests for Coggins, and all his export papers were drawn up. This time, I left the paperwork to Mario Sivilieri and Dino Gatta of Tast Cavalli in Milan. They ship over three thousand horses a year: they know the ropes. I washed my hands of the whole stupefying business.

I had lunch with Francesco in his Hotel dal Moro in Santa Maria. We had tagliatelle with mushroom and lemon sauce; cold pork with diced fennel and a green salad: a side plate of lightly fried and sliced aubergine, dipped in onions and tuna fish. A bottle of wine, delicious ice-cream, and I can't remember what happened after that.

15

Pioneer–Lead

I exercised Gonzales daily while waiting for the results of the Cogging tests and permission to export. While riding around, I found the Italian reaction to a mounted horseman similar to that of the Turks. They were always friendly, always smiling and shouted, 'Bello Cavallo! Bellissimo Cavalilni!' and offered wine and food.

I had been warned about theft in Italy, but I lost nothing. In the weeks that followed I often left Gonzales, saddlebags and all my kit untended for hours at a time, only to return and find nothing disturbed.

When I met Gonzales' owner, Colonello Federico Caldari, he took me for a drive around the villages. On the way he told me about himself. He had joined the carabinieri (rural police) with the aim of going into the cavalry side of the force but, on account of having a background in aviation, he was transferred straight into helicopters. He had retired young, having distinguished himself in the service, rising rapidly to the rank of colonel. He was a tall, handsome man with twinkling bright eyes. He had an air of fairness about him, was a popular figure in Assisi, a matto di Gubbio, a special honour conferred on citizens who have set themselves apart from their fellows in unusual ways; he had walked away from ten helicopter pile-ups with his life. In the village of Collepino, he pointed out a well where young mothers were encouraged to drink since the waters stimulated milk flow, and made 'the tits bigga-boum-boum – a gooda-placa-for-ladies eh?'

We went to Spello, saw the home of the late king of Bulgaria. But it was the Colonello's home which typified Italy for me. He lived near the steps of Duomo San Rufino, whose façade is the most majestic piece of architecture in the city. The interior of his house was painted white, furnished in that withheld style which is so peculiarly Italian. Old oil paintings in oak frames hung on walls beneath brick fan-vaulted ceilings. It had an atmosphere of unassumed sophistication, all quite natural.

His wife cooked a delicious meal, we drank a stirrup cup, and he introduced me to Verdi on horseback – which I learned to play on my harmonica: it's a wonderful combination. His wife wanted to know if Gonzales was up to travelling, and whether once back in Galles (Wales) he was assured of a good home, or whether I would sell him. I appreciated her concern: it told me much about the family. I asked a lot of questions about the horse and what he told me confirmed what I had already felt.

Whenever he rode Gonzales, he said, the horse always wanted to lead. On the day of the cavalcade from Nocera to Assisi, commemorating the return of St Francis, Gonzales would lead the other forty horses all the way. He was difficult to handle in company, sharp in a stable. On the face of it, he sounded a real liability – a horse who needed hard schooling. But it told me something altogether different about him.

I found him independent from the minute I met him. True, he was basically a wild horse and he shied a lot, leaving wide margins between himself and anything he regarded as suspicious. To me, he acted like a true lead horse. Many horses will become leading horses. Some refuse flat: but most, with persuasion, will. As leading horses they over-react: they are strong to ride, showy, sharp and nappy. Even the most demure horse will do this if put into lead position with other horses. Some horses are more subtle about it than others. This is why Ahmed Paşa became such a brute to ride when Şimşek joined. But Ahmed Paşa took on the part, unlike Gonzales, who was a natural born lead.

A lead horse will dominate. A herd without a lead will instantly accept him, and any group of horses will follow a born leader. It's a chemistry we don't properly understand. You can sometimes tell them from others: daft in stables, impossible to handle, they always pull, and add up to a serious pain in the neck most of the time. But put them in a field, and they'll lead the others. Invariably, they are brave, independent, greedy, they have good feet, seldom go ill and look after themselves first. They make the best travelling horses you can expect to find. If you can get close to one of these; if you can get him to trust you – and you'll have to go to him, because he won't come to you; you'll have a horse who'll spin the world beneath his feet for you. These horses look for new ground. They become bored easily and you can ruin them by trying to submit them to your will under pressure. It's in their character to be as they are. When I returned to England I was lucky enough to speak to a leading British event rider who told me she selects her horses on this principle, only she had never given it a name. I call them pioneer-leads.

On the night before collecting Gonzo (my shortened name for him), I rode a beautiful horse called Zanzibar. He was a big Lipizzaner cross Arab, who floated at the gallop as if he ran on feathers. Beside him, Gonzo looked like a lugger by a schooner, each with a different job to do. But he was flashy: he liked his home. Gonzo had fourteen hundred miles to walk before he reached his. At six that evening, I collected Gonzo from Snr Vignati's stables. In the meantime, I had cut a strand of hair from his mane, put it in an envelope for Patrick Kemp to work his radiasthesic healing on Gonzo's spine. I've never had any problems with this horse since.

In the twilight, the Colonello, Snr Vignati and three of his friends were there to see us off. We drank some sparkling wine, and as the sun went down, we all toasted Gonzo's feet. He was nervous – that was easy to see, but I had long got used to horses getting wind of what was going on, and reacting to it.

As I rode away, he whinnied, just a tiny little noise, and that was the last. In Santa Maria degli Angeli, Francesco prepared a stable for him and we arrived in darkness. After a light supper with Francesco, I thanked him for all he had done, paid a visit to Gonzo at midnight, and turned in.

Never walk past good grazing: this verdant pasture lay just below Priene

Ahmed Paşa getting some new shoes in the old holy city of Priene

Şimşek was offered a drink by a kind local on the track to Milet

Villagers at Develikoy

Milet, best known for its gigantic Hellenistic amphitheatre.
There was no-one there where we rode through

We had Ephesus all to ourselves

The hill above Izmir where we camped and a nightingale sang all night

We swam the horses whenever we could – it cooled them down and cleaned them off

Above: On the coast road to Candarli

Right: With Gonzo and map, lost in the Alps © Marco Windham

Chumpie

Parting with the horses. Şimşek is tried out by his new owner. It was a terrible, emotional day

Penny haggling over Maria's price with the knackerman

Washing up in an
Alpine river

Buying Gonzo from
Dolonel Federico
Caldari in Santa
Maria degli Angeli,
just outside Assisi

With Gonzo in the
Alps. Gonzo was
by far the best
travelling horse

© Marco Windham

Saddling up after a lunchtime stop in the Alps – though where we were I had no idea © Marco Windham

Sharing a pizza with Gonzo outside Lanslebourg Mont Cenis

16

Beautiful Italy

We slipped away from the stables at seven o'clock, past the Great Basilica, turning north-west on a compass bearing of 350 degrees. Gonzo walked away without any hesitation. The saddlery all fitted well, although I had to lift up the panniers because of his high withers. As we rose up the hill, the Basilica fell from view and the bell tolled again. It sounded like a good-bye: it felt fine, like good luck.

The country round about was glorious with large, lonely farmhouses in spectacular settings overlooking long plains below. Little valleys hid houses lying crumbling in abandoned silence. Round others chickens strutted, scratched and dogs dozed in shade, flat out.

We moved steadily northwards, spending our first few nights together in the open, Gonzo rapidly accustomising himself to being tied on a long tether at night. I found the longer the tether, the less likely a horse is to tangle: it's the short lines of five yards or less they hook up in. Gonzo's rope was twenty yards, and he never did.

The rural Italians were charm itself. They were always helpful, always smiled and produced delicious spaghetti, for which I developed a craving: I hunted it down, sought it, thought about it, dreamed of it. Plates of spaghetti, delicious dripping garlic and olive oil, a handful of parmesan. With that, a bottle of Chianti, the benign Italian sun, lovely Umbria, the Italians and a horse like Gonzo, I walked in paradise.

Umbria rolled on even more bewitching with low undulating hills, fields of sunflowers and maize. All the buildings were fine constructions, varying from the quiet vine-cloaked farmhouses of the mountains to small painted houses in the plains. The colours were always good, always pastel, lime-washed and peeling. Quietly by the Tiber, near Umbertide, we rested beneath poplars where the air was humid and hot. We must have crossed the Tiber a dozen times, caught between a motorway and the river. But on the whole, motorists were very thoughtful towards a horse on the roads – particularly Italian truck drivers, who showed an understanding of a horse's reaction to heavy goods vehicles. Every now and then we would stop in a transport cafe, where I unpacked Gonzo, and let him graze about while I stuffed myself with spaghetti. None of the truck drivers I met were rough or uncouth and, as a travelling horseman, I became part of their camaraderie. Often they would stop, having passed me in some other place, and give Gonzo carrots or some other treat. And always I found the transport cafes rather better than English restaurants, with white linen table cloths, nice glass and good cutlery.

We passed Trestino and spent the night beside a monastery in Conoscio, where the ground was marked as sacred, and where no mortal – except those cognoscenti who've got a special deal with God – is allowed to set foot. Gonzo and I spent the night bedded down in a dunghill lest we defile the holy ground. The stars shone bright over us that night, then the wind blew up, black clouds raced in the sky and it poured from dawn on. We must have trampled on the holy ground.

We walked all the following day in the rain. We picked up signs for an agri-tourismo place – a farmhouse bed and breakfast, where they'll cater for horses. I longed for a change of clothes, something dry, a meal. When we got there it was shut. We definitely must have trodden on the holy ground.

We went on. A storm welled, then broke over us, the rain howling around with curtains of fog and mists in the mountains. Lightning crashed in multi-coloured flashes. I panicked on a hill top when I saw the same tree hit twice in rapid succession, not a hundred yards from where we floundered around, Gonzo in his iron shoes. I promise not to tread on holy ground again, OK?

Italy was not easy to ride through. The further north we went, the nearer the mountains closed in on us, and all roads went to Rome. Nothing went north west. We were crossing the country at an angle across all the mountains, and we met every obstacle they threw at us.

Then, following the rain, came the sun. Blackberries were out in hedgerows. It took Gonzo two minutes to figure out how to pick blackberries. He cottons on fast. We spent hours up in the bushes on a little via bianca on the way to Marcignano past Citta di Castello, scoffing blackberries. We begged some water from a sixteenth century Italian woman living in a solitary cottage miles from anywhere. Toothless, black frocked, she gawped at us, tut-tutting. Gonzo laid a monster sized dongo on her freshly swept courtyard, which she beheld in silent fascination.

We pushed on later that afternoon, and all the time the track we were on edged away from our bearing. It took a nasty swing off to the south, but just at that point stood a burned out cottage beside a stream, recently swollen from the rains. A vague track struggled up the mountainside opposite, going north. We'd been caught like this before. You follow a tiny track, then it peters out leaving you on the edge of the world, or else it goes off in a long circle and brings you back exhausted hours later, having been nowhere in particular. Up we went.

It was a hot climb. I walked beside Gonzo in a pair of shorts; I wore just shorts most of the time. It's the good thing about proper empire-builders: they're so long, you can wear them with chaps when you are riding, then when you get off, you whip your chaps off and hey presto, there you are, in the pink of fashion. We stopped for a blow every now and then, swatted horse flies. As we came to the top, we saw a number of abandoned houses: an old settlement. Round the next corner was Peter Cushing reading a book.

'Fee fi fo fum ...' It had to be. Who else would you be likely to meet in an abandoned house in the middle of nowhere in Umbria but a nice barking English professor and his wife? I don't know who was more surprised, them or me. They thought I was Italian at first. But I got them as English in one: the GB on their Rover. They were camping in the shade of old pear trees in an overgrown garden. There was a tent, saucepans, bottles, bags, odds and ends: just like a couple of bedu.

'Have a glass of wine.' It was three o'clock on a hot afternoon.

'Love one: just park Gonzo.' I tethered him in some long grass where he could see us. You have to be mindful of a travelling horse, they get lonely fast. I sat down beside Peter. He poured out a glass of deep red wine. An awkward moment, couldn't think of a thing to say. Nor could they. We sat in silence rolling glasses in our hands. Norma spoke.

'Hot.'

'Yes.'

'Come far?'

'Turkey.'

'Poor horse.'

' .. er .. no .. no .. different horse .. we .. I ... couldn't get into Yugoslavia.'

'Hungry?'

'No, Yugoslavia.'

She frowned.

'Hungry food?'

'Famished ... I didn't bring a bottle.'

'It's all right. We've got a wine lake.'

This was the smooth. The last few days hadn't been easy. We'd found ourselves on roads in amongst traffic, unable to break free. The people near the big roads are never as kind as the people inland, away from the rush.

'Extraordinary thing happened coming up the track.'

'Oh?'

'A mouse – like a gerbil – ran out from the grass just in front of Gonzo's feet, with a viper right on his tail.'

'Extraordinary thing! What happened?'

'He got very close but the snake saw Gonzo's feet, did an about turn and the mouse got away.'

'Saved by the cavalry.' Norma said that.

'In the nick of time.' Peter polished it off.

Peter was a professor of English literature and had decided to take early retirement. He and Norma bought this tumbledown stone house up in those lovely hills, with a view all across the mountains. They planned to live there for six months of the year, when Peter would complete the book he was writing on Machiavelli.

The house hadn't been lived in for years, but it had a lot of feeling about it, warmth, conviviality. It had tiling on the floors upstairs, which gave it a cool feel. There was a lot of work to be done: Peter had already started and had cleared a stable below for the dining room. It was cool in there too, dark. All stone with big flags, stone mangers and an old wine barrel in the corner.

'That's empty, we drank it.'

There were some other cottages dotted about, all abandoned.

'Speculators bought a pair of cottages over there,' Peter pointed at collapsed walls. 'They intend to sell them to more English people – make a community up here. Just a few of us. Won't be too bad, I mean that track's hardly a motorway.' We swigged the wine.

'You're our first guest,' Norma mused, looking over the mountains. 'We'll lend you a lilo and a tent if you like, or you can sleep in the stables, or upstairs or anywhere you like.'

What luxury a lilo is. After nights of hard ground the thought of an air bed was dreamy.

We had supper in the cleaned out stable. Prosciutto, biscuits, canned meats, cheese and wine. It was one of the best dinner parties I have ever been to. All huddled in there, in the cool, unpainted, dry homely stable. Just an oil lamp burning, hanging on a nail. We seemed more like three desperadoes on the run who had found a good bolt hole. It made you all light headed, bubbly. They loved that house, those two. So did I.

Gonzo and I spent some of the night in the stable, then moved out later so he could graze. I watched the early dawn steal away the little stars you can see when the sky is dark. Then as it gets lighter, the big stars go, then the planets and it gets flooded with a blue phosphorescent light. You can see cobwebs all threaded about in the grass, with globs of dew on them and then the sun comes up like a big orange. Gonzo had cobwebs all over his nose.

Norma made some coffee at eight and we talked again. I'd slept really well. It had been such a joy to find those two; they put new drive into me, new hope somehow. They said they'd keep a room free for the odd itinerant horseman: I bet they do.

It's always awkward leaving, and I felt nervous – I don't know why. I found it difficult to say goodbye, cheerio. Just wandered off, waving and rode away in silence.

We spent the night with Pietro Malvisi having crossed the road to Sansepolcro where I saw signs for Il Bandito Maneggio Catigliano – The Bandit's Riding School. Either it had to be a bandit, or had bandit clients, or someone had an unusual sense of humour. Either way it was intriguing. It was four in the afternoon which is quite late enough to start looking for a night's lodging. I found that if you weren't settled by five, you were not likely to be settled by dark. It was an odd thing. The worry of where you were going to stay always took the thrill out of the afternoon ride.

The morning rides were easy because you were relaxed, it was cool, the horse was going well, and there was a prospect of a nice picnic lunch somewhere, by a stream or river, somewhere shady. I'd buy oats and barley for Gonzo too, so he'd be looking forward to it as much as I was. We usually took two hours over it. Time enough to do your laundry, clean the tack, while Gonzo ate whatever was going. He ate everything. Pine needles, banana leaves, hay, herba medica (lucerne), straw, maize, oats, fragmites, bamboo, got fat on it, and never bunged up.

Gonzo looked wonderful with his silver pelt all polished and shiny, his big strong feet and Italian shoes; not quite Gucci. They put ten nails in them in Italy. The Greeks put six nails in, and the Turks put in whatever happened to be around at the time. Italian shoes are long on one side, and very hard metal. He'd been well shod, they'd done it the day before we set out from Assisi. And like Ahmed Paşa and Maro, it took no time to build up that special bond between us. If I left him outside a shop, he'd howl until I reappeared, so I tried always to tie him so he could see through the glass. He'd pinch my lunch sometimes and discovered how to undo the saddlebags. He never went soft on his feet, never funked anything and had this wonderful alert strapping gait. He never needed urging. All that Tschiffeley said about Creoles, I found too. Somehow he was a blend of both Ahmed Paşa and Maro, being neither black nor white, but silver grey. He was neither stallion nor mare, but gelding, neither short nor tall, but middling, neither young nor old, but eight. Like them too, he became malleable, good to handle, dependable, a real travelling horse. It's funny how they get. When you sling your hook at night, that's it: home. The saddle, the pile of clobber is home. You don't even have to tether them. I walked often with him, never riding for more than two and a half hours at a time. I got stiff otherwise, and he got bored. So we'd stop for a while, gawp about. Little and often. You go a long way like that.

I don't know any long distance rider who doesn't walk a lot. This way the horse never goes lame, he never gets back sores, and you don't fall out with each other. Besides, much of the journey is in the stopping anyway. People come up to you, to chat, have a drink. You can ask directions. And it's astonishing how many people are completely ignorant of their immediate surroundings. I don't know how many times I was advised to take major routes in completely the wrong direction.

It had been dead easy in Turkey. Easiest riding of the lot. There were no fences, the people were wonderful, there was food everywhere, every village had a blacksmith and no one was proprietorial. It was far more difficult in Europe with motorways, railways, fences, tight field margins and grazing livestock, horses running around. In Turkey, everything had been tethered. So a night with Pietro Malvisi, the Bandit. Everybody thought he was one, so he advertised it. Sensible man.

Claudio the groom cooked a delicious supper of spaghetti and chicken breasts stuffed with fennel. After supper, Pietro showed me his horses. There were Marremanos, Arabs, English, Irish, Native Mountain Italian, Avilignese, Argentines, Uruguyan, Andalusians, Egyptians and his favourite – Sardinians.

They import horses from all over the world in Italy, and are far more dynamic than we are in Britain. They ride them in all sorts of tack, using Western saddles, classical Italian – which are glorious: the Italians make the world's most beautiful saddles – English, German, Spanish, French, American McClellands and the saddles of Appaloosa in Vicenza, who make the best saddle pack combination money can buy.

There is a lot of long distance riding in Italy: they have the room to do it. But nobody rode the route I seemed to be on, going obliquely across the country. The Romans never went that way for sure. I expect they went up the motorway on the coast, like everybody else.

Pietro fed the horses a breakfast feed of crushed biscuits and oats next morning. The rest of us tucked into prosciutto, eggs, bacon, bread and to my surprise, thick red wine. No tea, no coffee. A normal breakfast thing, all perfectly natural. Four or five glasses of that stuff and I was ready to carry Gonzo to Mars.

We left at nine, went up on a bearing going 300 north. I would like to have gone to Sansepolcro to see the frescos, and the birthplace of Michelangelo at Caprese. I should like to have spent longer talking to a family of Romans who'd bought a house in the mountains to escape from the city. He'd been an airline pilot for Alitalia for twenty years before finally chucking it in. Now he taught children in a Rudolf Steiner School. 'Believe me, it's harder than flying a jumbo. Nicer though.'

We slogged on and on that day up into the mountains. We saw no one, passed no houses, heard no birds. Just us and the mountain. We holed up high above the world with Protomagna on our right and all the ranges of hills to cross, marching off like frozen waves in some gigantic sea. It was a beautiful landscape, terraced and green, strung with vines and made grey by olive trees.

I watched the sun go down, watched the hills go a kind of mauve. Tried to make out how Protomagna was made, if it was rocky, or steep, easy or a pig of a climb. I couldn't tell. Thought about Pietro Malvisi, how he'd pushed back the money I offered, and given me a blanket: said I'd need it in the Alps. I looked down at the river, down in the valley. Didn't know it then, but I was to have a very bad time down there next day. Another mountain, another river, another tin of sardines.

17

The Rough and the Smooth

Gonzo raided my larder in the night. He stole my bread, divided the prosciutto amongst the ants. He left me a tin of sardines and a chewed packet of polos. What a miserable breakfast that is. I called him a rotten thieving so-and-so, standing there all full of my bread and half the grass in Italy. I didn't know whether to eat the sardines or the polos first, so ate them both together. It's not good.

I packed him, bellyaching. We set out on the road down to the river. I aimed to skirt Protomagna, then up through northern Tuscany. Down in the valley, the river had cut itself into a deep gorge, with high rock banks. Running along the length of the river was a busy main road. I wanted to cross, but there was no bridge, no way down to the river. We walked along the road. I tried to walk on verges, but kept meeting obstacles, fences, ditches, and vines strung right up to its edge.

On the right-hand side of the road was a cliff face. On the left was the river, sixty feet or so straight down, behind a motorway crash barrier. We followed the road north for a short distance before it swung away to the right, following the course of the river. I dared not walk on the correct side since the traffic was moving fast, hugging the cliff. If anything met us on that corner we would have been mangled. So we walked against the traffic. The road was polished, very slippery. Gonzo slithered about, barely able to stand in some places. I found a break in the crash barrier, and got behind it. So we were between it and the river, right up on top of a cliff. Anything had to be better than the road. There was a small path running parallel to the road along the top of the cliff, although I couldn't see all of it. I was leading Gonzo along the path which narrowed, leaving a bit of green between us and the drop, with the barrier hard on our shoulders to the right. We walked round the corner and there was a tree slap in the middle of the path. I could swing round it: but Gonzo couldn't.

Nausea swept over me as I realised that the 'bit of green' was overhanging old man's beard, and we stood on the very edge of the drop down into the river. Gonzo had his right shoulder against the motorway barrier. We couldn't go forwards, we couldn't go sideways, and we couldn't go back for fear of Gonzo reversing straight over the edge. And all the time the traffic roared past. I could see it all happening. One of these lorries would spook him, he would step back, lose his footing, scrabble frantically on the path and slide, I could feel the lead rope burn my hands as it slipped through, then he would crash down through the scrub and smash against the rocks below. Gonzo had two minutes to live.

I didn't know what to do. He couldn't jump at an angle over the barrier onto the road. It was too high for a start, and besides, he would be bound to reverse. I couldn't think. And the lorries pounded past us. He stood perfectly still. I will never know why I did what I did, but I let go of the reins, got up onto the crash barrier into the traffic, walked until I was level with his shoulder, and called him, quietly.

I froze. My mouth went dry and I couldn't swallow. He looked at the barrier, then suddenly reared right up above the barrier, cutting his chest on it as he did so, then pushed himself round on it and landed foursquare facing the opposite direction. It's impossible for a horse to turn like that. He'd spun 180 degrees on one foot.

I led him back the way we came. It left me shaking, full of self rebuke. How could I have been so unobservant? In those few minutes he'd figured out how to save his own life and the traffic had roared on. Creole!

It hadn't ended. Forced back onto the main road, we slithered along into oncoming traffic which hooted and howled at us. We found another break in the barrier, this time on a sharp grass slope that went down to the water. We took it. It wasn't an easy descent.

At the bottom, we wound up on wire mesh reinforcement cages for the river banks. There was another six or seven foot drop from them into the river. I could just make out the bottom, all covered in football sized rocks: leg breakers. I won't jump a horse down onto rock: I especially won't jump a loaded horse down onto rock. We turned to look for another way and he snagged his foot in the wire, ripping off a shoe.

A good bit of hoof came off with it: that's when ten nails in a shoe don't help. Now there was no question of getting down to the river: I couldn't afford to have him break up his foot on rock. It meant the road again, it meant having to climb back up that miserable slope into the traffic.

As we struggled up, the heavens opened. Everything conspired against us. The rain was freezing, the traffic didn't give up an inch. You get to detest motorists, thoughtless, and brutish. Not only were we soaked by rain, but had all the spray from the traffic. We turned south and after two hours of terror, which is absolutely what it was, we got off the road.

Clop, clop, clop, thud. Just like firing on three cylinders: the only mercy of Gonzo's shoeless foot was that he no longer fell around on the road. From the opposite bank, having crossed over at Sabatino, the path that nearly cost me Gonzo looked innocent. What would I have done had he fallen? How would I have felt? I shuddered.

You can get to loathe somewhere when things go wrong irrespective of all the good that may have gone on before. No one helped us that afternoon, the heavens raged all round, we were wet through, and I was shaken. Then just as suddenly, as though a spell was lifted, the curse taken off, it all changed. The rain stopped, a little boy gave Gonzo some barley and took us to a blacksmith. The sun came out and we wound up in the Managgio Vecchio, belonging to Paulo and Giuseppe Cipriani, and that was the smooth. The rough and the smooth in one day.

I cleaned up the cut on his chest that evening. He still bears the scar, although it can only be seen when his coat is short. From that day on, I frequently left it to Gonzo to chose a route to lead us away from trouble. He had a sixth sense I totally lacked.

We skirted Protomagna and northern Tuscany arriving a little north of Pistoia in sunshine. En route, I discovered that eau de cologne deodorant is an excellent fly repellent for a horse. Rub it on, and it keeps flies off for days. It's about the same price as a proprietary compound, smells a lot better and does a more lasting job. The roll-on stick is the effective version.

In the mountains I met Vasco, and his pet pig Cymbeline. I heard him singing Lili Marlene at the top of his voice, and when I called out, he said 'Pronto!'

I called again, and he came out.

'Stanko?' he said.

It means exhausted. I thought it meant he could smell me. I nodded. We stayed with Vasco for two nights in amongst his sheds and collection of animals. He had two beautiful Marramano horses, six rabbits, four chickens, one thrush, one blackbird, two puppies and Cymbelini. They all lived together in a glorious muddle.

His sheds were full of junk and heaps of trophies for horsemanship. He was a Caprilli horseman – that's old school Italian, once regarded as the world's best; still is by some. Being the man he was, his trophies were not on display, for all to see and admire, but were propping up shelves, full of earth, nuts and bolts, spanners and plants.

The buildings were thrown together with bits of wood, iron stakes, old signboards, corrugated iron and a good quantity of string. He had devised a system of channelling water to his animals so that each got the measure it required. The birds received drips, the horses buckets, Cymbelini a bowl and the puppies saucers. How he did it without the aid of stop cocks beat me.

I met Vasco's son-in-law who was an architect in Florence, responsible for the restoration of old buildings, a marvellous craft. I regretted not having visited Florence, but towns and horses are not a good mix. I noticed what beautiful hands Maurizio had and how alongside his mine looked like badly salted hams with the wrong sized pork sausages stuck on anywhere for fingers, and I tried to hide them.

A couple of days later Vasco led me away up through the mountains from Cireglio on his stallion, riding beautifully with a relaxed grace – the mark of a real horseman. He hardly touched that horse at all: they were old friends, understood each other. As we went through the village, Vasco shouted to a friend that he was showing the tourist the quickest way to Wales, and they wished Gonzo and me, 'Buona fortuna, buono viaggio!'

We weaved our way through vivid green chestnut forest with sunlight yellow in the leaves, coloured on the wild flowers, reflected in mountain streams. He borrowed my mouth organ, played *Lili Marlene*, then after three hours, pointed the way out through the forest and wished us God speed. I watched him go back through the trees, singing in time to the footfalls of his horse on the soft forest floor. I suppose Vasco was a man of fifty, but he had an evergreen spirit, radiated warmth, goodwill; somehow, everything round him reflected his shine. Even Gonzo looked more buttery after our short stay with him.

We walked on through mountains which were beginning to look very Alpine. Great peaks loomed around us in granite twists of land. We passed more pretty hill villages, got tangled up in another bottomless river, caught between two mountains and then I lost my map.

We went on compass bearings without any clue as to what obstacle lay in our path. We turned up a sign-posted track, which read 'Aipi Montagna Pisciola-Trekking.' I don't know who devised it, but that blooming track took us everywhere except forwards. We were sent through chestnut forests, down through pine woods, over gorges, up into the very last stop before heaven, down again to the centre of the earth, round and round, up again above the clouds to where Zeus was having a bath. It was exhausting.

There was nowhere to get anything to eat, and the two times we tried to get off it, we wound up by floundering around on cliffs. All the way along, I wrote letters in my head to the man who'd thought that route out. Threatening letters. I was going to sue him, pelt him with eggs, call him names. After two hours I hated him. After five hours of it, I had him skinned.

We arrived in Abetone at eleven that night, one centimetre from death's door. Both of us fell asleep on the spot in someone's barn. I didn't discover whose it was until the aching morning. They gave us a marvellous breakfast, and I found my map. I'd put it in the pocket of my numnah. When I found it, I remembered putting it there. Sometimes you can make yourself angry can't you? I tried to strangle myself.

The country we were in now was hard-going. We found ourselves on hairpin bends, going up and down mountains, which, if you try to straighten out with a short cut, you find yourself fooled. You walk fifty kilometres a day, advance maybe fifteen. The nights were getting cold and damp, and each morning my sleeping roll would be just a little more wet than the day before.

The architecture became Tyrollean. Houses with great deep eaves, all constructed of wood. Advertisements in villages showed off ski boots, ski pants, ski hats, ski lifts, and all around the Apennines grew mightier.

We slogged on and on and on. I wondered if it would ever end. My belongings had become tramp-like. Everything I possessed seemed to be parcelled up into grubby little bundles, dirty blue polythene bags. I hate polythene. The saddlebags smelled of cat pee, my clothes stuck to me. Shoes were mixed up with bread, sardines, rope, grooming kit, head collar, shaving kit and olives. Bits of cheese stuck to the inside of the saddle and I found three rotten pears in the panniers, together with some barley and a handful of mouldy lucerne.

We needed a bit of a sort out.

In a small icy stream, I scrubbed up as best I could and round about us clovers, eyebright, cushion calamint, buttercups, daisies, heathers and alpine plants I didn't know, stirred in surface breezes. Maples, sycamores, beech, birch and pine rustled on hillsides all about. But there were no birds. Terrible not to hear birds. Signs everywhere read 'Divieto di Caccia,' yet I saw people shooting. What is it that drives people to do this? What have the song-birds done that grieves them so? Then we tottered along some ravine or other and had to turn back because the way was barred in all that exasperating huge dominant land. We found ourselves on some tiny road then suddenly face-to-face with a hole cut in the rock, and couldn't see the other side. The far end of a tunnel is a long way on a horse. There's little more horrifying than riding through.

As we walked through it got darker and darker, colder and colder. The hooves beat a hollow echo that disappeared in the blackness in front. All we knew was the ringing blackness, and lines of light held in trickles of water that rolled down the tunnel sides. Clip, clop, clip, clop. Then Gonzo got windy because it was pitch black, couldn't see a thing, I hit my head on the tunnel roof where it arches on the sides. Then the noise I dreaded most. I couldn't tell which way it was coming; in front? behind?

There wasn't a thing I could do except go on walking. Where was he? I prayed he had his lights on.

It was a lorry. What was a lorry doing on this tiny road? The noise hit the tunnel with a roar, the sound amplified in the hollow black. He was coming fast. I wondered if we should gallop out – I could see the end, maybe a hundred and fifty yards. Dare you gallop in there? What happens if he falls? What happens at the other end? Maybe the road swings violently to one side, and we'll go straight over the edge. Sound rushed down on us. The horse swung his hind quarters out. Not now Gonzo! No! No! I heard the engine whining, the horse spooking, then he hit his brakes. Sounded like a bomb going off. The horse made to bolt. Hit my head on the roof again. Terrified. The lorry squeezed past then hooted. Shatters your ear drums, and he's gone. You live those seconds, every one.

At the far end I swore I'd never go through another. We cut down across a field, wound up nowhere. I unpacked Gonzo: hell of a good horse, Gonzo. Found him some good grazing. Why did he always want to eat the bit I was sitting on?

At times like that, exhausted, you just sit, empty your mind. Then you wonder how many horsemen are walking round the world with their horses just then. Where are they going? How do they feel? Anybody been squashed in a tunnel? Have they got food for their horses? Maybe they're cold, tired, hungry. You get to know these things.

Wherever they are, your best wishes go out to them. When you are cold and lonely on a mountainside, and all you've got is a tired horse who is looking to you to provide his supper, you have to go and find it. It can't wait. So you leave him, walk off, maybe for hours, come back, give him something, barley, oats, oranges, stale bread. Something. You can't rest until your horse has got all he needs. Then it's time to feed yourself, then maybe you can't be fashed. Too whacked. And your bed is a wet sleeping bag with a broken zip on an Alpine hill, and what do you do? You lie back, and think of all these other guys who walk a long way with their horses because they know exactly what you mean. Sometimes you want it to end because it's hard going and you're tired. You look at your horse, wonder what you're putting him through. But you know something special, some little treasure that no other horseman or woman can possibly know unless they travel with their horses: you know about that bond, something strong, real. You think of the way he is with you, you know the noises, the sounds, what they mean, the little ways of understanding and trust.

So you doze in your wet sleeping bag, because that night, it's the rough. Tomorrow, could be the smooth. You don't know. You get on your horse and ride, and you get off him and walk. Together you go on, roughing it and smoothing it and you don't want it to end.

Then you find a patch of grazing by one of these beautiful mountain streams and you unpack your horse, watch him eat the grass. You sit in the shade under the leaves, get all lost in yourself. The water calms you, the green quietens. No one else is there, just the crickets singing. Then you remember you've got a bottle of Chianti in your saddlebag. So you drink a bit, play a bit of Verdi on your harmonica, drink a bit more, think about Machiavelli, think about going to England. What can you do when you get back? Then you drink a bit more Chianti, and you've forgotten how to play the tune you were just playing or even what it was, so you lie back, go to sleep.

18

Spirit of the Mountains

We left Febbio at eight in the morning with a thick mountain mist rolling down behind us. It was chilly and damp as we wound on to Villa Minozzo and we had a nasty shock trying to avoid hairpin bends. We were up high and I could see the road running well away to the left then re-emerge straight in front of us, but a mile or two further down. A short cut would save us a needless walk. There was an opening into a field, and down we went. It was a steep descent, and we arrived above the road in to time, easily two miles saved. The bank down to the road was very steep, but, being experts at bank slithering, mere child's play.

What I hadn't seen was that the bank didn't go down to the road. It stopped about ten feet above, being buttressed up by a high concrete wall. We walked along the top of it, over more wire mesh squares, which dropped awkwardly down to the road, which we followed. What had been obscured from my view was a wide concrete drainage channel which ended in a six feet square hole right on our line of descent. The sides sloped in to a central cavity of three feet or so. Easy for me to step across. Not so for a horse.

The alternative was turning round on the wire mesh, and going all the way back up. I gave Gonzo the reins, got off, walked down to the hole, stepped across, and called. I turned to watch, terrified I had made a disastrous mistake. I watched him walk carefully down the wire, look at the hole, put his front feet on it, slide, then just before they disappeared down, he jumped and joined me on the road. Then he wandered off; that was our last mountain short cut.

We arrived in Villa Minozzo, stayed a night there, where Gonzo was looked after by two wonderful old farmers who had six cows, and who grew maize and vines. They fed Gonzo ten kilos of powdered maize I discovered next day for breakfast. No, I said, never. 'Si! si!', they replied.

Deci kilo! Mama mia!'

Ten kilos! No! Never! 'Si! Si! Multo fame cavallo !'

Strewth, I'd got a dead horse. What would ten kilos of powdered maize do to a horse?

That day, we went miles and miles. Didn't do anything to Gonzo. Isn't maize supposed to de-mineralise them? He looked good on it. They were a nice couple of old boys even if they did give Gonzo ten kilos of powdered maize. They didn't speak much, just watched in silence as I packed Gonzo up before we left. I shook hands with them: wide, strong hands. Looked into their deep, clear eyes. If I can look like them when I'm seventy, I reckon my life will have been worthwhile.

'Arrivederci! Buono fortuna!'

I gave them ten thousand lira: too much, I know. But they knew it was worth it for me.

The landscape grew softer after that, the wine sweeter, Lambrusco. It was good to be out of the big mountains. They were magnificent, but something about them was oppressive, dark; they were breathtaking and grand, but I preferred the landscape in Emilia and Romagna. It felt more Italian somehow. The people were warmer too: not so much the dollar-a-ride mentality of the people in the Apennines where there was skiing. There were geese and chickens everywhere again. People are better for having animals about.

Between Mantachie and Migliaria, up on a hillside as the sun was going down, I saw an empty house way below us, on its own, in a valley. Looked as if there was some grazing round about, and since I had a bite for both of us, it looked a good place to spend the night.

It was in silence, abandoned. Wasn't a big house, more like a long Devon cottage with stone mullioned windows, smashed in. I looked inside, walked in the rubble, the collapsed roof, thought it a shame so many houses lie abandoned in Italy. Behind the house was a perfect night-sized patch of grazing and nearby a well. I tried the water – it was fine. There was a barn too, with some old bales in – a bed for me. A peaceful place, restful. Just the sound of the crickets and the wind. I watched the sun go down just like every time we slept out, since I had no book with me. They are too heavy to carry, a diary was bad enough. I gazed round the rafters of the barn which looked like chestnut wood, not oak. I dozed off early while Gonzo grazed about between me and the house. I was woken by a voice at midnight. It jolted me awake with a start. For a moment, I held my breath, not certain whether I had actually heard it, or if it was a sound in a dream, on the cusp of sleep, making it real, as if someone had called out. Gonzo was on his feet, ears pricked, close to me. Had he heard it too? He was alert. Then he lost interest, grazed. Must have been a dream, I settled back to sleep.

Just as I was drifting off, I heard it dearly this time.

'Antonio!'

Then again, quite loud.

'Antonio! Pronto!'

It came from inside the house. It wasn't abandoned! There must be someone in there! Who? Why? What did he want in there? Maybe it was a madman, a hermit? I lay still waiting for someone to appear.

Gonzo was edgy, he'd heard it. Then there was silence. Not a sound.

But slowly, thinly, through the darkness came the sound of two men talking, low and in whispers, something arcane. It made my scalp crawl and I had to find out what it was, so slipped quietly out of my sleeping bag, crouched in the shadows, moved over to the wall of the house.

My heart was pounding, sounded liked grenades going off. What if it was a madman? Now there was silence again: just my own heart, my own breath and the wind. Gonzo stood stock still.

Then came the voices again. A dismembered sound, from within the walls of the house.

'Antonio!'

Then the whispers. Shivering, I moved to the decayed door, looked in. Black. I went round to the other side of the house, nervously peering round corners. Nothing.

I returned to my sleeping bag and spent the rest of the night listening. In all that time, from then till dawn, there was a presence in that house: something moved in there. Something strange.

At sunrise, I fed Gonzo the rest of his barley and went into the house. The only footprints were mine. The only marks were the ones I had made. In the morning light it appeared friendly and warm: not a hint of the distracted sounds and feelings of the night just passed.

Encounters like that are peculiar: echoes on the ether from the emotional charges of another time. Strong sensations stamped in the air, returning when conditions are just as they were when whatever it was, happened. I wondered what it could have been. What passions stirred the man who cried out? Why? Who were the others who spoke? I know Gonzo heard it. He wouldn't go near the house, not for bribes nor tugging.

Animals are sensitive to these things. I know people who maintain that spirits account for peculiar behaviour in animals. They'll send a horse right out of his way, stop him dead in his tracks. They'll drive a dog shivering into a corner, while you gaze on, blind to it, puzzled. They come in all forms yet we hardly ever see them: I suppose we are not sensitive to them. We are not as close to nature as we were: we live by light nearly always, and it's in darkness we can see the better.

You can feel them sometimes: something unsettling in the air. And if you are sensitive, you'll hear the air shudder, like the flutter of the wing of a bird, hard and fast, a glancing sigh and you'll know. That, or you've got a moth in your ear.

But children notice them, and as we age, our sensitivity fades. I believe in them. I believe them to live, to haunt a different dimension from ours, split off, neither good nor bad, just different. Then, for some reason, in a loophole of time, a quirk of understanding, you snatch a glimpse of them, half there, half impressed in the air around, like a seal held in melting wax, then gone.

We walked away. I left a few coins inside the door of the house.

'Grazie Antonio, arrivederci!'

We followed a path down to the river Enza, buying a few things in a tabacchi for breakfast. It was hot even beside that broad pebbly river, and everything was all in a kind of a haze, and soft, and limpid. Round there Hannibal moved with his forces right back in 212 BC. He'd come over the Alps. He was never beaten on the field of battle in Italy. Spent twelve years there, shadowed by the Roman army, never faced. You could picture the forces, with its huge train of cattle, horses, dogs, goats and elephants. I expect you could smell them ten miles off. I remember smelling the Hadj going through once in Saudi: they stank, and there wasn't that many of them.

Gonzo and I followed a line of footprints on the river bank which looked like big horses. Then we arrived in a huge mannaggio, so I made a short day of it, and they gave Gonzo a big airy stable, plenty of grub. A man took me up into San Polo d'Enza, to a smart hotel. I was the filthiest bloke in town.

It was good to have a scrub up with hot water. And a good meal in a chic restaurant with linen tablecloths, nice cutlery. There were dignified-looking people eating quietly, an old girl with a book and a bottle of Lambrusco, a young man smoking a cigarette with an artistic flourish. The huge napkin and later a bed with crisp linen sheets were in sharp contrast to the night before. The night before I slept on bales, sort of, and had a tin of sardines. It cost me about 45 pence. In the hotel they rushed me £35: but then I did go over the top. Nice once in a while but I couldn't bear it all of the time. The day after, Gonzo was on good form, and payment for his night's livery refused. They wished us 'Buono fortuna' and we forded the broad river Enza, and set out toward Parma.

Just like every other day, we walked with the sun on our right shoulders catching the corner of our eyes, then as the day went on, the sun swung round behind and to our left. So at the end of the day, we walked into it, shadows playing around behind.

We walked through great avenues of Lombardy poplars, substantial farm buildings and great courtyards, shuttered and quiet. Acres of lucerne rolled away on either side. There were willows in ditches, ploughed land, straw in barns, harvested grain. There were bananas too: surprising to see bananas and poplars together. Everywhere pig units ponged the air with porcine pooh. Parma ham.

Along we went at 310 degrees zigzagging round field margins going north west. To a motorist one kilometre of highway cost us four at least around field headlands. We crossed groves of vines, rode up streams that went our way then cursed the one we were following which had steep banks, and a tree fallen across it, too high to jump, too low to walk under, so we had to go right back. But it's good to walk with the bare earth beneath your feet, see things go slowly by, ditches, farms, great houses, the open patterned brickwork of the barns, the soft colour of stone and quiet sleepy villages. Then you stop, talk to a stranger in a language you barely know. You wish each other well, and you sense a great feeling of calm moving over the land.

So, come five in the evening, you reckon you've done your thirty kilometres for the day, which is plenty when you do it every day. You look at your map, and see maybe you've advanced just twenty, but if you were asked to describe it, you could recall every step.

That night we holed up in a hedge where a man was gathering snails. He shared some wine. He told us about the owners of the land he rented; the landlord lived in Parma. He spat the words out: absentee landlords. I didn't ask him what his quarrel was.

Then, leaving the kit and Gonzo, I went off to the village to buy us some supper. I bought bread, Chianti, cheese and oats. On the way back I jumped over a stream, the bottom fell out of the paper bag and everything fell in the water, smashing the Chianti, drowning the bread. The snail gatherer came to look. He watched the bread float down the brook. 'Uno fiasco.' Never realised it was an Italian word. I bought some more.

We were joined later by a small black dog. He was starving. He presented a problem. Did I ignore him, let him starve? Then he wouldn't follow us tomorrow. Or did I feed him, hope he'd blow after a meal? I didn't want my own personal revolving dog just then; I'd get to like him, and he'd get squashed in a tunnel, or he'd hold us up. Then I'd have to quarantine him in England and he'd have to come to jail in Oxford with me. I decided it was too much of a risk ... so I gave him bread, cheese and oats. Same stuff as the rest of us. I christened him 'Spud' and introduced him formally to Gonzo, and we'd picked up a hitch hiker.

Next morning we three set out for England, Spud weaving around behind us peeing on every single tree he could find. Where do they get it all? He stuck with us all the way to the Tano River, then for some reason, stopped dead, turned round, and went back. Just watched him jog away.

We were put up by a one-handed cavalieri in Noceto called Luigi Siliprandi, who fed me a stupendous risotto, prosciutto and water melon and Gonzo had a stupendous oats and barley mix and water melon.

After that we headed off for Fidenza, finding ourselves in a scrap yard. An oily crane driver came towards us, wiping his hands on an even oilier rag. I saw him running a look at Gonzo's feet. Surely not? He didn't think I was there to dispatch Gonzo for the price of his clogs did he? Know I looked like a tramp, but there are limits. He never said a word.

Just gazed at me as if I was mad. Then he pointed a way out through scrub, down to Il Torrente Stirrone, which was a brute to cross – another of these deeply gorged rivers. It was hot and muggy and we collapsed in amongst some poplars and I lost heart. It all seemed so pointless all this endless slogging on. Where to? What for? All I had back in England was Chumpie who'd probably run off with another bloke, if she'd got any sense; Punch, my bull terrier, who probably preferred living with Min in Norfolk anyway; and my mother who was probably glad I wasn't around whining about things. And then this prison thing for not paying a stupid parking fine. What could possibly be gained from crossing Il Torrente Stirrone to go to the nick?

It was a real effort getting going again that afternoon. I think Gonzo felt so too. And he didn't have to go to jail.

A few night later, we wound up in a castle. I had a four poster bed and enough material hanging off the posts to make curtains for the entire population of Mumbles. Silk shirt, perfectly tailored trousers, and had a meal with a Count, I think. Never found out who he was, what the castle was called or where it was even. It's just that I thought it was a village when we arrived in the dark. I knocked on this great door and the next thing I knew was that Gonzo was in a stately stable beside a horse with a title, and I was having a bath. Then I was lent these clothes and sat in an enormous room full of old men with grey hair and cigars. It all dripped in nobility. I felt just like a potato, all red and earthy, full of nicks and scratches. Couldn't think of a thing to say. Whatever I said sounded trite, absurd. I had no idea what was going on in the world, what day it was or anything else. I would have preferred to have been with Gonzo in his stable and his aristocratic friend. But you can't go on living with a horse, can you? Maybe you can. Why not?

I went to sleep gazing at angels trumpeting clouds on my ceiling, half clothed figures wrestling with dragons, Medusas, harpies and Gorgons. What a crew to fill your head with just before you go to sleep. I had nightmares.

19

Wine Harvest

In Pianello, Gonzo and I shared a stable with two calves and four rabbits, the property of Snr Carlo Barbieri. I had to get up to Milan to Tast Cavalli to collect my papers, so I hopped on a Pullman early one morning leaving Gonzo with the calves, and went to town.

It quickly became obvious to me how far separated from the reality of things you can get, even in Europe, if you travel by horse. I hadn't been on roads like that. I didn't see Italy like that at all. I hadn't seen all the miserable tacky side of advertising, hoardings grimly shouting loud slogans at the world on garish sign boards, all the roadside nicknack pull-ins, string upon string of tin-pot development laddered on dirty verges. In contrast to my meanderings through a rural Italy, what a trite lot of nonsense it looked. Whimsical, impermanent, depending on a chance that was likely to spurn it. How grim is the route of a bus to a town.

I had avoided towns as much as possible, but when we did go through them, Gonzo and I snuck in through a back street with no idea of where we were, just going through on a compass bearing. As we wiggled through there would be a sudden, 'Aaaahhh bellloo cavallloo ... Bellissiimmoo Cavvaalliinnniiii!' And Gonzo would meet the younger generation in a flurry of pear drops and apple cores, surrounded by children stroking him, all smiles and eyes.

In this way the towns became full of charm. We'd find little patches of green, tiny patches of grass where Gonzo would graze, get treats, and I could snatch a cappuccino. Or we'd walk through a park and only ever see the town through the trees. In this way it becomes bewitching a little, enchanting a bit. We slipped through like shadows, left no mark. I didn't anyway. Gonzo always did. But usually the towns were too difficult for us so when we wanted something, we would head for a village, buy it there. Our needs were always small so we found what we wanted. In either place for us, we met unquestioned goodwill and warmth.

In Milan I collected the papers from Mario Sivilieri in Tast Cavalli, and had ten days to leave Italy. We had no time to lose. I stayed in Milan for as long as it took to wait for a bus back out. I didn't want to see any of its jewels, I wanted to be back in the snug little stable in Pianello.

There was quite a long way to go to the French border, and someone told me the best way would be to follow the River Po, since it was flat riding the whole way and despite its twists and turns, I could make the frontier in six days. We crossed into Lombardia, slap into the grape harvest.

It was impossible to travel on the field margin technique because of all the vines. The roads heaved with tractors and loaded trailers full of grapes. There was an atmosphere of excitement, the air sharp with the scent of pulping grape, grape haulm and new wine. Everybody was working flat out.

I had never seen inside a winery and when I found a small private winery on a little road I asked if I could look around. The man who met me was three parts sloshed, in expansive mood. He handed me a large glass of white wine, although I didn't actually want any, being thirsty as indeed was Gonzo. I asked the man if Gonzo could have a drink and he said 'Si, si, uno momento .. .' disappeared, returning a moment later with a bucket half full. A quarter of an hour later when Gonzo started to behave very oddly I began to suspect something. The man looked at me.

'Bello cavallo ... ' he said, and going up to him, collected the bucket which Gonzo had nosed about the yard. He got another measure. Light white wine it was. Like a Riesling. Gonzo loved it. A bucketful of that stuff and he was anybody's. He stretched his neck, rolled his eyes, snorted and wrinkled his nose. There was no question of riding him, particularly after the next bucket, and the five more glasses I had. I still haven't seen inside a winery.

'Boone viaggio Marco Polo!' the man hailed as we staggered away, I saw him waving, or I saw two of him waving four arms as Gonzo tried to walk on a double visioned road swirling around six inches lower than it should be. He walked with his neck stretched out, then pulled his head in, kept on leaning on me, whinnied at a tractor and ambled benignly sloshed all over the road. I walked beside him in no better state, and when we arrived in a village a couple of hours later, he had a far-away look in his half closed eyes, tried to piddle and dump at the same time, made an awful mess of things, so we stayed where we were before any accidents happened.

The following morning he was fit for nothing. We walked away very slowly past acres and acres of vines, and people picking mushrooms, which they store in jars having dried them on strings first. We went through Bruin which was a beastly place, arriving at the old lppodromo, where the Nervi family all live amongst their horses. I slept in the back of a truck, Gonzo in a box.

At one thirty the following day we reached the mighty river Po. It reminded me of the Severn and its low surrounding landscape, being wide and muddy with greasy brown water. We arrived on an embankment, had some lunch, rested for an hour or two, then I mounted and we walked through dappled sunlight on a soft earth path beside the broad slow river. You can walk all day for miles and miles on paths like that.

We went a hundred yards. It might even have been a bit less; a tributary joined the river which was utterly uncrossable. It was little more than a shallow brook, but it had cut itself into a gorge about sixty feet across and fifteen feet deep. We had to go due south for five kilometres before we could cross that wretched thing.

Having done so, we met another. None of these streams was marked on my map.

The Po is unrideable – just in case anybody is in danger of falling into the same trap. If anyone tells you it is, don't believe them. We had wasted two days aiming for it, a further six hours trying to ride along it, and it had advantaged us a hundred yards. We were back on the tarmac.

Italy seemed determined not to be crossed. Or perhaps I had picked the one and only route that no one else was daft enough to attempt: why wasn't I privy to this information? Either the country was made of huge mountains and crashing ravines, or it was boiling hot plains, or totally unreadable rivers. Why couldn't it be nice rolling landscape with pull-ins for horses? Still, I suppose it would have been all right had I been walking alone: but you can't ask a horse to jump fifteen feet down into mud. Then again, perhaps this landscape accounted for the success of the Roman Infantry: a natural assault course in their backyard.

By nine thirty that night we were homeless. After a forty-five kilometre struggle, we'd drawn a total blank. I met my one and only nasty Italian too. He'd kicked us off a minute patch of grazing we'd found on the roadside, and we had nowhere to go. He was just like the horrid man in Greece: he had the same bad tempered look, the hard mask, unlovable eyes. I thought him a chinless drip. He did it from sheer spite. He'll get his come-uppance I expect. Or maybe his wife had just smashed up his car? We wandered along in darkness to San Gaudenzio. A young couple appeared from a restaurant, immediately understood our problem, and within minutes had found a home of a sort for us. I was given a stone slab to sleep on, and Gonzo a bush to hide in. He got hay: I got bread. There were a lot of chickens about the place, cows in pens. It was all pretty whiffy.

I slept soundly until four o'clock when I was woken by a cockerel crowing right down my ear. He was accompanied by six others. They all had varying pitches and intensities in their voices: like a sort of avian Morriston Ladies Male Voice Choir. One of them sounded exactly like a negro spiritual singer and he crowed with passion, gusto, a throaty warble none of the others could match. Seven cockerels around your bed at four in the morning is one hell of a way to wake up.

As I got up and stretched, I considered which one of them to boot when I saw with horror the carnage I'd slept in. There was offal lying around everywhere. Lungs and windpipes lay beside me, guts and bones scattered willy nilly. It was appalling. I had slept inches from the entrails of some disembowelled mammal I was at a loss to identify. It absolutely reeked. I don't know what sort of a place it was, but we beat it fast, Gonzo making such a swift exit he damn nearly left me behind.

Then it was back to the steady slog, the long hard grind. It can lose its colour then. You have to be careful when it's just hard work, because when it loses its colour, you lose your cool, your horse loses his head, and you could both wind up losing your lives. You have to go on steady, roughing it and smoothing it, guts and all.

20

Last Days in Italy

We didn't have long to be out of the country before the export licence expired and had arrived in Mulino di Mattie, south east of Susa. It is a lovely place, run as a riding holiday centre in the Italian Alps, where the mountains rise straight out of the plain. The Alps are extraordinary: they don't start nice and quietly in little folds of land, then grow into big mountains. They start as socking great mountains and get even bigger. But the villages on the Italian side were pretty, with stone slab roofs, cobstone walls, balconies and all dotted about in narrow, donkey-streeted-braying-chuminess.

The rock was soft coloured and granitish, with drystone walls, hill cottages, frothy watercourses, mills, little green fields and leafy trees. Il Mulino di Mattie is a maneggio offering everything for the travelling horseman. There are a string of these places through the Alps a convenient ride apart, from the south in Ventigimilia to the top, near Switzerland. In Britain we tend to think of it as a big deal crossing the Alps, but there are dozens of Italian horsemen who have crossed them stacks of times, thinking nothing of it.

Georgie and Anna who run the Mulino put me in touch with the local vet for a final inspection for Gonzo, and helped me locate the local Tast Cavalli agents in the Autoporto in Susa. We had to go there of course, queue up with lorries. But it was all done very efficiently by ltalsped and Mario Sivilieri. So I went back to the Mulino for a day or two more.

There were fourteen girls staying. Fourteen scheming, giggling, sloe-eyed fifteen-year-old school girls. It was exactly like being in a party of highly strung chimpanzees. They'd all been let out of Turin for the week, let loose on the Alps on horses. Poor horses. Poor Alps. They were wildly pretty, fun, crazy, full of beans. Made me feel like a whale, all clumpy and awkward, banana fingered and stiff jointed.

Georgie had restored the mill with architectural 'good manners' as Alec Clifton-Taylor would have put it. It had lots of dark cobwebby corners, good old wood joists, leaning walls, shadowy doorways. Anna's cooking was the very best.

From the Mulino, I went to stay at Cascina Parisio, nearer the customs point, while waiting for the OK to leave. It was a huge old house set low in among a tangle of rocks in its own valley, where Bruno, the owner, kept a lot of animals. He ran the farm as a kind of rehabilitation centre for young offenders, young people gone off the rails, with booze, drugs or something, not 'bad' enough to send to an approved school. There wasn't any disciplining. He just let them get on and sort themselves out with the dogs, donkeys, ducks, guinea fowl, geese, peacocks, pullets, cows, goats, pigs, sheep and horses. And in that tranquil setting, without ever pushing, he had a group of young kids who were good to be with, learning by themselves something about self-respect, which is the only way. He was a· retiring man, with a gentle manner, kind blue eyes. He explained how Susa had been the last Roman settlement before the Alpine ridge and had once belonged to France in old Savoyard. It was here Napoleon had crossed the mountains from France.

There used to be strong Celtic traditions in these parts historically, and he showed me the Casa Druido up in the mountains, behind the Cascina, and the sacrificial altar where a triangle of stones pointed to Rocciamelone, the highest peak. A sacred mountain. He pointed out the church that stands on the foundations of a Roman temple, on a pagan altar.

It all felt calm under that great mountain, with an air of peace. The weather had become cooler, touched with Alpine breezes, and goat bells. Fruit trees hung heavily with apples and pears. Grapes swung in smoky blue dusters, almonds were ripe and chestnuts fell to the ground with a dry thud. Walnuts, plump in green skins, pulled down the branches of the trees they hung in. The air carried a scent of thyme, sage and curry spice and took me straight back to Turkey.

Someone had a cutting of a newspaper exhibiting a twenty-two kilogram cat. Looked like a very fat jaguar. Bruno said it looked tasty. Celts like cats, he said. Years ago, in the little villages higher up, they used to eat a lot of cats. What better than mashed potato, roast cat and swede he asked, picking his teeth, grinning like the Cheshire ...

Our papers came through in the afternoon, and Maurizio Fabrizio of Italsped handed me my clearance form from the customs. All my papers were in order. Tast Cavalli had done a good job: it hadn't been easy, since I was going north and on foot.

At seven next morning Gonzo and I walked down into Susa, through the back streets taking the road up to Moncenisio. We followed the tarmac until we reached the final control point before leaving Italy, past the sign that says, 'Arrivederci ... Buono Viaggio!'

Vennaeus lay hidden down in the valley beneath, and higher, higher we climbed. The mountains rose with us, striding upward, reaching for heaven. Soon we were in conifer woodland. The mountain sides steepened, we broke off onto a track, followed it for six miles or so, it narrowed, disappeared. I hadn't got a due where we were. Way behind in the foggy distance was Susa somewhere, and ahead I imagined was Moncenisio.

There I made another fatal mistake, the sort I should not have. I wandered off in a fug, not thinking where we were going. In minutes we were in trouble. The ground was very steep. Rocks were overgrown with a layer of mossy earth and laurel, hiding nasty deep holes. Real leg breakers. I kicked myself for being so stupid. I took the bridle off Gonzo, said 'sort it out', left him to it. He went straight up in a direct line, taking us to a path, safe and secure out of the woods. He'd found the best way in seconds, taken no risks, and he turned round giving me a really old fashioned look. I was getting used to being made to look small. I put his bridle back on, despite wondering who ought to be wearing it. The scenery became wide and breath-taking, the sun sank, throwing us into cold shadow. There wasn't a soul anywhere. We were lost. Lost on the Alps. Brilliant. For three more hours we floundered on, Gonzo picking at dry grasses here and there, and finally, I saw a man on a scrambler motorbike.

'Scusi,' I asked, 'Dovay Francia?' It's terrible Italian.

'Ici c'est la France.'

21

France

We'd missed the frontier post. I had a good mind to push straight on, forget the whole business, hope it could be sorted out the other end. But bureaucracy isn't that obliging. They'd send us back: or guillotine us both. They couldn't get Gonzo to stick his head in a guillotine: he's not that daft. I would though, I expect. We had to find the border post.

The snag now of course was that we'd be approaching the French control point from the French side, saying we'd come from Italy. On the face of it, even I could see problems with that one. They'd never believe it. They would definitely guillotine us.

We found a track, followed it, staying the night in a big hotel, where, wrapped up in blankets Gonzo spent the night on the lawn and ate a sackful of stale bread. In the hotel, I telephoned England, delighted to hear that Marco Windham, a chum from Gloucestershire, planned to join Gonzo and me for a week's walk in the Alps.

Marco is a photographer: he's brilliant. I was flattered to think he intended taking up a week of his time slogging around these bruising great mountains taking snaps of our little adventure. We arranged to meet in Lanslebourg – anywhere in Lanslebourg, leaving it to chance – it seldom fails.

Next day, Gonzo and I walked up to the control point on the wrong side. They didn't like it. They made me wait. Rang people up. Came out to look at us. Someone came over and prodded Gonzo. Then, after three hours' interrogation with thumb screws they told us to go away.

The saddest part of the morning for me was the constant flow of trucks full of horses, beautiful horses, going to Italy for meat. And as

Gonzo and I walked away, another truck carrying maybe twenty horses went past, and I heard one of them whinny. Glad I had Gonzo with me, walking the other way.

I rode the long dam wall on Le Lac du Mont Cenis towards Lanslebourg. The scenery was grand, high and rolling, with the great mountains reflected in the lake. I saw brown Swiss cows with big bells and hawks up near the clouds and felt a hollow cold wind. The Route Napoleon. How he managed to provision his army there is quite another thing, considering the Hotel du Mont Cenis had enough meat for only one sandwich when I got there, so when Napoleon arrived with his outfit and asked for thirty thousand rounds of ham and lettuce they must have been a bit stuck. I wonder if they ripped him off too?

I asked a bloke the quickest way to Lanslebourg, and he said helpfully, 'Suivez la merde des éléphants d'Hannibal,' so we did, and arrived in the town four hours later.

We passed the war memorial which told of the Combatants de la Guerre 1939-1945, and of *les combats furieux* which had taken place there between the Germans and the French Alpine regiments. Strange to think of all that there, that on that peaceful mountain men blew each other to bits. And all the other armies that had marched through before. The madness of man.

It was like a final farewell to Italy. Rocciamelone slipped out of sight. I lovely Italy: loved the Italians, the country, the food, the humour and warmth. I was glad to have passed through it in the way I had: to have been drawn into the country like that. I found it every bit as enjoyable and friendly as I thought I might. I'll go back again. With a lorry, pick up all the furniture I saw lying on the roadsides: I could furnish a castle of my very own with all that. And I want to see the Colonello again, Vasco, Pietro Malvisi – everyone. I looked forward to being in France too. I had an idea we might try to push up through the wine growing regions, through Beaujolais, Sancerre, Beaune, then over to the Loire and Orleans, west of Paris then to the sea. Looked a long way on a map: six weeks maybe.

We arrived in Lanslebourg at 3.30, and I found lodgings for Gonzo, with difficulty. I booked into the first place I saw, called the Vielle Post Hotel, picked up the telephone to ring England, and in walked Marco.

'That was clever Marko, how did you do that?'

'First place I saw.'

See? It was good to see him, to talk in my own language instead of the constant struggle for words, and absence of understanding. You feel all the richness of your own tongue when you've been deprived of it for a while, all its twists, angles, nuances, blind alleys. I don't think you ever get to find out all these things in another language even if you speak it fluently.

We had dinner together, were both tired, turned in early. We were up early, and Marco had brought a sensible sausage-shaped bag with him, which I threw over the saddle, and we three, our little gang, with Gonzo in the middle, set off on Le Chemin de Petit Bonheur, a fitting name for our starting point. Wonderful to have a travelling companion and exciting to be able to see things with another pair of eyes, in another way, from higher up. Marco is very tall. Made me feel like Humpty-dumpty. There he was striding along with his six foot two foot steps, tall and elegant, looking cool: and Humpty-dumpty. We walked through pine beside the river, stopping to take photographs while sunlight arced and shot beams of light through the trees. He took atmospheric photographs and clouds rolled around above.

We walked until lunchtime, and he produced a delicious lunch, with brie, camembert, bottles of white wine, baguettes, thinly sliced meats and fruit. Not the sort of lunch I tended to buy: it was delicious, and I wolfed it greedily as he talked quietly about Krisnamurti, Sophocles, why the sky is blue, why the common cormorant or shag lays eggs inside a paper bag.

We camped that night beside the crashing river Arc, near Bramans. We were surrounded by paperbark birch, the dwarfing Massif de la Vannoise. I washed clothes in the river, Marco read *I Claudius*, Gonzo grazed. It was a lovely setting. The sun disappeared throwing us into shadow and darkness. We swapped campsites because of the dampness of the river, settling a little further away from the noise of rushing water, chatted as the night grew dark. Marco rolled out his sleeping bag, lay back, gazed up through the dark grey-green-silversided leaves. He didn't speak: I wondered what he thought. You do that with Marco: you wonder what he thinks.

Having a friend there, just then, meant all the world to me, just there. And I don't know why, but looking up at Orion, I was reminded of the passage from Job, when God speaks to Job out of the whirlwind, which I struggled to remember, and could only in part.

We were up early and left as the sun chased a shadow up a valley, and we walked to Aussois. Marco chatted about this and that, philosophy, theosophy, Gurdjieff, Buddhism, biscuits, baguettes, cameras and coffee. We had lunch under a high tumbling waterfall, took photographs of mysterious, unnamed, unknown buildings where Gonzo posed in swimming trunks with hooves on his hips. Then we galloped up banks, down banks, looking like the lone ranger – Sloane ranger (never) – we looked smart, looked silly, did somersaults, hid behind trees, posed in fashion outfits and then it rained.

We reached Modane, which isn't a pretty town. It specially isn't pretty in the rain. In a pet shop, buying oats for the big furry bloke in the middle, we wound up having to pay a lot more than we bargained for on account of an equine fit. With that and the sudden appearance of the gendarmerie outside who wanted to know what we thought we were doing in a pet shop with a horse, we were left tongue tied.

They told us to behave ourselves, sent us away with a surly nod, and we were stuck. No home. Marco asked a butcher if he had any ideas, which led us rather too directly to the abattoir. Gonzo was given the condemned cell. We got the second condemned cell, so to speak. Decided to stay there with Gonzo rather than a hotel, firstly because it was cheaper, and secondly because we didn't want to risk arriving late in the morning to find Gonzo already dispatched, being sold as salami in the market.

It was, nevertheless, an uncomfortable feeling and when Gonzo received a prodigious dinner, I did wonder if it was his last. Would he be popped out of his box and executed in the morning by a conscientious knacker man? So we slipped out for an early supper, and on our return Gonzo was still there. We all slept about as well as you can in a slaughter house.

The chief knackerman accepted a few glasses of early morning white wine in the café – they get stuck into their drinking bright and early on the Continent, don't they? And we pushed off through more of the Alps. They do go on a bit. You can get fed up with slogging up hills all the time. Particularly since we seemed to find ourselves crossing, double crossing and meeting a fearful main road which shared the valley with a jumble of railway lines, a river, and dozens of hydro electric power stations. From these things, laddered off at intervals, were skiing resorts and dull architecture. The Modane valley was a bore. We bashed on to Chambéry, and found some nice people who said they had just the place for Gonzo. We found a hotel. Chambéry was a thoroughly pleasant town. It felt French. Everywhere else we had been in France so far didn't feel like anywhere: certainly not France. But here were genuine Frenchmen speaking real French to each other over glasses of pastis, onions and berets. They smiled: they were friendly: they talked to us. Little girls doted over Gonzo, which he likes – don't we all? – in his fine stable at Le Centre Hippique. It had great high ceilings, and 'défense de fumer' signs, but Gonzo doesn't smoke anyway.

It rained all the time in Chambéry. Seemed to have been raining for months. Then Marco said he had to go back home. I was sorry to see him go. It made me lonely. I left him at the station in Chambéry and as he left it was as if a light had been withdrawn. Thrown down, I hoofed about Chambéry, then discovered the launderette. I shoved all my stuff in there in one big mouthful, including my sleeping bag. Ruined it. After I put it through the driers, all the feathers hung in wet lumps all over it: felt like it was full of dead birds. Clean though. I had a Chinese meal that night all alone and ate ban hoi which was some sort of meat, sliced, boiled and served on a mat of hair. That and some tsing tao, which was either a drink or a game and I thoroughly enjoyed knocking about the wrong end of town for the rest of the night.

A Polish fellow had been looking after Gonzo: I like the Poles, they're very nice. He showed us the way out of Chambéry, put us on the road to Novelaise. He wished us 'Bon voyage! Bonne chance! Bonne route!' It's so nice. Gonzo stepped out well after his two days' rest and soon we were on the road for San Sulpice, our first stop. Coffee and buns for me: grass and buns for Gonzo. Then, on Col de l'Epine, an extraordinary thing happened. We walked into autumn.

On the road a mist held white in front of us and as we walked into it, we left summer behind. I know exactly where it was: I could go back there. The leaves turned to autumn shades, damp air dripped a fine dew through the trees. Little beads of water formed on Gonzo's mane and fetlock, on my hair, my face. It was a strange silent place. The grey mist advanced before us as we walked on, objects loomed obscure, then clear, passing into the enveloping mist that folded in behind, fogging and hiding our path.

A great sinister building, towered and empty, rose and disappeared in silence: just the steady clip-clop of the horse's feet on the wet road. Three hours it took to pass through that place and we arrived in Novelaise, chilled and damp to the core.

We spent the night in a farm, with lovely old buildings, where they reared good strong cattle. I didn't catch the name of the breed: they looked a bit like Hereford Ayrshire crosses. They had milkers, rather like Jerseys but with Devon colouring and a raised tail head. Very pretty. The young farmer kept a trotter – un trotteur – sixteen years old, and he spoke with a rolling brogue, detectable even by me. It was a comfortable manner of speech, and the short 'oui' ,of the Alps became 'oh weigh!'

That night was the first time I had been really cold since the beginning of March that year, just before I started with Ahmed Paşa. Many of the houses in that area are constructed of compressed mud, cut into large squares, bound with grass and small stones. They are a perfectly wonderful colour: cool in the summer, warm in the winter so they say.

We were heading up the Rhone looking for a marechal – a farrier – when in a little bit of a place called Les Nappes le Bayet, I met a German girl called Claudia and her boyfriend Philippe, who could help. They told me the best farrier in France lived in Culin.

I looked on the map. It was south. A long way south. Two days' ride. I never go south to go north. No, I said, have to go on looking. But Gonzo badly needed new shoes: his were finished, though they'd done well. Claudia said they had a truck. No, I said too much hassle. Best farrier in France, maybe the whole world.

They called that truck 'Le tube'. It was a grey tin Lizzy Citröen horsebox, with the chummiest dimensions I have ever come across. We all seemed to be looking out of the windscreen, horse and all, all seemed to be driving, squashed up in there, Claudia, Philippe, Gonzo, the engine and me, wheezing along to Culin. We arrived in the dark, met by Philippe the maréchal, who put us up for the night into the bargain.

The next day, I had the pleasure of watching the finest piece of farriery. He spent a quarter of an hour just watching how the horse moved. He trimmed his feet, cleaned them up, cut the frogs clean as a whistle. Hot shod Gonzo with shoes he made, tipped them with borium and tungsten, told me they'd be good for eight hundred kilometres or more, and they were. He touched the sole of the horse's foot with turpentine, ran a light dressing of cod liver oil over his feet, told me never to use anything else. Best thing you can do for horses' feet he said, goes right in, and also tends to stop rheumatism.

He put new fire under my kettle, that man. To have a well shod horse is one thing. To have a perfectly shod horse is another: he'd even allowed for the way Gonzo screws his nearside hind. Best farrier in France, maybe the whole world. That we were now quite a long way south from our original position hardly mattered: we were further west, so the route pointed to Lyon.

On our way, we spent the night with Pascale up in the hills, near Frontonas, in his cottage, surrounded by sheds and chickens. He spoke good English. He was wearing an apron when I met him, standing outside his door. He asked me where I was staying and I told him I didn't know.

'You can stay here,' he said, 'but it's not for you, it's for the horse.'

He explained that he lived alone, was going to sing madrigals, would be out for four hours, but would leave me the house, a bottle of wine, some fish, and bread for my supper, a field of grazing for Gonzo. He would be back, he thought, at midnight.

'The house is yours,' he said. 'Don't burn it down, it's the only one I've got.' Just before he left, he took a French hunting horn outside, and purple-fit-to burst, played a rousing aria from Mozart to the mountains.

Gonzo and I ate well. I drank the wine and crawled into the put-up in his sitting room. I heard Pascale tip-toe in at I don't know what time. I was woken at four by a jaunty French air played on a bugle and he appeared on the top of the stairs announcing that it was four o'clock and all was well. Then he went outside and I heard him talking to his chickens in a high squeaky voice and play them a loud lullaby on a trumpet. He went over to Gonzo, and on returning said the horse had an ear for music and went to bed.

Nothing was mentioned of any of this in the morning. He talked airily about an English madrigal they had sung the night before from 1599 and did I know it? I offered to pay for my night's lodging, but he wouldn't hear of it. 'It's free: not for you, it's for your horse.' I liked Pascal.

As I rode away into the hills, I heard him play the horn again, another rousing melody as he shattered the morning quiet, giving voice to an indomitable spirit that spoke of goodwill, and art and the unreserved delight to express it right out loud.

22

A Night at the Zoo

They say the Rhône is exactly like the great grey-green greasy Limpopo, except the two times I've crossed the Limpopo, it's been dry.

Everything had become intensely French, with sharp sloping roofs, signs that said 'défense d'afficher' (no posters) and 'défense de chasse' (no hunting). There were auberges, epiceries, vins de table and croissants. 2 CV Citröens whirred about in their corrugated hundreds. Lovely old French towns with fairy tale chateaux hiding in woodlands, dignified French mi-lords with taut olive-skin faces under Napoleon Buonaparte haircuts, old peasant farmers in faded denim, holding little pigs under their arms. Even the chickens clucked in French.

Gonzo and I spent the nights in everything from campsites to farmhouses, auberges, woods, barns and lean-tos. Being out at night became a cold experience since having ruined my sleeping bag in Chambéry; it was a miserable thing to curl up in at night. The dark air was damp, unfair on Gonzo too. Sometimes winter's fingers would feel in around us at night and steal all our warmth away, leaving us chilled and frozen-footed in the morning.

The patched blue and white glossy skies of summer became always grey and overcast. But the sun might occasionally struggle through the autumn sky and throw us a ray of light when we pulled up for our lunchtime brie and baguettes. Then grasshoppers would bounce around again and little beetles hide tiny in the grass. I saw reeds and toadflax, the flowers of the late year and under the dripping autumn leaves we would hear les églises françaises pealing long sad bells in stone villages out of sight.

I saw birds: herons, storks, woodpeckers, doves and hawks above pointed towers and vanishing chateaux. Lots of lakes, lots of horses: lovely houses with wood-stacked balconies, ready for winter. Fields had been harvested but for maize, and most things had flowered and gone to seed.

The hedgerows hung with the fruits of the fall: sloes, hawthorn, blackberries. And spindleberry lit dark patches with bright little pink lanterns. Gonzo and I had crab apples, buns and kisses. We walked past fields of Charolais cattle with their broad faces and raised tail heads, and we clip-clopped past Lyon, St Maurice de Gourdans, Perouges, Versailleux, Neuville-les-Dames, where we stayed in a Centre d'équestre where everything hummed in orderly precision and horses were fed with hydroponically-grown barley.

We crossed the Saône and spent the night in the zoo at Maison Blanche, the sign for which caught my eye just before all the signs for 'les routes des vins'. Georges, the owner, found Gonzo a stable for the night and leading him past the giraffes, elephants, apes, wallabys and ant-eaters Gonzo pulled a set of faces I had not seen before.

He refused to believe in elephants. I could see it. Giraffes proved to be the most horrible creatures that he had ever heard of and much to my surprise, he and the zebras scared the living daylights out of each other. Not that they even got that close. Gonzo was given a stable between the camels and the wallabys, both of which he eyed suspiciously as he ate his dinner of zebra nuts.

I had a wonderful night with Georges, his wife Florianne, her brother Denny and two of the sweetest children. Georges told me how to formulate rations for hippopotamuses, how to calculate the correct diet for a tapir, how much meat a tiger can eat and what to do about a fly-away parrot. All this was accompanied by the background banter of lemurs making eyes at us in the trees above. Georges and his family were dazzling. Not only because they were all so good looking, but they shared a charismatic glow which was reflected in the animals. Personally, I have never much cared for zoos, but that one, *Touro Pare en Beaujolais*, was lovely. All the animals had big generous quarters, and they all looked very well.

Into my deep ignorance of wines, Georges and Denny tiptoed delicately, trying me out on the Fleuries, Romaneche Thorins, Ville Morgan, St Lager, St Juliens, the Moulins a Vent. They gave me the vin du paradis, which is Beaujolais before its last pressing: pure nectar: sadly unbuyable. We rounded off the night with Marc du Bourgogne: a sharp concoction, guaranteed to send you tumbling into a depth of sleep, inches from rigor mortis. They gave me maps in the morning, pushed back into my hands the money I offered, set me on a course for the Loire.

'Bonne chance! Bonne route! Bonne promenade!' they waved and Gonzo bounced me into Fleurie, Beaujolais, full of a zebra's breakfast.

The grape harvest was in full swing. Bottles filled every corner of every shed, every window in every chateau, every trailer on every tractor. I sampled the wines, Gonzo the grasses, he wouldn't drink red wine: not a bad thing: not sure if it's a good thing to get your horse into drinking habits.

We stayed with Gerard Gautier and his goats, ate his fromage du chevre, drank his vin biologique, which, produced without any chemicals at all, gives a light resonant wine with a high flavour and the astounding advantage of leaving you without a headache.

Gonzo bolted the following morning because I was daft enough to mount him in a headcollar only, after a breakfast feed of powerful black oats. He went downhill at the speed of light with me clinging on, once again snagged in the saddlebags, bedroll and panniers. Just like the time in Turkey when Ahmed Paşa had taken off downhill, and turned me on my back like a beetle, waving arms and legs around in the air, clawing for things to grab.

He composed himself and we walked through Bourgogne, Burgundy. I liked the small-scale stock farming: farms with six cows or so, pigs, sheep and goats, but they must have been hard to earn a living from. Such a contrast to the vast grain farms I passed later on.

We passed an intensive pig unit which looked exactly like I imagine a concentration camp must have looked like from the outside, even down to the watch tower, lest one pig escape. They're dreadful places. I'd worked as a pigman once in a unit like that and found it so desperately cruel I let the pigs out and was sacked on the spot. At least the pigs had a bit of a run-around. Sacked from the next job too: not much good really.

The maddening thing about France was that everything was always shut. I kept running out of money and whenever I went into a town it was either Monday and shut, or Saturday and shut because it shouldn't be open, or Sunday and shut because it should be. On Tuesdays everything was abandoned, and on Wednesdays you couldn't buy anything because no one had been around on Tuesday. On Thursdays if you were lucky enough to find a boulangerie open, the fellow would just be selling the last morsel of food to his friend, and on Fridays I gave up. It drove me completely berserk, and I spent days without any food at all.

And trying to draw money with my cash card that I carried all the way seemed to confuse the banks so completely, that I began to wonder what the point of the thing was. I had to wait hours and hours to get my francs, despite assurances in England that plastic money fixes things fast. Well, it doesn't. That's a figment of the imagination of the advertisers. You turn up skint in a tiny French town on a horse with a plastic card and see how long you've got to wait if you don't believe me.

I saw people shooting again. Grown men in bandoliers, camouflaged jackets, army webbing and game pouches off to kill little birds. Really brave men. A young chap, with a shotgun broken over his shoulder, swaggered down a village street in butch army fatigues wearing a smug self-satisfied grin. He swung a dead leveret from his hands. He was proud of that: to have shot that young thing to pieces with his high velocity gun.

It was quite extraordinary how many people can't ever have walked any distance. Sometimes we would turn up in a village, ask for a centre d'equestre, to be told of one fifty kilometres away, having arrived on foot with a horse at five, an hour before dark. They had no conception of what it is to walk fifty kilometres, how long it takes, how knackering it is.

Then others would swear blind there was a place in the very next village. We'd arrive and find nothing at all. Not even an epicerie, and if there was one the damn thing would be shut.

Of all the countries we passed through, I would never have believed that in France Gonzo and I would go hungry.

23

Marcel and Raymond

If a man does not know and does not know he does not know: leave him. But if a man does not know, but knows he does not know: enlighten him. And if a man knows, and knows he knows: follow him.' – Arab Anon.

I aimed to reach the Loire, then ride along its banks to Orleans. I was told it was easy riding. After my experience with the Po, no assurances gave me any shred of confidence that this was true. It might be all right if you are in a helicopter, or balloon: but I doubted it.

The ride across to the Loire took us through St Aubin en Charolais to a welcome of nothing. There was only one cafe with only wine. There wasn't so much as a stale baguette. Four people said there was an auberge in St Aubin, and that we should find a bed and a stable. We didn't. We slept out on a cold uncomfortable night, hungry again. In the morning, I was able to buy a little barley for Gonzo, but nothing for myself.

We passed through Viry, a very pretty village then to St Vincent Bragny, where a homely madame put us up for two nights in the filthiest weather. Gonzo was given a huge field to stuff himself with, which he shared with three aged cows, who were standing round in the middle when we arrived, discussing knitting patterns. Gonzo eyeballed them, then broke away to graze. An hour later, the owner of the cows came dripping to the hotel, and gave me a filthy look.

'Vôtre cheval est une bête très désagréable.' (' Your horse is a most unpleasant animal.') He squeezed the words out between his teeth, with a lot of contempt. 'C'est le plus méchant cheval et il a tout cassé. ('He is the meanest horse and has broken everything up.')

He wasn't pleased about something, so I grabbed the groundsheet, wrapped up in it and found Gonzo quietly grazing, minding his own business. The picture of content.

'Mais je ne comprends pas.' I said as Frenchly as I could. 'What's the problem?'

The man snorted out his retort in a florid oath, 'Mes vaches ont disparu et votre cheval diabolique et complètement merdique!' ('My cows have disappeared and your devilish horse is a complete shit.')

Crumbs, was he wild! The cows had gone, and Gonzo was responsible. It took three hours to find the man's cattle and restore harmony, by way of chocolates, apologies, promises to have Gonzo executed, bottles of Ricard and every other mortal thing to appease the man's hot indignation. We had a rowdy dinner together that night, and Gonzo was forgiven.

By now it was raining constantly, and I couldn't stay in one place hoping for clear skies. We pressed on to Geugnon, told that at Vendenese we'd find a night's lodging. It was a pretty village spanning the river Arroux with a well-proportioned stone bridge, and a fine old church. We lunched on the river bank, in the company of two tipsy fishermen who were impressed with Gonzo's fondness for fish paste sandwiches, and any other morsel that could be loosely described as food.

They told me a story about a Welshman who had parachuted into the village in the last war – at least I think he was a Welshman, they described him over and over again as a Gallois, which is how I described myself – baled out of a burning plane, and was hidden by a girl, who found him. 'Et, pour lui avian était un oiseau d'amour! Parce qu'il est tombé dans les bras d'une fille formidable!'(c'est avion était pour lui un oiseau d'amour, car il était tombé dans les bras d'une belle demoiselle)

So he'd fallen out of his 'plane into the arms of a beautiful young girl. I think they meant 'arms'. Isn't 'bras' French for 'arms'? Or is it French for 'bra'? Anyway, he got lucky wherever he fell, married her after the war, and lived there until he died. They told me it was 'une histoire incroyable' since she not only hid him from the Bosche, but also from her parents.

The weather cleared up that afternoon, and they put me on the road to Issy L'Eveque, only 15 kilometres away. In Issy L'Eveque, I met Marcel, proprietor of Hotel des Voyageurs. He watched me for a while before coming to talk to me asking rather incongruously what books I read as an opening gambit.

It seemed an odd question from a total stranger, but it was in earnest. He had very clear eyes, and went on, 'because, if you don't have any books, I can lend you one that will change your life.' He showed it to me: *The Life of The Masters*, by Baird T. Spalding. I'd not come across it before.

'Esoteric writing,' he went on, 'this has altered the nature of all my thoughts. And near here is the Tibetan Monastery at le Boulay. You should go there. They'll show you how to think, how to marshal your thoughts, to meditate. Go with your horse: they'll look after you both.'

He talked on in the Risqué Bleu smoky atmosphere of that place, asking questions about my trip, and was deeply interested in the writings of Mevlana, and of Ibn Arabi, *The Bezels of Wisdom*, that I left on the riverbank in Turkey. I told him how I sensed a connection between St Francis and Mevlana.

'Of course,' he said, 'they lived round about the same time and Francis actually visited the Sultan, walking through Christian battlelines to do so. They must have talked for days, otherwise it wouldn't have been recorded so well. And I bet they impressed each other – things happen that way.' I hadn't seen it like that. And it seemed so odd to hear all that stuff there, in France somehow. Yet there was a compelling side to Marcel, and it was good to listen: I have rarely found a man who holds my attention as completely as Marcel did then.

'No encounter is just by chance,' he said. 'Stones are not turned and left unobserved. Even from our brief meeting like this, something will spring, just wait.' When I left the following morning, I asked if I might take an apple for Gonzo. He pushed a dozen on me.

'Thank you Marcel: I'm sure you'll get these back in their hundreds.'

'Thousands,' he said. 'It's worth learning, that if you give, don't give the least you can: give the most: au revoir – à bientôt.'

It's beyond my powers of description to say how Marcel affected me, and how what he said all sounded so right. Maybe it was just that our chemistry matched in some way as it does from time to time and you really hear someone: maybe another would not have understood him in the way I did. He lived by what he thought in the pretty little town of Issy L'Eveque on a principle obedient to God as he understood Him, and it made him a good man to be with. He felt he had no right to judge others or what they did, and if everyone who meets him is affected, touched in the way he touched me, then he is doing his bit for God, just as undoubtedly he would like to think he was. When I collected Gonzo from the farmer, I could turn left to go to England, or right to the monastery. I got on Gonzo, gave him the reins, closed my eyes. He went left.

We left Bourgogne, crossed into Nievre into a strong westerly wind through flat landscape, past La Node Maulaix, then through long woodland to Fours. Fours is a typical main road town. Usually I made an especial point of avoiding main road towns because they are the worst. They are lorry ridden, noisy, seldom have horse places and are expensive. But as it happened, I found a hotel painted in powerful primary colours, over-fussy shades, too many flowers, poncy garden furniture and an air of the very worst in decor. I decided to stay.

In that hotel, someone had gone berserk with carpet. It was everywhere. On the floors, up the walls, round the beds and even all over the bog cistern. Where there wasn't carpet there was paper with huge floral swirling designs, each wall howling another garish pattern, contrasting in every single way to the one adjacent. In amongst this, goldfish mouthed in lurid green fish tanks, a spiteful Dobermann Pincher slunk about, and the whole place was set off in a suffocating fug and reek of wet knickers. It was quite a place. I hung in there for the night, glad to get out in the morning, since all the windows had been nailed shut and not a breath of air stirred the dust under the divans.

Gonzo spent a good night in a classy joint at the far end of town and in the morning we bounded up to Decize. I had been told of La Crinière en route, that it was where the Loire, the Aron and the canal all meet.

We cantered up the canal bank, and I saw the sign. I dismounted, walked in the yard and was met by Raymond, grinning through his beard, and his wife Monique, who smiled a half smile, and, stubbing her cigarette under her foot, greeted me with a coy 'bonjour'.

Gonzo quickly had a stable and I sat talking to Raymond, Monique, Gaitane, Violane and Aurora, their three pretty daughters. What Marcel had been to men, Raymond was to horses. Although quite untrained, he had a natural understanding of them. He had a strikingly simple and straightforward philosophy with a quick wisdom, and when I said how appalling had been the lot of draught animals in Turkey, he answered immediately that animals reflect the wealth or poverty of a country anywhere. They are the first things that suffer when things go wrong.

They kept fourteen horses in La Crinière, all shapes and sizes, and endurance riding was their speciality. In the summer, they went on long rides en famille, taking paying tourists with them on randonnaise all over France. It's a very good country to take horses across, and many people do it. I heard of one girl who rode over 110,000 kilometres on her horse all round France, and Evelyn Cocquet who rode from Paris to Jerusalem in the early Seventies, and who set out for China while I was riding through.

The French are good horsemen, and have an equestrian touring organisation set up, with the names of all centre d'hippique, marechals and so on. Something we lack in Britain: needs doing.

They look after horses rather differently in France to us, and I came across a lot of animals kept on deep litter. Nobody seemed to clean much tack. Raymond had a knack with horses which one seldom meets. A kind of intuition with them, but he wasn't the first who I have heard say 'show me a horse and I will tell you about his master'.

In many ways he reminded me of all I had heard about Hubert in Greece. Like him, he believed that a singular discipline could be learned from horsemanship, and that, if learned correctly, riding could teach you to use your body properly, your mind fully and create a harmony within. His instruction had echoes of the Alexander technique, yet he had no knowledge of it. His skills were innate, somehow pure. 'Doucement' was a word I heard him use with his horses over and over again. It means 'gently'.

I spent several days with his family, during which time it poured, and approaching winter stripped the leaves off the trees. The rivers swelled with muddy undertowing currents, frothing brown over the weir at Decize. I met his friends Jean Jacques, a writer, and his wife Helen who lived in a pretty small chateau called Les Eschots, and had a goat cheese lunch with cousins in Morvan, one of the woolier regions of

France, where they hunt wild boar.

After four days, Raymond and a friend Jean-Claude rode with me up to L'Etrier Magny in the middle of the forest of Sauvigny. The voices were different in those parts and the 'R' was rolled as in Welsh, the *patois* a Gallic melody to it. In the bois de Cigogne I bought a pair of Camargue stirrups, which I had searched for all the way through France. They are marvellous things, covering the whole of the front of iliefum (the foot).

Somewhere along that track after a long lunch, I fell off Gonzo, landing at his feet like a pile of tripe. Who should happen round the next corner, but the only English horsewoman in France. She eyeballed me in silence, as one does a fellow countryman who has just made a spectacle of himself. My pride grovelled around in the mud at Gonzo's hooves.

Raymond left me at Herry on the banks of the canal that follow the Loire. He told me it would be far better riding than by the river, since there was a tow path the whole way, dead level going.

Then came the moment to say goodbye. I don't know why it was always such a wrench, but my emotions hit my eyes before the words came. He left me standing by the water under a grey sky, holding a little china horse from his daughters, a keepsake. While tethering Gonzo, I dropped it, and it shattered: all that I salvaged was its head, the only bit intact: just like Ahmed Paşa's.

I went off to look for a night's billet and looked across to La Charité. Seemed a nice sort of a place. So did a lot of the French towns I steadily avoided. Interesting how fond one can get of a place by looking at it, afar off, just imagining what it must be like.

Herry was a delightful place. In the evening I went to Mass. No idea why, I'm not a Roman Catholic. There was no organ music. They played Mozart on a cassette recorder in the church, which gave it a warm, soft feel.

Then a man with a quick nervous smile and a wandering unconcentrated eye found a home for Gonzo for the night. A doting blue-denimed-strong-handed old man offered his stable. Gonzo stood in literally three feet of straw, given no less than five bales of hay. The old man called him 'mon petit', much to my surprise, and to Gonzo's. Seemed an unlikely name to me, for this very jumpy, highly intelligent, alert horse who wouldn't think twice about giving you a boot into the middle of next week if you crossed him.

But Gonzo played the part. Looking all starry-eyed, he greased up to the old man with an oily Latin charm that was disgusting to watch. And of course, he got everything he wanted and more besides. The old chap didn't have to ride him. I knew next day would be thirty kilometres jogging and canter at the end of which Gonzo would look as if he'd just got up, there wouldn't be a drop of sweat on him and I'd be exhausted. I knew what to expect of Gonzo.

In the morning I gave the old boy 50 francs for livery for the night: £5. He wished us 'Bonne route,' kissed Gonzo goodbye, tears in his eyes. I think he'd spent all night in the stable with him. Must have reminded him of a horse he once had. Tender emotions like that break me up inside.

And just as I thought, in the quiet of the morning air, Gonzo cantered long stretches on the water's edge. He carried me light and easy. What freedom it is then! The sun shone on the smooth water where a low mist blurred the distance, the far trees soft and vague. To ride and listen then to the even rhythm of hooves falling hollow on the grass, the sun warm behind, clear blue above: heavens, it's lovely then!

To see the sprinkling of fine houses, pretty farmsteads and homes shuttered in Sunday morning silence, barges passing on the canal murmuring quietly, their marine diesels ticking over, and, all laden with grain, heading north. There, in the region of Sancerre, a pretty village straddled the canal: a jumble of slate and tile on double pitched roofs, casement windows and old stone houses: a little boulangerie, a patisserie, a tabac, the iron bridge over the canal, and we stopped for our lunch time break.

Each time I stopped, I found it harder to get going again. Although so much of it was glorious, the riding kind, the people friendly, I longed to be able to stop, to finish, to put my hand on a door handle, turn it, walk in and call that home my own. I wanted to reach into a barn for a bale of hay for Gonzo, not have to look for it all the time.

Though the Loire was graceful, the chateaux splendid, I longed then for the wild mountains of Wales, my home. For Rhandirwywn, Abergwesyn: to see the buzzards on Mynydd Eppynt, the Mountain of the Horses, the red kites at Llyn Brianne. I wanted to speak in my own tongue, listen to them talk about the sheep sales in Builth. I wanted to be in my own little cottage where the wind blows sharp, and only the sheep, peewits and dirty old crows break the silence.

And yet I knew how wonderful it was to ride the land I was in and to have had the great good fortune to have been able to do it. In many ways, I was sorry not to have ridden all the way from Turkey nonstop; yet I never set out to break records and took things as they came. For me, they'd been pretty cushy. I know of no more satisfying way to travel than on a horse, and I knew then, on the Loire that I had spoiled myself for any other way of travelling. That somehow too, I had been changed by the experience in little ways that would stay with me. I knew I should always be content with less in life, disinterested in material success. Perhaps that had been something to do with what Marcel had said, and that was echoed by Raymond. That is that you can never make the wrong decision in life, that all things will work to teach you in one way or another, and that the only thing to fear is ignorance.

I spent that night at La Ferme Equestre de la Matairie, Sort de Boulleret, near Lere, and again, was not charged. All you can say is thank you. Or was it teşiqur ederem? Epharisto parapoli? Grazie mille? Merci mille fois? It comes from your heart. These people touched the quick of my soul. They never questioned whether I could or could not pay, and often in Turkey, I had been better equipped than they. Always it was a gift, it asked nothing in return, only that I remember. And how can I forget?

Many nights I had lain awake just thinking about the places I had been, stayed in with my horses. Thought of the nights under the stars, fears, laughter, little tender moments, the rope burns and my temper. How, in effect, they had carried me and my grubby pile of kit across a continent. And because of them, I had met the very best of human kindness and warmth. I had seen people through the green of the trees, with barley running through their fingers, and through arms full of hay. People who wished to live in peace on their farms, with their animals.

24

Last Days in France

The next day's ride was easy, with big tourist barges ploughing up and down the canal, their occupants snug in autumn outfits, rosy-wine faces flushed with bonhomie and saucy encounters.

Then on the aqueduct at Briare, I thought our end had come. It's a long, elegant construction spanning the Loire and barges pass along quietly, one at a time on the central waterway. The footpath on either side is metal – not so good for a horse.

There is about a forty feet drop from the aqueduct down into the river. Half way across Gonzo realised he was on a metal bridge with water in the middle and a river underneath and he didn't like it. I quickened his step to get across when a barge came oozing steadily towards us, with a liberal sprinkling of tourists on top who wanted to stroke the nice horsey as they glided by. At that moment, a man with a road drill, or a machine gun, or riveter, chose to start boring into the fabric of the aqueduct, sending up a rough tremor. Gonzo lost his head.

I thought he was going to jump over the side and then all at once he reversed, and dropped a hind leg into the canal and I was certain we were going in, to be run over by the barge and just quietly drowned, but he scrambled, jumped and made a bolt for the far side which we met at a hideously out-of-control gallop. We scattered the onlookers.

I tried to get out of the town as fast as possible, the aqueduct leaving me feeling as I had with the tunnel – no more fancy waterway crossings for us. But could we find somewhere to stay? We lost the canal, following the Loire, which just there is bordered by trees and scrub, and everything worked against us. I lost count how many times I had given up hope at that time of night, feeling that everything had gone wrong, only to find somewhere, somehow, and an open door. That night, it was the Theatre L'escabeau. It would have been the very last place that I thought I should find to stable a horse. Gonzo grazed their lawn, was given buns and maize, and I dined with Dan and Philippe, the owners, who made the theatre their life and home.

They talked of Voltaire, Victor Hugo, Rabelais and Shakespeare, and the quality of Philippe's English proved how frequently he must have translated Shakespeare into French. It's puzzling to be told your destination to be a 'mere two leagues hence'. I don't know how long a league is. They struggled to keep the theatre alive, just for the love of it. They had no grants, no grand patron and being short of funds, begged, made or borrowed all they had, turning a ramshackle set of buildings into a lean and fit cultural enclave and I admired them for it.

The next night we spent in St Benoit, having come up through Sully, a town largely rebuilt after Allied bombings during the last war and a final flattening by a flying fortress in 1944. I checked into a small hotel in St Benoit, and while I was thinking about supper, I heard chanting, Gregorian chanting. I had stumbled on yet another saint. Here lies – in part – St Benedict.

Benedict was not a priest, nor had he intended to found an order: he set out to write a Rule. His outlook was characterised by balance – work, rest and pray, and he is regarded as the father of Western Monasticism, Patron Saint of the Occident. St Benoit is a delightful town and luckily it had a stable for my furry friend, who couldn't give a hoot about St Benedict, being far more interested in the other horses, and the carroty mixture he had for supper. When I went to collect him in the morning, he'd gone.

I was stunned. What could have happened? Had he legged it all the way back to Italy? I asked a groom. He hadn't seen any grey horse, knew nothing about one. Another groom came round the corner, 'Oh,' he said, 'Le cheval gris?'

'Oui!' I was alarmed.

'Mais il est vendu!'

'What?'

'Oui. Un camion pour l'abbatoir est arrive a six heures pour le cheval gris.'

'What!?'

'Oui. Et maintenant, c'est le diner pour les gens de St Benoit!'

'Who's eating him? What?'

'Nous avons reçu un bon prix.'

I nearly died. Then they took me into an inner stable, and there was Gonzo. They laughed at my expense. It took me a moment to see the joke, serving only to draw me closer to Gonzo, vowing never to let him out of my sight again, not as long as there were people around going to eat him.

The ride after St Benoit took us up by way of little roads, tracks and paths, all pretty muddy. We went through Fay-au-Loges where I was told of the French shepherd who was reputed to be responsible for huge areas of forestry in that part of the country.

Apparently, whenever he went out to look at his sheep, he took a handful of beech mast, acorns, conkers and any other tree seed with him and, while he walked through his sheep, he pressed them into the ground, one by one. In this way, he planted thousands of trees in the seventy years or so of his lifetime. It's a nice little story. We should all do it.

We passed la Blaine Poteau, following forestry tracks, then up to Loury, which was stone dead – not a soul stirred there. A biting wind buffetted us, grew in strength, and we walked in swirling cold gales all day.

The countryside was devoid of animals: we had arrived in the granary of France, and there was nothing for us. We made for Bougylez-Neuville, where no one had hay, no straw, nor took the slightest interest in our plight. In Villereau, winds lashed us with stinging rain, and Gonzo tried constantly to tuck his backside into the wind.

In Villereau, we were turned away: no one had anything for us. We went east to the nearest town, hoping to find something there, but saw no animals, and there was nowhere to stay. I asked in no less than six farms, and six times was turned away. It became darker, rained harder, and an old man stepped out of a barn.

'Suivez-moi!' he shouted above the noise. Blue with cold and drenched, he showed Gonzo into a stable, where we quickly made up a bed, giving him the last feed on lucerne hay he's had to this day.

'Pas bon, le temps.' The old man said, through chattering teeth.

'C'est un bon cheval.'

I blessed that man.

I found a bolt hole in Neuville aux Bois, where the landlord sloped about sucking Gitanes, knocking back Ricard Pastis, playing cards with a bunch of fousty-looking lushes hanging onto the bar. It was the filthiest joint I've been in since a soup shop in Benghazi. My bedroom was cold, my clothes clung to me, the meal was foul, my bed was lumpy and I had the best night's sleep I had for months. Felt sharp as a razor next day.

A thick cold fog enveloped the land and I have no idea what it looked like round there, but judging from the ground we walked on, it was flat as a witches' tit.

We wandered through Aschères le Marché when, south of Toury, Gonzo started to react to something out in the fog. By now, I had begun to recognise his reactions, and I knew he had scented horses. Ten minutes later, we walked into a beautifully appointed yard, where some twenty horses were stabled in magnificent surroundings. A man appeared telling me I was fifteen or so kilometres from the nearest riding school, but that we could stay and have lunch with them.

Gonzo stuffed himself on a boiled linseed and barley mix while I prattled on about how nice the horses looked. The man said nothing, simply that he bought and sold them. Usually good horses. Only later did I discover I had had lunch with Yves Lemaire, France's top dealer. We'd been to an Olympic stable. Can't help being thick, just comes naturally.

He telephoned the riding school and I spent the night with Gerard Delestre in Le Centre Hippique d'Arbourville, near Rouvray St Denis. Gonzo and I were given first prize. I have no idea why. They presented me with a handsome plaque, which I still have, saying 'Centre Hippique D'Arbourville Rally 1987, Premier Prix'. There's a drawing of a fellow smoking a fag, sitting beside his travelling horse. It's the only thing I have ever won: it's pinned to Gonzo's stable door.

Gerard was another intuitive horseman and Elizabeth was the first person I met on my way who recognised Gonzo's breed.

'Mon Dieu! Sacre Bleu! Un Créole d'Argentan!' And he looked very especially proud to be recognised so correctly.

They'd just bought a nervy young horse from a man who was unable to handle him, and Gerard said that by the morning that wild little horse would be eating out of his hand. I've heard some claims, but none so swift. I was intrigued.

In his box, they pushed the young horse, and half a dozen goats: it was all a mighty squash. Like he said, in the morning that little horse was eating out of his hand. It was remarkable. 'Never fails,' he said. 'Squash a pile of goats in with a crazy horse, and in the morning the horse is fine.'

'What about the goats?'

'They go crazy.'

All his horses were like him. Happy-go-lucky, full of life. Elizabeth rode with the fluidity of a gaucho and they were the cheeriest bunch you could chance on. I watched them carry off the prizes next day when I met them up in Chateau Saronville where there was a gymkhana. Then they put me on the Roman Road right across country. Dead straight grass riding, north of Chartres. The country was uninteresting. Mile after mile of flat ground. Small units with huge agricultural machinery, all claiming EEC grants to beat the band. How on earth they managed to buy these vast machines on the size of farms they had beat me. The French have an understanding of the EEC that wholly eludes us. I stayed with two families on that ride. The first in Chateau Neuf en Thymerais, and the next in Boisvillen, the Henaults.

They told me they knew one person in England. When I asked them where he lived: they said Hertfordshire. I don't know anybody in Hertfordshire. Of all the millions of people in England, I would not be likely to know this one man. When they pulled out a photograph album later that night, I gazed at an old snap shot in disbelief. Not only did I know him, but had fagged for him at Monmouth where I was at school, when I was an urchin and he was a prefect. 'Vraiment, le monde est petit,' Denis Henault said.

By the time I reached Normandy, I had only six days left in France and had to make arrangements to be shipped out. Sarah Hayes of International Horse Services booked Gonzo on a lorry from Deauville on 6 November. My last few days I spent with Raoul Cotteret in La Ferme du Chateau in Courteilles. He was a classical dressage instructor, who had an abundance of Gallic charm which epitomises Frenchness.

He ran a kibbutz of a sort for young horse enthusiasts just outside Verneuil, having moved there from Deauville.

Raoul told me a few little secrets of horsemanship which he implored me not to let on, and I won't. He helped me with many things, not the least of which was securing another lot of papers from the veterinary service for Gonzo's exit, and a meeting place in Deauville where the BBA horsebox would pick us up. On 5 November Gonzo and I went to Lisieux, where we stayed with Christian, who runs a riding school. I went to look around the Basilica of St Theresa, which is a beautiful building: but my mind wasn't on it.

I met the BBA box in Deauville as arranged, overwhelmed by what a vast contraption it was: how thoroughly professional, and what a marvellous thing for transporting horses. There was nothing it didn't have. Maybe it was because they were countrymen of mine, or maybe because I hadn't spoken English myself for the past few weeks, or maybe it's just because I'm not much of a horseman, but those guys seemed so efficient and calm about everything, I began to wonder why I had bothered to do any of it at all. Gonzo is a brute to load into a box, but they had him in there before he knew it. There were no sticks, no shouting, no hassle. They shut the ramp door. We were off.

'Right,' Mick said, 'let's bugger off. Got all your papers?'

Up in the cab, I handed him the wad.

'Cor,' Bob said, 'you've got a T2L. How did you get a T2L?'

'Have I?'

'That'll make life easier. Bet that was Mario in Italy. Wonder how he managed to swing that?' I didn't know what he was talking about.

'Got any guns, drugs, contraband?' he asked. I hadn't. Although someone in Italy suggested I buy a gun to shoot the horse just in case he broke a leg. Very dodgy idea I thought. Far more likely to have shot myself. Or put the muzzle of the thing to my temple, and pulled the trigger, just to see if there was life after death.

'No, no guns. Nothing'.

We set out for Le Havre with Bob at the wheel and they talked about flying horses round the world. Their passports were covered in International stamps. They'd been everywhere: twice. In Le Havre we met another couple of Peden International chaps, who also flew horses all over the world. I had no idea how many horses flew. But the interesting thing about their chat was that they rarely talked about horses. They talked about the red tape, customs, airports, lorries and my T2L, whatever that was.

'How would you like to fly a bunch of Tennessee mules to Sandy Land?' One of them asked me.

'Where from?'

'Tennessee, of course.'

This thickness thing is definitely not good.

We were loaded onto the ferry at 10 that night, sailed at 11.15. I visited Gonzo a few times, but he was quiet all the way: and he had the company of a little filly in the back of the box.

The sea was mirror flat. The ferry throbbed a deep hum, and I felt sick as a dog. Here it was all ending, and all I managed to fill my thoughts with was Oxford County Council jail.

25

At the End of a Rainbow

We rolled off the ferry at 6.15am. International Horse Services had done their job and we were met by Jean, their woman-on-the-spot, who processed the paperwork with efficiency. Bob handed over the veterinary documents, pointing out that Gonzo had a new Coggins test, with Mallein, Dourine, Glanders – the lot. He had a full house of papers, been through fifteen vets in the time I'd had him, to get to England. The customs people went through my baggage and checked up that Gonzo was who he pretended to be, and wasn't a counterfeit Ahmed Paşa, who would not have been allowed entry. They checked up too that we hadn't been anywhere near Spain, which, at the time had a bout of African Horse Sickness, and no Spanish horses were allowed entry.

As all this went on, I gazed into Chumpie's eyes. It seemed a long time since I had seen her: times when I was certain she'd forgotten all about me, times when I felt I'd asked too much. I don't know any finer feeling in the world than a friend who hangs on, a girl who waits.

'Well,' she said, 'where's this horse?' She's a big romantic.

All those feelings and sounds from Turkey came tumbling back, the heat, the flies, the horses, all those rides on dusty tracks, Şimşek and his unjumpable tree.

We were through the customs in an hour and Bob tipped us out at the Redlands Riding Club, Fort Widley, just north of Portsmouth. As he was led up the long corridors in the stables in Fort Widley, I thanked Bob and Mick for their help and off they went, only to return to Switzerland in two days to get another load.

Chumpie took me to lay a wreath on her grandfather's grave and how strange it seemed to hear all those English voices. I don't know why it was. I've been away for much longer periods, and never noticed it.

We stayed in an hotel in Selsey for the night and I slept a deep sleep, half caught in the past, half in the present, as in the eye of a storm with all things now and then whirling round. How everything had gone easily, from all that might have happened. With what fortune had we moved so freely through Turkey, Greece, Italy and France. And save for one or two exceptions, we had been every night in the best place for us, then. And now just there on the edge of Portsmouth, an easy ride out.

Chumpie took me to Fort Widley in the morning, I saddled and packed Gonzo, ready for the ride north to Wales. She told me the night before, that all the gales we had walked through in France were the same ones that had devastated southern England, and within twenty minutes of riding away, I saw the terrible damage I had only half believed.

Whole woods were hurled down; great swathes of timber lay felled raggedly about, as if some colossal beast had gone berserk in there. I noticed how sodden the air in England was too, and how only just across the channel where the weather was similar, the air had been dry. There were a lot of birds, and I hadn't heard so much bird song since March; we have a lot of birds, and what a treasure they are.

The lanes wiggled on. We passed other horsemen, who looked at us as though we were stupid. I did feel horribly out of place, in leather jerkin, battered felt hat, saddlebags and this peculiar coloured horse.

We didn't get far that day, winding up in the Little Uplands Motel, Garrison Hill, and Gonzo was stabled nearby. It was the first time too I had been asked about the welfare of the horse before my own: it was a question I appreciated to the full, understanding all its implications. I watched television, appalled to hear about the bombing in Enniskillen. After all the kindness I had met, it sounded like something from another planet. I listened to people struggle to find adjectives to express their feelings for what the bombers had done. But there isn't a word for that: never has been. I didn't know it then, but I only had two days' riding left. Wind and rain gusted constantly. We moved on through Winchester, spending the night in South Wanston, then up to Penton Mewsey, and I ended my ride in pouring rain.

I pulled in at 5-30pm, drenched and worn out having got lost on the industrial estate in Andover. I couldn't find a way out of that wretched place, and went round and round for an hour in amongst lorries, vans and fences. I lost my will to continue.

I didn't feel anything when I decided to chuck it in. Didn't know if I was glad, sad or indifferent. All I knew was it was over, and if I couldn't convey that to myself, I certainly couldn't convey it to others. I drank too much whisky that night and went to bed half-cut. I don't remember much about the evening except sounding as if I was talking drivel. Nothing new. A friend took me to Gloucestershire next day by Land Rover and trailer.

A box waited for Gonzo at the Long Distance Riding Centre in Bourton-on-the-Water which Joan Davies runs like clockwork, a highly efficient yard. Gonzo didn't know what had hit him. He received his meals regularly, was despatched of his worms, had his wolf teeth cut, was groomed until he glistened like a piece of marble. We wintered in Gloucestershire, a sometime home for me, and I didn't have to go to jail. Mark Leon put Gonzo up for the last few months of bad weather; and catered for Gonzo's near impossible peculiarities. Being treated like an English hunter has given him a high opinion of himself.

In the spring we completed our journey by box. Gonzo is up behind my cottage now, with Chatterbox, a Welsh pony, who keeps him company. They're browsing around, like Hengist and Horsa, wondering whose place to beat up next.

And I can see right across the roof of Wales, can ride him up into the wide silent hills, see the lambs. Come back, stare at this strange Argentinian horse in Welsh twilight. No sum of money would part him from me: his price is above rubies.

And I've heard that Maro has grown. She's learning to jump, still listens to bazouki music, lives under the trees in Ktima Litsas, safe. But I don't know where Ahmed Paşa and Şimşek are. Good Saint Hippolytus, look after them. Not a day goes by when I don't think about them: good saint, protect them.

There's two pairs of buzzards nesting down by the river, and the red kites have a home again, above the Towi, near Llyn Brianne.

Love horses: tend them well, for they are worthy of your tenderness. Treat them like children, nourish them like friends of the family, clothe them with care. For the love of Allah do not neglect to do this, or you will repent for it in this house and the next.

(Exhortation of Omar, general of The Prophet.)

Other Merlin Unwin books that might interest you

The Byerley Turk   Jeremy James £8.99 paperback / £6.75 ebook

Vagabond Jeremy James £16.99 hardback/£6.75 ebook

The Yellow Earl Douglas Sutherland £20 hardback / £6.75 ebook

Right Royal John Masefield £20 hardback

The Racingman's Bedside Book (anthology) £18.95 hardback

Hoofbeats through my Heart David Edelsten £7.99 paperback

www.merlinunwin.co.uk